PRAISE FOR *CHARACTER*

"As we walk through the world, we can start to feel a collective sense that something isn't right — or worse: something is very wrong. In such moments, we can either resort to hopelessness, cynicism, and desperate self-preservation, or we can answer the call to courageously step into our fullest potential as human beings. Gerard Seijts and Kimberley Young Milani's *Character* is the road map (and inspirational rocket fuel) for that journey. Its cutting-edge Leader Character Framework is built for the trenches, for the real-world challenges we face, for our everyday decision-making. Through the deeply inspirational conversations, we're invited to consider a transformational possibility: I could do that too. Can you imagine a world in which every individual was acting with character as their compass? That's the path to the future we want; that's the path we need to be on." — PETER KATZ, JUNO– and Canadian Screen Award–nominated singer-songwriter, keynote speaker, and facilitator

"Gerard Seijts and Kimberley Young Milani have written an insightful and incisive book which deserves to be read by leaders in the public, private, and not-for-profit sectors. Their thought-provoking argument that competence and commitment mean nothing without character, and that character can be developed through concerted effort like other leadership skills, is crucially important at a time when we need great leaders to solve boundary-crossing problems." — GOLDY HYDER, president and chief executive officer of the Business Council of Canada

"Character lies at the very heart of leadership and its absence has never mattered more than it does today, in our uncertain, high-stakes world. This magnificent book describes what character means and how to develop more of it. Its beautifully written case studies bring the author's ideas to life. Better still, the book is grounded in research and full of actionable advice related to recognizing and developing the character that is so desperately needed in leadership roles across sectors. If you want to be a better leader, this book should be at the top of your reading list." — AMY C. EDMONDSON, Novartis Professor of Leadership, Harvard Business School, and author of *Right Kind of Wrong: The Science of Failing Well*

"Gerard Seijts and Kimberley Young Milani have delivered a masterclass on the importance of character in shaping leadership decisions. Their analysis, based on years of impressive research, casts a rare beam of light on the most consequential factor of our essence as human beings. The light shines brightly through the book's ingenious collection of interviews of personalities from around the world who offer inspiring examples of the power of character. *Character* deserves a special place in the canon of leadership scholarship." — THOMAS D'AQUINO, founding CEO, Business Council of Canada, and author of *Private Power Public Purpose: Adventures in Business, Politics, and the Arts*

"A remarkable book that will grip you from start to finish. The demonstrable strength of character in action will challenge your thinking and exemplify strong leaders who stand up for injustice and work towards peace, hope, and reconciliation."
— KEVIN MCAREVEY, principal of Holy Cross Boys' Primary School featured in the award-winning documentary *Young Plato*

"We've never had more tools available to improve engagement, results, and organizational productivity. Yet one of the most determining factors for success — leadership character — has been one of the most elusive. Artificial intelligence and other innovations may push the boundaries of what's possible, but they can't compete with this core tenet of leadership and the 'echo effect' it has on teams and organizational success. Gerard Seijts and Kimberley Young Milani show why character is the leadership skill to be cultivated. The world needs more of it." — SEVAUN PALVETZIAN, president and CEO, UNICEF Canada

"This book uniquely challenges you to examine and develop the core of your character through the lived experiences of leaders and their personal calls to action. Inspired by each page, I began to reflect and embrace this book's resounding message: to invest in developing who you are as a person and as a leader — not just your skills or talents; to believe that you have a unique contribution to make for the betterment for your organization, community, or society; and to muster the courage to take action with intent." — CHERYL POUNDER, two-time Olympic gold medalist in women's ice hockey, TSN analyst and broadcaster

"The importance of leadership character is well known but few studies really add much value beyond the intuitive. This book provides a deep and innovative analysis of leadership character along with a method to assess and develop it. A must read for any ambitious, responsible leader." — ANDREW BURKE, chair of Business Studies at Trinity College Dublin

"Gerard Seijts and Kimberley Young Milani give us leader character in a way that is grounded and practical, while also building on responsible research. They choose great leaders to bring their ideas to life. We all should be doing more of what they are trying to help us do: to develop, support, and be leaders and citizens committed to tackling the boundary-crossing grand challenges of our time." — RYAN QUINN, chair and associate professor of Management and Entrepreneurship and academic director of the Center for Positive Leadership, College of Business, University of Louisville

Gerard H. Seijts
Kimberley Young Milani

Foreword by Steven C. Preston,
President and CEO, Goodwill Industries International

CHARACTER

What contemporary leaders can teach us about building a more just, prosperous, and sustainable future

Published by ECW Press
665 Gerrard Street East
Toronto, Ontario, Canada M4M 1Y2
416-694-3348 / info@ecwpress.com

Editor for the Press: Jennifer Smith
Copy-editor: David Marsh
Cover design: Ian Sullivan Cant

LIBRARY AND ARCHIVES CANADA CATALOGUING
IN PUBLICATION

Title: Character : what contemporary leaders can teach us about building a more just, prosperous, and sustainable future / Gerard H. Seijts, Kimberley Young Mliani ; foreword by Steven C. Preston, President and CEO, Goodwill Industries International.

Names: Seijts, Gerard H., author. | Milani, Kimberley Young, author.

Identifiers: Canadiana (print) 20230584470 | Canadiana (ebook) 2023058456X

ISBN 978-1-77041-730-4 (hardcover)
ISBN 978-1-77852-258-1 (ePub)
ISBN 978-1-77852-259-8 (PDF)

Subjects: LCSH: Leadership.

Classification: LCC HM1261 .S45 2024 | DDC 303.3/4—dc23

This book is funded in part by the Government of Canada. *Ce livre est financé en partie par le gouvernement du Canada.* We also acknowledge the support of the Government of Ontario through the Ontario Book Publishing Tax Credit, and through Ontario Creates.

PRINTED AND BOUND IN CANADA

PRINTING: FRIESENS 5 4 3 2 1

Gerard Seijts

To Aiden and Arianna,
may the stories in this book inspire each of you to become
a person of strong, well-developed character.

Kimberley Young Milani

To my daughter, Evangeline,
my life's greatest gift,
&
to my sister, Tricia, whose generous heart and
profound strength of character are a constant inspiration.

CONTENTS

PART III: CHARACTER IN ACTION

ACKNOWLEDGMENTS

We would like to acknowledge the many leaders from the public, private, and not-for-profit sectors who participated in our research on leader character and contributed to our intellectual stimulation over the past fifteen years. A special thank-you goes out to Ian O. Ihnatowycz, President and CEO, First Generation Capital Inc.; Bill Troost, President and CEO, Peel Plastic Products; Walter Zuppinger, Chairman and CEO, Domco Group of Canada Limited; Barbara Stymiest, corporate director; Don and Marion MacDougall; and other donors for their ongoing interest in and financial support of our work that led to *Character: What Contemporary Leaders Can Teach Us about Building a More Just, Prosperous, and Sustainable Future*.

We are grateful to the membership of the Leadership Council of the Ian O. Ihnatowycz Institute for Leadership, the Executives in Residence at the institute, and our Ivey colleagues for the insights they shared with us. A special thank-you to Kate Palmer-Gryp, Dawn Oosterhoff, and Lindsay Hobbs for their transcription and editing support. We are indebted to Don Loney for his thoughtful and helpful guidance in getting the book written, and Jennifer Smith, acquisitions and business development at ECW Press, for her encouragement along the way. We are grateful to the Social Sciences and Humanities Research Council for the funding that has supported much of our research on which the book is based.

This book also came to life through the direct involvement and advocacy of many people who connected us to the leaders featured within its pages. We are deeply grateful to Michael Flynn and Trinity College Dublin, Anna Maria Tremonti, Andriy Rozhdestvensky, Rahul Bhardwaj, Richard W. Ivey, Sevaun Palvetzian, Karen Huiberts, Ted MacDonald, Sukhinder Singh Cassidy, Pierre Bisaillon, Sue Dopson, Laura Louden, Matthew Wallen, and Julia Hoggett for their kind support.

FOREWORD

When I was younger I was an avid windsurfer, engineering trips to windy coastal destinations whenever possible. On one such trip, I joined a group of people to windsurf from Cape Cod to Martha's Vineyard off the coast of Massachusetts.

As we took off, it was clear that the weather would be challenging. The October sky was gray, the wind was cold and blustering, and the waters were choppy. After a complicated and arduous journey across much of the Vineyard Sound, I could finally see the shoreline just a few hundred yards away.

But things changed quickly. My line had somehow separated from the mast and my sail collapsed, leaving me with nothing to power my board. By that point, the wind had become more erratic, the chop had reached three to four feet, and I was unable to rerig my sail in the water.

In the distance to the east, I began to hear the faint sound of a bell ringing. I didn't pay much attention at first, but the sound became louder, and within a short time I had drifted to the buoy that housed that bell. The strength of the current became more apparent to me as it quickly swept me past the bell buoy; the ringing becoming increasingly faint, and now to the west of me. I realized that I was on my way to Nantucket Sound, beyond where anyone would see me. Thankfully, I was eventually spotted by a ferry and rescued by the coast guard.

Before I had the fixed reference point of the bell buoy, I had no idea how quickly the current was pulling me, how far I had drifted, or how alarmed I should have been. I was not able to get my bearings or a sense of movement in the large body of open water. It took that immovable standard to show me how far I had drifted from solid ground.

This story has served as a metaphor for the moral drift I have seen at many points throughout my life in banking, business, government, and nonprofit. Few people go from being anchored in the right thing to doing the wrong thing in one fell swoop. It happens gradually, like erosion. It is often imperceptible. The crowd migrates and we move with it, until we find ourselves at a place far from where we began, often far from what we once believed to be acceptable.

As the CFO of a publicly traded company, I had a front row seat to the crisis of confidence in corporate ethics that led to the passage of the Sarbanes-Oxley Act, a law that significantly increased accounting and oversight requirements for US companies. Over the several years prior, the gradual relaxing of standards among accounting firms, corporate leaders, bankers, and equity analysts, fueled by a strong stock market, had led to a lack of integrity in the financial reports on which investors based their decisions. We saw the collapse of companies like Worldcom and Enron; the disintegration of Arthur Andersen, a storied accounting firm; and the resulting realization that the financial statements of many US companies were not trustworthy. Investigations ensued, corporate leaders went to jail, employees lost their retirement savings, and trust in our institutions was deeply shaken.

Later, as the Secretary for the US Department of Housing and Urban Development, I had a clear view into the near collapse of our financial system, caused in large part by deteriorating practices in mortgage lending. Trillions of dollars in investment value were obliterated, millions of people lost their jobs, and a wave of mortgage foreclosures swept the country, removing people from their homes and resulting in neighborhoods full of abandoned properties. Again, over several years, we saw the erosion of standards and oversight, along with unethical behaviors from financial institutions, rating agencies, regulators, law makers, and individuals.

In both cases, institutional leaders lacked a commitment to strong principles, allowing their organizations and the people within them —

often seeking their own personal gain — to drift to a place that resulted in great loss to millions of people. Also in both cases, strong character-based leadership could have averted these crises.

Thankfully, we see great change for good through the steadfast perseverance, often in the face of great difficulty, by leaders committed to something bigger than themselves.

Consider Paul Farmer, who co-founded and led Partners in Health, a company that delivers lifesaving health and other support services to millions of people each year who live in the world's poorest places. Farmer came from a family that, at one point, lived in a school bus and supported itself by picking crops. He has since become a visionary who has transformed our understanding of medical justice, and of what is possible in the delivery of care to people who we once thought were unable to be helped. His lifelong commitment started as a student when he made multiple trips to Haiti to work in a clinic and with communities to improve healthcare practices. While many people doubted the possibility of improving successful medical outcomes with the rural poor, Farmer undertook remarkable efforts to advance what was possible, going door-to-door, and often walking hours, to ensure that patients complied with health treatments. Through his work, infant mortality, disease rates, and nutritional measures improved dramatically, providing a model for the effective delivery of services on a much larger scale to communities around the world.

Also consider those such as Harriet Tubman, Nelson Mandela, William Wilberforce, and Mother Teresa, whose lifelong missions, though starting humbly, advanced justice, freedom, and/or human rights for millions of people.

Among these people, I believe we see two dimensions of character. First, we see the *strength* of one's character that provides the steadfastness and resilience needed to persevere through difficulties. It demonstrates the depth of our commitments and our willingness to sacrifice our own comforts and well-being to achieve them. When one's character is strong, it is the bedrock upon which they stand.

In addition, we see the *nature* of one's character, shaping how one engages with the world. It describes who we are at our core with respect to our ethics, integrity, selflessness, empathy, curiosity, optimism, and accountability. It reveals what we believe in and what we value. It determines what we are committed to.

It is important, however, to consider that people of laudable character, with deeply held convictions and positive intentions, may believe in, and even fight for, very different things. For example, people who seek to serve the poor, advance the value of human life, and to achieve peace in our world may believe in different pathways to reach those ends. In a culture that is increasingly combative, losing sight of good intentions leads to increased division and hostility. Rather than seeking to understand others, people are often filled with contempt for those whose convictions differ from their own; and, in some cases, even seek to impugn the character of others who are not aligned with their own beliefs and principles. In opposing the viewpoints of others, assailing their very foundation has become a destructive tactic that divides us further and, ironically, reveals a diminished character on the part of the assailant.

Because of our considerable divisions and the magnitude of the issues we face, I believe now, more than ever, we need people of strong and good character to reach out to others with humility, extend them the respect and dignity they deserve, and seek to build understanding, and even common ground, wherever possible. I hope that in the pages of this book, you will find such people, as well as the inspiration to lead and live in a way that brings understanding and purpose to our world.

Steven C. Preston is the president and CEO of Goodwill Industries International, a nonprofit social enterprise whose mission is to help people reach their full potential through learning and the power of work.

PART 1

Exploring Character

CHAPTER 1

A CALL TO CHARACTER

Mia Amor Mottley is the prime minister of Barbados, an island country in the Lesser Antilles of the West Indies, with a population of approximately 287,000. It is one of many island nations in this part of the world whose survival is at the mercy of the Atlantic Ocean. During the 2021 United Nations Climate Change Conference in Glasgow, Scotland, Prime Minister Mottley delivered an impassioned speech that grabbed headlines around the world. Observers described the speech as a "break-out moment" at the conference.

In her speech, Mottley refused to allow her country and other island or vulnerable nations to be collateral damage to climate change — damage caused by greed. She expressed frustration at the absence of world leaders who are failing to act quickly enough to cut carbon emissions. To those present, she said:

> Today, we need the correct mix of voices, ambition, and action. Do some leaders in this world believe that they can survive and thrive on their own? Have they not learned from the pandemic? Can there be peace and prosperity if one-third of the world, literally, prospers and the other two-thirds of the world live under siege and face calamitous threats to our well-being?
>
> Or are we so blinded and hardened that we can no longer appreciate the cries of humanity?

> For those who have eyes to see, for those who have
> ears to listen, and for those who have a heart to feel,
> 1.5°C is what we need to survive, and 2°C, yes, S[ecretary]
> G[eneral], is a death sentence for the people of Antigua
> and Barbuda, for the people of the Maldives, for the
> people of Dominica and Fiji, for the people of Kenya
> and Mozambique, and yes, for the people of Samoa and
> Barbados. We do not want that dreaded death sentence.
> And we have come here to say: "Try harder."[1]

Mottley is also one of several women leaders who have been acknowledged for their outstanding response in containing the spread of the coronavirus. Further, time and time again, she has urged regional solidarity to recover from the crisis and build more resilient economies and communities across the Caribbean so they can more effectively address pressing issues. What lessons can we draw about leadership from the prime minister's impassioned and bold words? Why do so many people consider her a role model for future politicians in Barbados and the world?

In an era of converging crises and challenges — climate change, global health, economic uncertainty, social unrest, the direct and collateral damage of national and international conflict, human rights, and Indigenous reconciliation — acts of leadership are consequential. This may seem like an obvious statement when viewed through the lens of political leadership, but it is also true of individuals whose leadership is enacted within other arenas — large or small — whether they are social or civil, business, economic, or environmental. For example, business leaders have a significant role to play in helping to shape a just and sustainable future, in addition to meeting the responsibilities they have to their shareholders.

Leadership creates a powerful ripple effect, for better or for worse. A leader's influence is like a stone dropped in the water, with the concentric circles expanding to impact much more than the initial sphere. Think

---

1   Her full speech can be accessed at pmo.gov.bb/2021/11/01/speech-at-world-leaders-summit
-opening-ceremony/.

of a time when you exerted or witnessed leadership influence, whether minor or significant, that called upon your competencies, commitment, and character. All of us face choices in life that reveal something about who we are: that is, our character. Perhaps you are faced with a crisis or challenge now that is calling for strong leadership.

The nature and importance of character in leadership, which is the central theme to be explored in this book, is a journalistic and social media obsession of late. It has rightly been said that if a crisis is a test of character, then not everyone has passed it. It has indeed been disappointing to see a serious lack in the quality of leadership provided by many of our public, private, and not-for-profit leaders. There are many reasons why this is the case, but in an age of uncertainty one of the most common pitfalls leaders face is the need to make decisions and carry them out while having incomplete information. Leadership takes judgment, a central component of character, to address pressing issues that present themselves in highly volatile, uncertain, complex, and ambiguous contexts. For example, Stephen Poloz, former governor of the Bank of Canada, made this forecast in his book *The Next Age of Uncertainty: How the World Can Adapt to a Riskier Future*:

> Populations age, technology progresses, income equality worsens, debt loads rise, and our planet gets warmer. None of these is complex, really, but their consequences are. And when they all are evolving simultaneously, their interactions have the potential, in theory, to generate what appears to be chaotic or inexplicable outcomes for the global economy. . . . This degree of uncertainty is, again in theory, incalculable. . . . For individuals, this means that the economic risks associated with ordinary decisions will be higher in the future. . . . Inexplicable events may appear to be black swans, but will be the natural product of the growing complexity of our environment.[2]

---

2   Stephen Poloz, *The Next Age of Uncertainty* (Toronto: Penguin Random House, 2022).

Thus, it is not a stretch to argue that leadership is a crucial factor to a nation's social, political, and economic development and well-being — for better or for worse. And, more importantly, no level of competence or commitment will matter without the foundational leadership element of strong, well-developed character. In his book *The Man Who Broke Capitalism*,[3] David Gelles, columnist and business reporter for the *New York Times*, makes the case that former General Electric CEO Jack Welch's ruthless cost-cutting and single-minded focus on quarterly earnings, while profitable in the short term, was ultimately unsustainable — and hurt both General Electric and capitalism itself. Welch was celebrated for his competencies while the organization was making money, but the short-term results may have hid deficiencies in his character that compromised his decision-making over many years. Interestingly, character — for example, transcendence, accountability, humility, temperance, or sense of justice — only gets the attention it deserves during or after a crisis.

It has never been more clear that character development must be included if we are going to help create leaders who are willing and able to tackle the grand challenges of our time and work towards a more prosperous, just, and inclusive society. Our purpose in writing this book is to share inspirational stories from a wide array of exceptional leaders who demonstrate character in action, and thereby learn to elevate our own character in service of building better leaders and citizens, stronger teams, organizations, and communities, and a flourishing society and world. A tall order, but in the pages that follow we do offer proof that it can happen.

Sometimes, inspiration and insight can be gleaned from fictional stories as well. In the movie *The Hobbit: An Unexpected Journey*, there is a poignant moment we feel reflects our current times and the role we must all play to help lead us to a better world. The scene does not depict an epic battle or a formidable fight with a dragon; instead, it shows a quiet moment before the start of a long and perilous journey. The

---

3   David Gelles, *The Man Who Broke Capitalism: How Jack Welch Gutted the Heartland and Crushed the Soul of Corporate America — and How to Undo His Legacy* (New York: Simon & Schuster, 2023).

character Galadriel, a powerful elf, asks Gandalf, an equally powerful wizard, why he included the diminutive, unremarkable hobbit Bilbo Baggins in a company of fourteen experienced fighters embarking on a dangerous quest culminating in a consequential task. Gandalf replies that Saruman, the leader of his order of wizards, "believes it is only great power that can hold evil in check, but that is not what I have found. I have found it is the small everyday deeds of ordinary folk that keep the darkness at bay . . . simple acts of kindness and love. Why Bilbo Baggins? Perhaps it is because I am afraid, and he gives me courage."

Gandalf's words struck us as being particularly relevant to the journey upon which we all find ourselves, where everyday deeds and simple acts of kindness can have a profound effect. And while the leaders featured within this book have an elevated profile compared to most of us (to extend *The Hobbit* metaphor, they belong to the "order of wizards"), we hope that their stories can help you (1) to connect to elements of leadership that are universal and in which you can see yourself, (2) to be inspired by their character so that you can weave their insights into your own leadership practice, (3) to stir your imagination about a world filled with possibility, and (4) to understand the importance of engaging in simple acts — those small everyday deeds — that can help us to turn the tide, to undo past harms, or to create new ways of being that can lead us towards a future with greater human and planetary flourishing.

CHAPTER 2

CULTIVATING CHARACTER

Mac Van Wielingen is a Canadian investment management executive, corporate director, entrepreneur, and philanthropist. He said, "I believe leader character is the bedrock of an organization. I believe that, over the long term, character becomes the destiny of the organization. Character helps to build and sustain a business over long periods of time."[1]

Recent research surveying members of the Institute of Corporate Directors — an influential not-for-profit national community of directors in the public, private, and not-for-profit sectors — indicated that directors believe character plays an important role in board governance, particularly with regard to how boards make decisions, recruit new members, lead their organizations, and work together to perform their fiduciary and other responsibilities. However, the results also showed that despite the perceived importance of leader character as reported by highly experienced corporate directors, character is seldom an area of focus or development as a means to improve the way boards operate.

Further, the directors echoed the findings from our study of leadership during the 2008 global financial crisis: the educational system does a poor job of developing character in students. The upshot is that business schools — and other academic institutions — need to address character as an essential aspect of not only good leadership, but good scholarship

---

1   Gerard Seijts, Alyson Byrne, Mary Crossan, and Jeffrey Gandz, "Leader Character in Board Governance," *Journal of Management and Governance* 23 (2020): 227–258.

and good citizenship. This will take a shift, because current education prepares students for jobs rather than life, and that is almost solely based on competencies. Interestingly enough, it was not always this way. Mary Woolley, a renowned American educator who in 1901 became the first woman president at Mount Holyoke College, succinctly captured the widely held belief that "character is the main object of education."[2] More famously, in 1947, Martin Luther King Jr., leader in the United States civil rights movement, wrote in the Morehouse College student newspaper, the *Maroon Tiger*: "We must remember that intelligence is not enough. Intelligence plus character — that is the goal of true education. The complete education gives one not only power of concentration, but worthy objectives upon which to concentrate."[3]

If board members do not see character as playing a role in the "destiny of organizations," then how likely is it that senior executives will consider character as an integral aspect of their leadership? How likely is character to cascade down the organization to influence managers and front-line employees? And how can academic institutions help to build awareness of the importance of character and bring it into conversations and curricula on leadership?

Reversing direction takes awareness. So, where to start? Actually, perhaps the initial question is not where or even how to start, but when? We believe it is important to first understand that character is not about inhabiting a title, but a way of being. This means that character development is important and impactful whether it is engaged in by young students or senior leaders. So, to answer the question of when: now!

To begin the development process, we suggest you start by engaging in the practice of introspection and consider the myriad ways in which character is foundational to who you are and, specifically, how it informs your leadership (and that of others). We seek to stimulate your curiosity

---

2   David Brooks, "Becoming a Real Person," *New York Times*, September 8, 2014, www.nytimes
    .com/2014/09/09/opinion/david-brooks-becoming-a-real-person.html.

3   The full article, "The Purpose of Education," can be accessed through the Martin Luther King,
    Jr. Research & Education Institute at Stanford University: kinginstitute.stanford.edu/king
    -papers/documents/purpose-education#:~:text=We%20must%20remember%20that%20
    intelligence,objectives%20upon%20which%20to%20concentrate.

and articulate that character *can* be developed. Character development influences your growth as an individual and as a leader — to the benefit of the teams and organizations you lead, as well as the communities you belong to. However, it also requires reflection and self-knowledge. What we want this book to achieve is to grow your self-knowledge through the leader character framework we have developed over fifteen-plus years of research and trial at the Ian O. Ihnatowycz Institute for Leadership. We illustrate this framework through a series of engaging interviews with respected leaders from the public, private, and not-for-profit sectors. Our hope is that you participate in a journey of self-discovery and learn from some extraordinary leaders by using the framework as a tool when reflecting on the interviews and stories we share throughout the book. If you become even more effective in your role, even incrementally by using the leader character framework, then our work has meaning.

The Three Pillars of Leadership

Through research, we learned that the foundation of good leadership always rests on three pillars: competencies, character, and commitment to the role of leadership.[4] It would be a mistake to privilege one of these *C*'s over another, because if any of these pillars is deficient, the shortfall will undermine the other pillars and, ultimately, lead to performance problems for leaders, organizations, and related stakeholders. For example, our research into the leadership failures in the lead-up to the global financial crisis revealed that the crisis was not due to a deficiency in competence or commitment but, to a great extent, to a deficiency in strong, well-developed character.

---

4   Jeffrey Gandz, Mary Crossan, Gerard Seijts, and Carol Stephenson, *Leadership on Trial: A Manifesto for Leadership Development* (London, ON: Richard Ivey School of Business, 2010).

Figure 1: The Three Pillars of Leadership

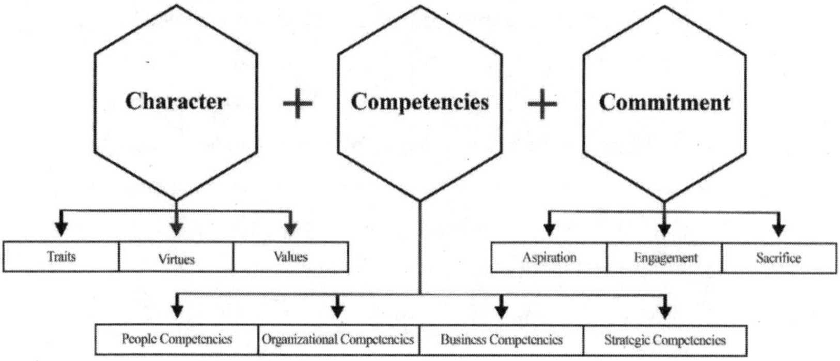

Together, character, competencies, and commitment determine courses of action — and our success or failure. However, it is important to note that character underpins competencies and the commitment to the role of leadership: it influences whether a leader will acquire the requisite competencies through training and development and make the commitment to lead in a sustainable manner.

> *Competencies* reflect what a person can do. They encompass the broad or focused skill sets that are required by one's particular profession. Competencies can include skills related to leading or working in teams in a variety of settings, such as communication, negotiating, strategic thinking, and motivating people, or they can relate to singular skills of specific occupation, such as coding, welding, conducting surgery or accounting.

> *Commitment* describes the degree of effort and persistence that a person applies to create forward momentum to make things happen, based on the person's level of aspiration, their degree of engagement with personally or professionally relevant issues, and what they are willing to give to reach a goal.

> *Character* involves a defined set of interconnected
> behaviors that satisfy a set of criteria as being virtuous —
> meaning, behaviors that contribute to sustained excel-
> lence and well-being of self and others.[5] Character is the
> foundation that individuals rely upon to help them enact
> good judgment. It is about how any individual — leader
> or citizen — can bring their best self to their endeavors.
> The stronger the character, the better the judgment and
> decisions you make, which means better outcomes for
> all: yourself, family, team, organization, and community.

Character is *not* innate — you are not born with character, nor is it set in stone at an early age. Character is built, ultimately becoming our habit of being. Habits are learned behaviors — and individuals learn or strengthen these behaviors through deliberate practice. In other words, through experiences we have in our lives . . . regardless of whether an experience is chosen or thrust upon us, positive or negative. Our charac-ter develops through our behavior within those moments and, through reflection, by the wisdom we glean from the lessons those experiences offer us. When left untested, character can be weakened and molded in dysfunctional ways by external pressures and contexts. Therefore, it's never too late to strengthen character; indeed, it is a lifelong journey.

Most individuals have a rudimentary understanding of character and have little difficulty talking about its importance when examining current events, whether in business, politics, or sports. But our extensive teaching and outreach initiatives have taught us that this understanding is often amorphous and there is no consistent understanding of what character really means or how it directly impacts leadership effectiveness. And without a consistent vocabulary with which to discuss it, character has been set aside or ignored as a critical area of professional development. For example, what are the behaviors that make up our leader character?

---

5   The construct of character — what it is and what it is not — is extensively discussed in Mary Crossan, Gerard Seijts, and Bill Furlong, *The Character Compass: Transforming Leadership for the 21st Century* (New York: Routledge, 2024).

The Leader Character Framework

Years of research by scholars from the Ian O. Ihnatowycz Institute for Leadership at the Ivey Business School in London, Canada, have led to the development and validation of the leader character framework shown in Figure 2.[6] This research — where we moved from looking at character through a subjective lens to a rigorous, scientific approach — was inspired by the 2008 global financial crisis, in which character was heavily implicated as a primary cause; the COVID-19 pandemic, which starkly displayed the character of leaders; and national and international politicians whose vices detrimentally impacted those they are meant to serve.

The leader character framework shown in Figure 2 is made up of eleven dimensions of character that relate to being an effective leader and the behaviors associated with each of those dimensions. It is important to note that these behaviors are observable, measurable, and actionable. Table 1 lists the descriptions of each of the character dimensions. Further, each behavior has an impact on the strength of the corresponding dimension of character. The easier it is for you to activate, or engage in, a particular behavior when the situation demands it, the stronger the associated dimension will be. For example, if you are able to conduct yourself in a calm, composed manner and maintain the ability to think clearly and to respond reasonably in tense situations, then you have strength of temperance (see Figure 2 and Table 1). In contrast, your temperance will be more fragile if you have difficulties in demonstrating these behaviors, thus making it more challenging to complete your work in a thoughtful, careful manner.

The dimensions and their associated behaviors independently *and* interactively influence behavior and individual, team, and organizational

---

6   The leader character framework is based on both qualitative and quantitative research involving over five thousand leaders from the public, private, and not-for-profit sectors in North America, Asia, Europe, and South America. The language embedded in the framework is based on research and — critically important — input from leaders from various sectors and industries, thereby enhancing the applicability of the framework to organizations from different sectors.

Figure 2: The Leader Character Framework

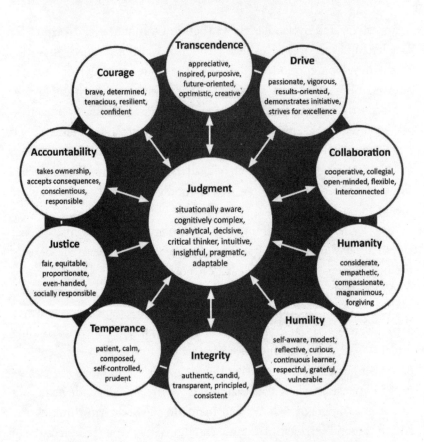

outcomes. For example, using candor (a behavior that supports integrity) when having difficult conversations on gender, race, or Indigenous reconciliation also takes courage, because we run the risk of having our words met with resistance, disbelief, or anger. Conversely, being asked to deeply listen to the experience of those who have suffered from discrimination or racism, especially when you are a part of the dominant group, will require humility, empathy (a behavior reflective of humanity), and calmness (a behavior that supports temperance). Demonstrating these dimensions of character increases the potential for meaningful change because it can invoke understanding and trust.

Table 1: Behavioral Descriptions of the Leader Character Dimensions

Dimension	Behavioral Description
Judgment	Makes sound decisions in a timely manner based on relevant information and critical analysis of facts. Appreciates the broader context when reaching decisions. Shows flexibility when confronted with new information or situations. Has an implicit sense of the best way to proceed. Can see into the heart of challenging issues. Can reason effectively in uncertain or ambiguous situations.
Courage	Does the right thing even though it may be unpopular, actively discouraged, and/or result in a negative outcome for him/her/them. Shows an unrelenting determination, confidence, and perseverance in confronting difficult situations. Rebounds quickly from setbacks.
Drive	Strives for excellence, has a strong desire to succeed, tackles problems with a sense of urgency, approaches challenges with energy and passion.
Collaboration	Values and actively supports development and maintenance of positive relationships among people. Encourages open dialogue and does not react defensively when challenged. Is able to connect with others at a fundamental level, in a way that fosters the productive sharing of ideas. Recognizes that what happens to someone, somewhere, can affect all.
Integrity	Holds oneself to a high moral standard and behaves consistently with ethical standards, even in difficult situations. Is seen by others as behaving in a way that is consistent with their personal values and beliefs. Behaves consistently with organizational policies and practices.
Temperance	Conducts oneself in a calm, composed manner. Maintains the ability to think clearly and respond reasonably in tense situations. Completes work and solves problems in a thoughtful, careful manner. Resists excesses and stays grounded.

Accountability	Willingly accepts responsibility for decisions and actions. Is willing to step up and take ownership of challenging issues. Reliably delivers on expectations. Can be counted on in tough situations.
Justice	Strives to ensure that individuals are treated fairly and that consequences (positive or negative) are commensurate with contributions. Remains objective and keeps personal biases to a minimum when making decisions. Provides others with the opportunity to voice their opinions on processes and procedures. Provides timely, specific, and candid explanations for decisions. Seeks to redress wrong-doings inside and outside the organization.
Humility	Lets accomplishments speak for themselves, acknowledges limitations, understands the importance of thoughtful examination of one's own opinions and ideas and embraces opportunities for personal growth and development. Does not consider oneself to be more important or special than others, is respectful of others, and understands and appreciates others' strengths and contributions.
Humanity	Demonstrates genuine concern and care for others, and can appreciate and identify with others' values, feelings, and beliefs. Has a capacity to forgive and not hold grudges. Understands that people are fallible and offers opportunities for individuals to learn from their mistakes.
Transcendence	Draws inspiration from excellence or appreciation of beauty in such areas as sports, music, arts, and design. Sees possibility where others cannot. Has a very expansive view of things both in terms of taking into account the long term and broad factors. Demonstrates a sense of purpose in life.

This places a special emphasis on judgment, the central dimension of character. The other dimensions work together to support judgment, which acts like an air traffic controller, activating the right balance or interactivity of the various character dimensions and their behaviors as necessitated by the situation or context. Good judgment does not allow the person to fall into extremes. Leadership is always context-dependent in that wise leaders — those who exercise good judgment — understand when it is appropriate to encourage collaboration and foster engagement and when to be more directive, when to demonstrate humility, when to be assertive, etc.

It is also important to note that each virtuous behavior can operate as a vice if it is in deficiency or excess (see Table 2). You can have too much or too little of a good thing. For example, bravery can manifest as cowardice if in deficiency or as recklessness in excess. Vindictiveness is the absence of forgiveness, whereas one is exploitable if one is overly forgiving. However, excess or deficiency is not simply about having too much or too little of a single dimension. As outlined above, the dimensions of character are interactive and integrated. Therefore, excess and deficiency manifest when you have too much of one dimension and too little of another, generating an imbalance. For example, bravery (courage) needs to be balanced or constrained by prudence (temperance) to avoid tipping into recklessness. Thus, to create positive outcomes or achieve any goal, we must be guided by the appropriate behaviors in the right balance, guided by what is required by the situation or context.

Table 2: Sample Behaviors in their Virtue and Vice States[7]

Deficient Vice	Virtue	Excess Vice
	Accountability	
Negligent	Conscientious	Obsessive
Irresponsible	Responsible	Controlling
	Courage	
Cowardice	Brave	Reckless
Unassured	Confident	Arrogant
	Transcendence	
Directionless	Purposive	Fixated
Pessimistic	Optimistic	Delusional
	Drive	
Apathetic	Passionate	Fanatical
Aimless	Results-oriented	Tunnel vision
	Collaboration	
Self-centered	Cooperative	Conflict-avoider
Confrontational	Collegial	People-pleaser
	Humanity	
Unrelatable	Empathetic	Overwhelmed by feelings
Vindictive	Forgiving	Exploitable
	Humility	
Braggart	Modest	Self-effacing
Disinterested	Curious	Transfixed
	Integrity	
Fake	Authentic	Uncompromising
Unprincipled	Principled	Dogmatic

---

7   The full table illustrating that the dimensions (and their associated behaviors) can become vices in either deficiency or excess can be found in Corey Crossan and Mary Crossan, "The Practice of Developing Leader Character to Elevate Judgment" in Toby Newstead and Ronald Riggio, eds., *Virtues and Leadership: Understanding and Practicing Good Leadership* (New York: Taylor and Francis Group, 2004).

Deficient Vice	Virtue	Excess Vice
	Temperance	
Anxious	Calm	Indifferent
Inattentive	Prudent	Overly cautious
	Justice	
Inequitable	Equitable	No exceptions
Biased	Even-handed	No differences
	Judgment	
Lacking logic	Analytical	Over-analyzing
Indecisive	Decisive	Impulsive

To achieve the vision of creating a sustainable, thriving world, as consummately articulated by Prime Minister Mottley, we need leaders with the judgment necessary to balance complex, urgent, and competing stakeholder interests, and the strength of character to use their influence wisely in navigating this journey. However, in almost every conversation on leader character, no matter the composition of the audience, a predictable question emerges: Can character be taught or developed in people?

Where Are You in Your Leadership Career?

Rashid Wasti is the executive vice-president and chief talent officer of the Weston Group of Companies. The Weston Group is Canada's largest private employer with over 200,000 employees and $50 billion in revenues and consists of several well-known consumer businesses. In his role, Wasti is focused on helping all the businesses in the group develop their current and future senior talent through effective succession planning, recruiting, learning and development, diversity and inclusion, culture building, and mentorship.

Throughout his many years of experience, Wasti has witnessed a number of cases where an individual who generally would be considered very capable, driven, and motivated did not grow into the role of leader and/or did not achieve the success that was within their potential. He asserts that a particular dynamic accounts for the lion's share of the reason that this happens. Here is what he told us:

> We all start out with a certain amount of talent and a certain amount of drive early in our careers. Many individuals are very smart, ambitious, and hardworking; they want to try to do great things. But their professional life is going to span thirty or forty years and in that time the world around them is going to change. As these ambitious individuals make progress and take on bigger and more complicated roles, the demands of those roles are also going to change. This means that the talent these individuals start off with is not going to be enough. One cannot rest on their laurels but must constantly seek ways to change and grow. Unfortunately, this doesn't always happen. When high-potential people get derailed, it's because they don't focus enough on their evolutionary growth.
>
> I teach a training and development course in our company and the headline words of that course are introspection and renewal. At every stage of your life and at every stage of your career, you have to have introspection. And what does that mean? It means you have to reflect on what you're doing right and what you're doing wrong, on how you can do something better and what you are doing that really works. It also means that you have to seek feedback from others, and you have to hear and receive that feedback with an open mind when you get it. It is critical that you identify those elements you need to shift, change or grow about yourself that will allow you to be more effective in your career. That's the introspection part. The renewal part is making an intellectual and emotional commitment to actually changing. What you need to understand is you don't grow just because you work hard.

You actually don't. Personal development and growth is a choice — a choice you have to make and you have to work at. And it's not easy. You have to make an intellectual commitment to it and you have to make an emotional commitment to it.

So, in short, when you're smart, ambitious, and hardworking, it is easy to fall into the trap of thinking those attributes will take you all the way. They are essential, but they're not sufficient. Your ability to learn, grow and change, and to recognize the ways in which you need to do that, is the biggest enabler. If not [present], it is also the biggest derailer of promising leadership careers.

As Wasti shares, a successful leadership trajectory is about growth and development, but it is also about taking responsibility for that professional (or personal) evolution and engaging in introspection and renewal. This advice taps into the behaviors associated with character dimensions of accountability (takes ownership, responsible), humility (reflective, continuous learner), drive (demonstrates initiative, strives for excellence) and transcendence (creative, purposive, future-oriented) (see Figure 2 and Table 1). We see four lessons to consider within Wasti's story:

- Understand the need for introspection in the learning-to-lead process and set aside time each day, week, or month to reflect on your areas for growth. Introspection helps to develop self-awareness, which is essential to good leadership and leadership development.
- Appreciate the importance of coaching, mentoring, and feedback for developmental purposes and your personal growth as a leader; this will require a level of humility because sometimes constructive feedback can be challenging to hear.
- Take ownership of your leadership journey and actively manage your career. Look ahead and identify what you will need to obtain to be successful in the next leadership

position. Then, take the initiative to find creative ways to grow and develop towards that role.

- Your ability to learn, grow and change, and to recognize the ways in which you need to do that, is the biggest enabler of leadership development.

Committing to personal growth and development is a deliberate choice; it is not a consequence or side effect of working hard or being busy. You have to work at it intentionally and consistently, because the only person who is truly capable of creating positive, lasting, sustainable growth in your life is you.[8] Let's take a deeper dive into the lessons Rashid Wasti teaches us.

Take Time to Reflect and Build Self-Awareness

In our very busy lives, we often get wrapped up in the seemingly endless list of daily, weekly, or monthly tasks and responsibilities that require our attention — both personal and professional, both large and small. It is easy to simply rush from one undertaking to another. But as one of our colleagues is fond of saying, "Who are you becoming while you are busy doing?" Have you become more patient or less patient? More compassionate or less? More humble or less?

By carving out some quiet moments to turn our consciousness towards our character, we can become (re)acquainted with the dimensions of our self that impact who we are and how we show up in the world. And, really, why wouldn't we want to know this? The French philosopher Simone Weil once stated: "Attention is the rarest and purest form of generosity."[9] If we

---

8   A detailed and overarching framework for character exercise and development — one that has proven itself in real-world contexts — is outlined in another book that was written by academics and practitioners associated with the Ian O. Ihnatowycz Institute for Leadership: Mary Crossan, Gerard Seijts, and Bill Furlong, *The Character Compass: Transforming Leadership for the 21st Century* (New York: Routledge, 2024).

9   This quote was taken from *First and Last Notebooks: Supernatural Knowledge*, which captures Simone Weil's most important thinking. The full citation is Simone Weil, *First and Last Notebooks: Supernatural Knowledge* (Eugene, OR: Wipf & Stock, 2014).

want to engage in developing our character — developing who we are — then we need to give ourselves the attention we deserve and require. In this respect, attention is not about engaging in a strained focus, but about creating a quiet expansiveness that allows us to hear our inner selves. We need to be generous to ourselves by giving ourselves time to reflect and time to invest in *our own becoming*. What is most important is that your practice of reflection is consistent so that, over time, it becomes habitual. Additionally, being reflective is a behavior connected to the character dimension of humility. So, by engaging in reflection, you are already strengthening one element of your character.

While "our own becoming" may sound like a quaint phrase, consider a recent crisis that you faced or witnessed. Would you call it a defining moment — a test of commitment, competencies, and character? These defining moments — whether brief or drawn out — affect those we lead and our own growth as a leader. Inevitably, each of us will face defining moments in our personal lives and careers, and we must seize the opportunity they offer to reflect, learn, and strengthen our character.

Defining moments happen to all of us; they may be tragic, traumatic, joyful, or inspirational. And often they are serendipitous. But, as Michael Bleich describes, what these moments have in common is that they unfurl a part of the human spirit that was previously unknown and change the way one thinks, views the truth, or acts with purpose.[10]

A Coach or Mentor Can Be Life-Changing

Did you ever seek out a coach or mentor, someone you can trust to have honest conversations with you and offer constructive criticism? A mentor will share with you their advice, wisdom, and experience, particularly when it comes to navigating career paths and strategizing to achieve career goals. A coach will pull from you your thoughts, ideas, and opinions, and will let you arrive at your own insights to solve a challenge you

---

10   Michael Bleich, "Defining Moments in Leadership Character Development," *Journal of Continuing Education in Nursing* 46, no. 6 (2015): 247–249.

face. Both of these processes are about helping people grow and learn, and what people discover about themselves often has ties to leader character: critical thinking, judgment, compassion, patience, etc. Individuals can engage in formal coaching and/or mentoring through relationships established intentionally for this purpose, or informally by harnessing points in time within a particular role when an opportunity presents itself to offer or receive help in problem-solving.

For example, as a leader you have opportunities to coach team members (those teachable moments that crop up during our day). Consider taking the time to ask questions about how their character played a role with a decision they made or actions they took in resolving a situation.

Sukhinder Singh Cassidy is a Silicon Valley executive with more than twenty-five years of global leadership experience. She currently is the CEO of Xero Limited. Sukhinder served as a mentor to many people with leadership potential and has publicly commented on the myriad ways in which promising careers derailed. For example, she observed that some people, no matter how smart they are, are always the victim; something is always being done to them. This can signal either a lack of accountability or outright arrogance (or both). It is never acceptable to believe that you are the smartest person in the room, *ever*. People don't truly learn if they don't show humility and take responsibility for mistakes.

Sukhinder also reflected on the leadership lessons that Bill Campbell, a mentor to many executives in Silicon Valley, shared with her during her leadership journey.[11] She recalled: "Bill supports a leadership style that centers on leading from the heart; that it is okay to show up as your authentic self and lead with what works for you. For me, it was very much an endorsement that it is okay to come to work as a leader who is not just fully packaged as a professional, perfect entity, but as somebody who leads from their own personal passion."[12]

---

11 Bill Campbell died of cancer on April 18, 2016, at the age of seventy-five.

12 Gerard Seijts, *Good Leaders Learn: Lessons from Lifetimes of Leadership* (New York: Routledge Publishing, 2014).

Harnessing the Lessons from Sudden Insight

Rashid Wasti talked about finding creative ways to develop your career. Sometimes they come from flashes of intuition and insight called epiphanies, which means sudden manifestations or perceptions. Such revelations teach us something new.

Douglas Yacek and Kevin Gary argue that epiphanies are a central means for transformative growth and development.[13] They see three distinct aspects related to such learning: a disruption of our everyday activity, a realization of an ethical good or value, and an aspiration to integrate this value more fully into our lives. Although epiphanies occur spontaneously within the mind, we can create the conditions that can help facilitate their emergence. These conditions can be generated through many different means: books, movies or plays, conversations, walks in nature, life events, and so on.

You can create the conditions for epiphanies about character in leadership to occur in the workplace. For example, use the stories in this book to (1) enhance team members' awareness of character-related challenges encountered in leadership; (2) deepen team members' understanding of the role of character in leadership effectiveness and how it shapes decisions and actions; and (3) help team members think about their own character, and offer them tools and strategies to further develop their strengths and address their deficiencies.

You can also act as a role model by sharing your own stories in which character provided you with insight into what steps to take to resolve a situation. It is expected of leaders to set a good example, and the respect and trust you establish with your team allow you to be looked to as a role model.

Tabatha Bull, president and CEO of the Canadian Council for Aboriginal Business, explained to students at the Ivey Business School how Indigenous teachings she was raised with continue to inform her leadership, and how inspiring leaders do not need to be powerful figures, but can be found in our families and communities. Bull explained that

---

13   Douglas Yacek and Kevin Gary, "Transformative Experience and Epiphany in Education," *Theory and Research in Education*, 18, no.2 (2020): 217–237.

her leadership, and more so her character, is consciously grounded in the Seven Grandfather Teachings: humility, courage, honesty, wisdom, truth, respect, and love. These teachings (also called the Seven Sacred Teachings by some) are rooted in Anishinaabe traditional knowledge, but many other Indigenous communities follow or adapt them as well. The Seven Grandfather Teachings are a way of being, a holistic set of teachings that can serve as guiding principles to living a good life, both individually and collectively. Every day, Bull strives to ensure that all she does is consistent with and reflective of those teachings.

During the class, a student asked Bull who served as her role model and inspired her leadership. Bull shared that her role model was someone close to home: her great-grandmother. She explained that her great-grandmother lived a life in service to the Indigenous community in which she had dwelt for her entire life. She served as the de facto midwife, often traveling by dogsled to deliver babies. She also ran a small business, akin to a convenience store, out of the back of her house. It was the only business in the community and was where everyone went to get their snacks and treats. Bull reflected: "She was never an elected person in the community, but everybody came to her house to talk and ask her questions. She always had time for everyone."

Her great-grandmother lost her husband when she was still quite young, but her house was always full of people, as she raised several of her grandchildren, nieces, and nephews. Bull shared: "To me, she's someone that I just admire for her real authenticity . . . She lived into her nineties and the number of people that came to say their goodbyes was a real testament to what she had done. And there's so many of us who still talk about her." Bull's story is also a testament to how a leader need not be larger than life but can be a member of our family or community whose tireless efforts to care for those around them change lives through the character or teachings they employ.

Most leaders we talk to acknowledge individuals who served as powerful role models, who shaped their thinking and character. These role models include parents, teachers, coaches, colleagues, and managers. Sometimes, people we spoke with told us they had a role model whom they didn't know personally, yet that person inspired them in a deeply personal way, like an author, scholar, athlete, scientist, politician, or leader of an organization. These days, with global and social media, it can also be simply another citizen — often a young one — whose words and actions galvanize others: people like Malala Yousafzai, Severn Cullis-Suzuki, or Emma González and David Hogg.

We assume that many of you — our readers —have worked with young people. In what ways are you sharing the wisdom of your experiences? How are you helping to unearth the ideas held within them? How are you helping others develop their character by not only exploring what they can do but who they are? As a leader, we need to bring the best of ourselves and bring out the best in others. This is critically important in any situation, but especially in times of crisis and disruption. How are you inspiring others to become their best selves, either by learning from your example or through the benefit of your encouragement?

The Great Enabler: Discipline

Jon Hantho, president and CEO of CBI Health, spoke about his challenges as a leader during the COVID-19 pandemic. He articulated to his employees that the stress of leadership is constant, and that the role of leader has been a burden for many in the organization.[14] We all want to be the best leaders we can be — to support and inspire our teams to perform their best. And in the midst of the many pressure points that leaders face, it can be difficult to remember that great leadership starts with taking care of ourselves first. Healthy leaders make better leaders. He went on to share some of his thoughts on self-care: the importance of being intentional in what we do and consistent in our actions, and engaging in deliberate practice to form virtuous habits.

But Hantho also explained that leaders inevitably make mistakes, and when that happens they need to have the discipline to "call their own

---

14   Liza Agrba, "How CBI Health Helped Create a Unified Culture — and Stave Off Employee Burnout," *The Globe and Mail*, September 16, 2022, www.theglobeandmail.com/business/rob -magazine/article-cbi-health-culture-prevent-employee-burnout/.

foul" and repair the damage. Hantho remembers an episode in which he "torpedoed" a Zoom conversation by addressing a colleague on the executive team in unnecessarily harsh language.[15] As soon as he got off the call, he knew he had blown it. He immediately called back the individual he had interacted with in that semi-public setting and apologized. He then connected with each of the other participants individually and apologized to them as well, telling them, "This is unacceptable behavior on my part" and "This is not who I am."

As Rashid Wasti told us, leaders who have the desire to grow and develop don't rest on their laurels, hunker down in their comfort zones, and become complacent. They engage in deliberate practice — a planned, concerted effort to master the elements of leader character. For example, consider how the following dimensions of character and the learning process intersect:

> *Accountability*: Taking ownership of your decisions, behaviors, and outcomes, and recognizing how you contributed to personal or organizational problems. There can be no learning if we blame others or the situation for mistakes. Unfortunately, there is a well-documented tendency for individuals to attribute the success of an event or project to their own actions while attributing failure to others.

> *Courage*: Openly addressing problems and opportunities and calling out bad behaviors; being brave enough to bare your soul first to establish an environment of emotional safety; showing an unrelenting determination, confidence, and perseverance in challenging situations; and being resilient in the face of setbacks. Growth and development require courage — courage to try new things, set stretch goals, and admit to one's mistakes and change course.

---

15 Jon shared this anecdote in the Learning from Leaders undergraduate class taught by Gerard Seijts at the Ivey Business School.

Humility: Embracing continuous learning and opportunities for your personal growth and development; being willing to identify and discuss your mistakes and biases; engaging in exercises that generate greater self-awareness and gratitude; and being open to feedback to help guide your development. In short, learning and growth require humility. Without it, we can slip into arrogance and hubris, mistakenly believing we already have all the answers.

Temperance: Conducting yourself in a calm, composed manner during stressful situations, and maintaining your ability to think clearly and respond reasonably amid candid or difficult conversations. Those who are unable to control emotions and responses in difficult, tense situations often fail to recognize the learning embedded within it.

Drive: Striving for excellence and having a strong desire to succeed; tackling problems with a sense of urgency. Bringing a sustained momentum around your specific learning goals facilitates and maintains the learning process.

Transcendence: Engaging in a future-orientation to set optimistic goals that will elevate your opportunities; tapping into and honing your creativity; being appreciative of the incredible body of knowledge and wisdom that surrounds you — in books, journals and other materials, online, and most importantly in those around you. By keeping an eye on the future you wish to create for yourself, family, team, or organization, you can anticipate the learning you will need and that can serve an overarching or specific purpose in your life.

Developing one's character is a lifelong journey. Opportunities to develop and strengthen character exist in everyday activity. The greater the understanding we have of the dimensions that define leader character, the greater insight we have into what can be achieved by being invested in those dimensions and the associated behaviors.

The recently retired tennis player Serena Williams is an extraordinary leader and role model who has long exemplified the behaviors associated with strong leader character. First, she is a role model for anyone invested in sports. She will be forever known as Serena — an icon who broke barriers and shattered records. She did so with absolute class — on and off the tennis court — while most of the world was watching. Her athletic prowess was unparalleled, characterized by tenacity, fearlessness, and self-confidence, and over her thirty-year career she was celebrated for her humility, grace, and honesty. We believe she is, in short, the paradigm of excellence in sports. She inspired millions of people, and in particular women and girls of color. Her resilience in becoming the person she is today should be admired. She faced countless instances of prejudice, racism, misogyny, and disrespect as people tried to undermine her, both as a person and tennis player.

Her achievements can be attributed to her raw talent, unassailable ambition, and the support from a visionary father and family. We believe people would be even more awed if they truly appreciated her life's trajectory from being a young Black girl in Compton, Los Angeles, to a global icon. There can be no doubt that Serena transformed sports in general, and tennis in particular, as well as the image of what it means to be an athlete, a woman, and a mother. She expressed the hope that people come to think of her as symbolizing something bigger than tennis. We believe she most definitely achieved that. Serena showed that women and mothers are strong, capable, and competitive in the world of sports.

At the same time she inspired millions of people with her humanity and vulnerability. For example, she has been open and candid about the life-threatening complications she faced following the birth of her daughter, Olympia, and how she had to self-advocate for the medical care she knew was needed to save her own life. Moreover, she has initiated many successful activities outside of tennis that include business ventures relating to fashion, beauty, and accessories that embrace diverse leadership and create social change.

In the pages that follow you will meet many extraordinary leaders who will give you their insights on their leadership journey. We chose leaders from a wide range of fields who we believe have exhibited exemplary leader character in their careers and lives.[16] A second important criterion for our selection of leaders was the nature of their work and the impact on society. Consider, for example, Cameron Bailey, Canadian film critic and the current CEO of the Toronto International Film Festival. The mission of the festival is to transform the way people see the world, through film. We believe the arts can help us to confront and redress issues surrounding societal injustice — from racism to poverty, war to climate change; and at the same time, the arts can inspire and uplift, can help us to dream bigger, love deeper, and show us the power of human flourishing. Let us give you some examples and a taste of what to expect.

On humility: In our interview with Mary Robinson, the former President of Ireland and UN High Commissioner for Human Rights, she told us:

> And then, finally, when I became UN High Commissioner for Human Rights and I began to see the need to address human rights globally — which frankly, at the beginning, connected to places I had never heard of! — I found myself being asked questions about countries or communities that I didn't know anything about. With this role, however, I didn't have any big stick, did not have any power at that time, so I decided the best way to address these issues was to be close to the victims. My colleagues in my office would always describe me as coming back energized from being in some of the worst and most dangerous places in the world. And I was indeed energized

---

16 We approached leaders through email, phone calls, and personal connections. We emphasized that we wished to make our leader character research come alive by weaving it into the stories of character-infused leaders who act in service of creating a more sustainable, just, and compassionate world. We requested sixty minutes of their time to conduct an interview designed to draw out their story of character-based leadership (but often the interview lasted much longer). The interview questions were provided in advance for their review and reflection.

by those I met — by the bravery of the people who were on the ground fighting for human rights — because I was in and out, [but] they were there permanently. That really taught me a huge lesson in the fact that human rights are defended all over the world by people who would describe themselves as ordinary. That was a big learning for me.

On courage: In our interview with Maria Ressa, a Nobel Peace Prize laureate and a fierce defender of independent journalism, she told us:

> I came of age during the golden age of journalism through reporting on air. When I was in a war zone and had to do a live shot, it provided the best training on how to not just focus, but to have clarity of thought. Even if bullets are whizzing by on either side of you, a journalist's task — my task — during those two minutes of live reporting is to distill everything into three points.
>
> Those experiences provided the best leadership training that I could have because I was in charge of my team.

On accountability: In our interview with the Honourable Murray Sinclair, a former Canadian Senator and Chief Commissioner of Canada's Indian Residential Schools Truth and Reconciliation Commission, he told us:

> The reality is that we must never give up the responsibility of doing what we can, when we can. The teaching that I learned when I was a young boy is that at the end of my life, I will be turned around on my spirit journey. They will turn me around, and they will make me look back at the trail that I created in this world, and they will ask me to account for everything I did, but also everything I didn't do that I could have done. I have to be prepared to speak for that. I want to be able to speak about this thing when I'm ready to go.

These are just a few examples of the many leaders who are featured within this book — all of whom deliver unique insights on and experiences of character-based leadership. We engaged in these interviews with the hopes of achieving three aims: (1) discern the many ways in which character guided their behavior and choices; (2) explore how character contributed to their success; and (3) learn how they developed dimensions of character. Purposeful stories often serve as powerful calls to action.

To get the most benefit from the interviews, we encourage you to pause after reading an interview and reflect on it. Use the leader character dimensions and elements described in Table 1 as a touchpoint in your reflection. What aspects of character emerged in the interviews? What deepened your understanding of the nature of leader character as a guiding influence? Are there parallels you can draw with your own leadership practice, where insights into character can spark new ideas, possibilities, confidence, and meaning in your lives? To acknowledge Rashid Wasti once again, what changed in the world of the interviewees and how did they adapt? How much was character an influencer in doing something better?

You will read stories of people from all over the world and things that happened all over the world. We also ask you to reflect on which stories inspire you the most. Which have more personal relevance for you? What key insights do you take away from the interviews that you will add to your own accumulated experiences as a leader? What are your character strengths and where do you see potential for further development of your leader character? This is the essential question because it has never been more clear that character development must be included if we are going to help create the leaders who are willing and able to tackle the grand challenges of our time and work towards a more just, prosperous, and sustainable future.

PART II

The Interviews

CHAPTER 3

CAMERON BAILEY

CEO, Toronto International Film Festival

Cameron Bailey, the Chief Executive Officer of the Toronto International Film Festival (TIFF), is also a voting member of the Academy of Motion Picture Arts and Sciences, which presents the Oscars, and a Chevalier in France's Order of Arts and Letters. For eleven consecutive years (2012–2022), *Toronto Life* magazine has named him one of Toronto's 50 Most Influential People.

Born in London, Cameron grew up in England and Barbados before immigrating to Canada. He began his career as a film critic, then joined TIFF in 1990 as a seasonal programmer. At TIFF he headed the festival's Perspective Canada program, devoted to Canadian cinema, and founded its Planet Africa section in 1995, curating a selection of new films from the African continent and diaspora.

For twenty years he worked as both programmer and critic, contributing to Toronto's *NOW Magazine*, CBC Radio One, TVO, and CTV's *Canada AM*. He has been published in the *Globe and Mail*, the *Village Voice*, and the UK's *Screen*, as well as in several books, including the Phaidon Press publication *Take 100*. Cameron has taught film curation at the University of Toronto and holds an honorary Doctor of Laws from Western University.

Where did your love for movies and stories come from? What were the defining moments in shaping your love for movies?

I actually didn't grow up with a great love for movies. I wasn't exposed to a lot of cinema as a child. I enjoyed books and was more into stories through literature. I was a voracious reader and eventually did an undergraduate degree in English Literature at Western University. It was there that I took an optional course in cinema — Contemporary World Cinema. The course began with us viewing Jean-Luc Godard's *Breathless* and then went all over the world, except for Hollywood. It was my first exposure to European cinema, Asian cinema, Latin American and African cinema — cinema that did more than just try to entertain. That was what did it. I realized that film could do so much more than just be a diversion. It could be about ideas, about the form of the medium itself, and that it could explore some of the deep, persistent social issues in the world.

I think this was the second year of my undergraduate degree, and I began writing about film for the campus newspaper. I then became a film critic after I graduated, and one thing led to another.

The mission of TIFF is to transform the way people see the world, through film. You said that film does so much more than entertain. Film can have transformative power. What are you hoping will transform?

When it comes to film, I think the idea of transformation goes in two different directions. It begins with the very medium itself. Traditionally, we would watch films in a movie theater surrounded by other people and on a giant screen that was so much bigger than ourselves. And so I think what this does — when you are in a collective space and being overwhelmed by picture and sound — is open people up. You surrender to movies when they are presented in that way because they are just so much bigger than us. And when you're opened up in such a way, I think empathy can be at the end of that path. So films, on the one hand, can show you experiences that are totally different from your own — worlds that are different from your own, places in the world you will never visit, people that are very unlike yourself — and because you're opened up to it, you can empathize with people who have very, very different ways of living. I think that's an important thing for all of us, no matter where we are in the world.

On the other end of it, the other thing film can do is it can be a very personal, singular experience. It can reflect your own experience back at you. There's nothing more powerful than watching a film and seeing something of your own life there — a moment that you had with your parent, or when you were falling out of love, or an experience that you had. You just see a moment in your life replayed up on-screen and you suddenly feel like this movie is speaking to you. That's also such a powerful experience, and it can be transformative because it gives you the feeling that you're not alone in the world, that other people share your experiences, that there is some common humanity, and that someone else gets you. There is nothing more powerful than that feeling. So what I find so transformative is that on the one hand, there is that vast exposure to the world and all its variety and, on the other hand, that movies can speak to us as individuals.

So, film is like a mirror *and* a doorway.

Yes, that's right.

Are there any of those film moments you described that have shaped you as a human being? From a particular movie? A particular scene?

There are many. The one that comes to mind is a film called *Moonlight* by Barry Jenkins that won the Oscar for Best Picture a few years ago. It certainly is about a very different experience than mine. It is set in a neighborhood in Miami that is mostly an African-American community, which is not the kind of neighborhood that I grew up in. It is about a man coming of age and coming in to his sexuality as a gay man, and I'm not a gay man. And yet, there is something about it that reflected

Black masculinity on screen as a rich, nuanced experience that involved a lot of vulnerability. It wasn't simply about being strong. I had never seen that in a movie before — not from a portrayal of someone who looked like me. So that is the personal part, but then also expanding out into a common experience. I believe this is something every person goes through: we all have a vulnerability, fears inside of us, but that is not the way Black men are usually represented in film. That was a really powerful experience for me, and I felt like, "Oh yeah, this movie is doing something that is going to be important." Not just for me, but for so many others who need to see that.

The world is changing. Can the arts help us to confront and redress issues surrounding societal injustice, from racism to poverty, war, and climate change?

For better or worse, I think the arts generally, and film and music in particular, can cut through the cerebral understanding of a political or social issue and get right to your heart, to your gut. With the movies that we show at TIFF, the way they most often do that is by showing stark injustice. For instance, migration is a pressing issue for the world right now, and there is a lot of injustice when it comes to how migrants are treated as human beings. But a movie can show you that injustice on an emotional level — the stark unfairness of the way people are treated. You see how we are all human beings and are made to question why one person on one side of a border is treated so much differently than a person on the other side of a border? You can put away all of the news coverage and the academic analysis and all that stuff — the argument — and you just get the feeling. And that feeling is a powerful motivator. It can drive you to act. Whether you decide that you want to learn more about this issue, or you want to help make a change, it can inspire you to want to be part of a movement. Art offers you a way to open your own heart in a way that other things often don't.

You are a very passionate advocate. In your opinion, are we investing enough in the arts given its significance that you just articulated?

The answer may be obvious — hell no! I have a humanities degree and I remain involved with Western University, and I'm aware that the humanities as a discipline, as an area of study, seems to be under threat and on the decline. Technology is incredibly important, but it doesn't help us understand the world fully. We need so much more than that. We need what we learn from art. I learned how to think critically through a humanities degree — through studying not just literature, but philosophy, and art, and music and film. I feel like I understand the world so much better than I would have had I just studied quantitative sciences. So yes, I think we need to support art much more. I think it helps us all become much more whole human beings. It's not art instead of science, it's art plus science. I think you need it all.

The arts have been a foundational element of human expression since time immemorial. They suggest the existence of meaning outside of ourselves and tap into universal elements of the human experience. What do you see as the role of film in creating a better, more interconnected and empathetic world?

There is a great film-making pair in Toronto — Jennifer Baichwal and Nicholas de Pencier — who make documentaries largely about climate issues. They have made films that explore water, and how industry is degrading the natural environment. They travel all over the world, and they'll show you how the climate impact is affecting glaciers in Antarctica and mining in Africa and how it's affecting forests, et cetera. That is useful because most of us are probably never going to go to these places ourselves, and we need to see what that looks like.

On the other hand, I think of films by Hong Kong film-maker Wong Kar-wai, which are about these fleeting, intangible moments between people, and about how people think and feel. Sometimes the camera will just rest on a character, and through the actor's expression you are helped to imagine what that character is thinking and feeling. Sometimes you don't even need words during that moment in the scene, because the structure of the film — everything that goes before it and after it — helps you feel like you understand how someone else is thinking.

That is a remarkable thing. Science has been trying forever to understand how the human mind works. Stories can help us do that. Beyond interior monologues in novels, film can do that in a way that doesn't need words necessarily, because the way that films are put together when they're done well, they work by image and sound more than by dialogue. That's the essence of cinema. Any art form can help you understand a human emotional state, and perhaps in a better way than much of what we have been able to learn through science.

You once said, "You can have all of the facts and figures and rational arguments in the world, but if you don't appeal to people emotionally, it's harder to win them over."[1] What have you learned about cinema's potential to help people to reflect, learn, and grow?

So many things. I feel like this is what we are striving for every day at TIFF. It might not have the same impact or the same scale every day, but that is always what we are aiming for. I'll give you what seems like a bit of a left-field example. A few years back TIFF hosted the world premiere of a film called *Knives Out*, which is essentially a caper comedy/murder mystery. [Spoiler alert.] It takes place largely in a big house, and follows a master detective investigating the death of the patriarch (and crime novelist) of a wealthy, dysfunctional family. The film and its

---

1   CBC Books, "TIFF CEO Cameron Bailey Reflects on Canada Reads — and His Emotional Connection to the Winning Title," CBC, December 16, 2021, www.cbc.ca /books/tiff-ceo-cameron-bailey-reflects-on-canada-reads-and-his-emotional-connection -to-the-winning-title-1.6278073.

structure are all leading towards a revelation. I hope this isn't a spoiler for you, but the revelation has to do with how we think about migrant labor. There is a shot at the end of Ana de Armas's character where she is drinking from the mug, and she has been underestimated and ignored and invisible through so much of the story, but really she was the mind behind so much of it. That was just a great thing to see.

People were taken on this joyful ride — the film is very funny and has a lot of entertaining things in it — but at the end there is still a poignant message, but presented in an entertaining way. People come out of the theater thinking about that. Maybe they start to question who is that character in their own personal lives that they may also be ignoring. That to me is what movies can do at their best. That is a broad, Hollywood version of it, but there are many, many examples that are similar.

So films can inspire us to change and become an agent for change — is that a criterion you use when you select your films for TIFF?

Yes! The other thing I would add is that we are not here to tell people how to behave through film — that is not what we are about at all. What we hope for or want is to get people to begin asking those questions for themselves. A great example from recent years is the film *Parasite*, which also won Best Picture at the Oscars. What is interesting about it is the directions it takes people's thinking. The film is a little bit of a Rorschach test — a lot depends on what you bring into the experience of watching it. It is very much about class, it's very much about how the servant class in the film and the ruling class in the film — the elite — are symbiotic in a way. If you ask people who have seen the movie, "Who are the parasites?" they will give you different answers depending on where they are coming from. To me, that is interesting because it opens the door to asking "How do we think about that symbiosis between classes? How do we think about how our societies are structured, and who is there to serve and who is there to rule? And yes, who are the parasites?" It's been fascinating to hear different people give you very solid arguments about how one family or the other family in that movie are the parasites.

What dimensions of leader character do you need to possess to deliver on the mission of TIFF? How do transcendence (creativity, future-orientation), collaboration, and courage interplay in your leadership and how you hope to create impact through TIFF?

The key word in TIFF's mission is "transform." So, to even begin to fulfill a mission like that, I think the first thing you need is the belief that people *can* transform. Not everybody believes this, but I happen to be very optimistic. I believe that everyone has the capacity to transform, and also that many people want to do so. Through our mission, we communicate that belief and optimism, or faith, in the limitlessness or infinite wellspring of human potential. Every year at the festival, and all year round as well, I see people get excited by things they didn't know would excite them. Confidence in human capacity is important, and then the ability to communicate that as well. I think anyone who leads will understand and tell you that communication is key. But communication, of course, is not a one-way street; it is not just how you talk, but also how you listen, how you observe.

I'm an immigrant twice over. I was born in England; I left there and went to live with grandparents in Barbados when I was young and then came to Canada when I was almost eight years old. I had to change twice — change my accent, my behavior, my dress, all of those things — very quickly. This taught me to observe, because the only way you can know what you're changing into is by really looking and listening closely. How do people speak? What is the cadence? All kinds of scientific studies will tell you that people speak at different speeds in different countries, or between city and country, so it requires understanding about what is the rhythm of how people talk. What is the idiom people are using? I had to do all of that as a child, and I do it as an adult almost naturally. I am always paying attention to how people communicate and, in a way, sometimes just try to mirror and find a common ground where we can communicate together. That is important to being a leader because it means you are really paying attention to the people you're working with. It is also important to be confident enough in what you have to say and what you have to share so that you're able to do it effectively. I think I, and many others, have learned that. You can gain it through experience, or just through conscious effort.

I'll tell you something else. We have a senior management team here, and we had a retreat last week. We were all sharing different things at the beginning of the retreat, and at the end of it, our CFO — who is the most rational guy around the table — said to me that he felt that I was most effective as a leader when I was the most vulnerable, which I felt was very interesting. Especially for a CFO, a pretty hard-nosed guy, to say that. But that told me something: that the emotional side, the openness, not putting up a hard façade as a leader, is really important. It's certainly important to the team we work with. It might not work in every environment, but for us, I think it's important.

What is the role of courage in your current position? In particular, for example, as you select movies where you have the possibility to set an agenda and signal things that are important. Can you talk a little bit about courage as an aspect of your leadership moving TIFF forward?

Absolutely. For me, courage is sometimes based on a projection of other people's expectations, right? Something seems to require courage because you anticipate a reaction by doing it, by taking that act. Sometimes you might be completely wrong about the reaction you're projecting, and sometimes you may be right. In the past here at TIFF, it has taken courage to program certain films that the majority of our audience might not like but that we felt were important, or that we thought advanced the form of the art of film in a way that maybe not all the audience would be ready for. Then, there is also the consideration of where you put those films, because you have expectations about the audience. If you put a certain kind of film in front of a big audience of two thousand people in Roy Thompson Hall who just want a good night out, that's different than an audience of two hundred people who are there for the most challenging film they can find. The courage comes in through the films you choose, how you choose to present them, to whom, and then also whatever expectations you're putting in front of yourself about how the audience's reaction will go.

I try as much as possible to be conscious about those expectations and sometimes question them. Is our audience really that conservative in this case? Are they ready for something more? I think that helps. Also, we are all part of different social groups. Even having an opinion about a film that is out of step with other opinions in your social group, the people that matter to you, takes courage too. That is something that I try to train our team to do, because if we just have groupthink when it comes to consensus around films, that is the death of our curatorial reputation. We need those strong, diverse opinions in order to do our job.

What do you believe are the great movies and stories that help us reflect and develop as leaders of character?

It's funny, because as you were just finishing your question, I was thinking back to the holiday season in late December or early January. My wife and I have a son who is thirteen years old, and we sat down and watched all three *Godfather* movies over a course of maybe four days. It was a lot for him, but he'd been asking about them. It's funny to me, because when I think of leadership in the movies, I think of the Corleone family. It is an example of a terrible leader, but Michael Corleone is a fascinating figure. He is someone who, in his youth, was doing everything he could to escape the brutality of his father, and his father's rule over that whole part of the Mafia, but then, he became even more coldly brutal than his father was. So, this is not a positive example by any means, but I think it is an illustrative example of leadership and how it is a kind of moral tale.

You watch the *Godfather* movies, and you realize what strength it actually does take to become a leader, and how sometimes the path of violence — whether that is literal or moral or emotional violence — can be the path that is the most seductive. I watch those movies now and I think, "Yeah, I learned a lot about what I want to do and to *not* do by watching the Corleone family." I don't have a great, sunshiny example, but I think *The Godfather* can teach you a lot.

Your passion for the arts is obvious. Is there anything else that you would like to share with the readers of the book around the arts and their importance to leadership, or the importance of leadership to arts? Any parting words as they pertain to leadership and growing? To develop not only as a leader, but a decent human being of good character?

That's a great question. We talked before about films that illustrate some of the big moral, ethical questions of our time. We show a lot of those films, and sometimes it's easy to say that the lessons for us, as people, for our teams — the leadership lessons — are there on the screen, and that's how people should behave. People should be nice to each other and that kind of thing. Actually modeling — that is a lot harder, right? I think that is something that I try to pay a lot of attention to so that there is not a lot of daylight between the films that we hold up as exemplary human behavior and how we, as an organization, behave.

The other thing that is important there, and this is a whole other conversation, is how does an organization behave in terms of its own ethics and its history and its priorities versus how does an individual behave within the organization, including the organization's leader? Those are very different things, and there is a lot of nuance there that needs to be explored. My job now, as the CEO of TIFF, is to make sure that TIFF is behaving ethically as an organization. But it is not going to have the exact same qualities that I do as an individual. I never believe that organizations are people — they are not people — but you have to hold them to standards that are similar to the standards that you hold people to.

It often seems right now that a lot of the media we consume is geared towards telling us our opinions are right rather than challenging us to think more deeply or even change our mind. We think the power of film to create curiosity and have people rethink things is more important than ever. Would you say that is something that goes into your leadership in terms of how you cultivate your team and your organization? And have you brought that into the festival itself?

You're absolutely right. It's funny — in our retreat, we talked about curiosity. That was one of the values that I said was most important to me and that I was looking for in my senior team as well. I look for it in our audience and also everyone we deal with. There are so many forces that are working to make our world smaller where it becomes just about you and your little circle and the things you care about. Whether it is the echo chamber of social media or the media we select or expose ourselves to, that is the momentum right now. What art can do, and what I hope that TIFF can do, is just push back against that and encourage people to make their worlds bigger, and broader, and deeper — and be curious about where that can take them rather than being satisfied with the comfort of a small world.

CHAPTER 4

ERIKA CHEUNG

Theranos Whistleblower and Co-Founder and
Executive Director of Ethics in Entrepreneurship

Erika Cheung was born in Los Angeles. She was homeschooled for most of her education until she started community college at age fourteen, and then went on to obtain a dual degree in Linguistics and Molecular and Cell Biology from University of California, Berkeley.

She was one of the key whistleblowers that reported Theranos, a health technology corporation, to health regulators. Her report helped lead to the shutdown of Theranos's clinical lab, which prevented the company from providing false medical results to thousands of patients. These events were covered by the book *Bad Blood* by John Carreyrou, *60 Minutes, ABC Podcast: The Dropout,* and Alex Gibney's documentary *The Inventor: Out for Blood in Silicon Valley.*

Currently, Erika is the Program Director of Betatron, a technology accelerator based in Hong Kong. She is a key entrepreneurial ecosystem builder in Asia. Her company supports technology entrepreneurs to grow their businesses all throughout Southeast Asia and China. She independently consults on healthcare and biotechnology projects.

You were attracted to the vision statement of Theranos: "Our mission is to make actionable information accessible to everyone at the time it matters. . . . We are working to facilitate the early detection and prevention of disease, and empower people everywhere to live their best possible lives." Can you describe what went through your mind when you began to notice significant irregularities in the testing and questionable results? Did you doubt yourself and what you were seeing? Did management attempt to gaslight you into questioning your conclusions?

I think especially as you start to uncover irregularities, the implications of what it could mean are so harsh that there is a part of you that wants to be wrong, and that does not want it to be the truth. I was very aware of the fact that I was young, that I didn't have a lot of experience, and the fact that there were many departments at Theranos, so maybe I wasn't getting the full picture about what was going on. I think that is what fueled my insistence on running more and more experiments. To say, "Okay, what is the validity of these machines? Are we seeing consistency of results — not just with one type of test but with many types of tests?" And then also to do a lot of error tracking to explore "What is the prevalence of this? Is it just happening with me, or is it happening with other people? What are we seeing?"

There was not a lot of infrastructure set up in the company to even figure out when there was an issue, how often those issues were happening, where they were happening, and all other relevant information. It could have been that I was doubting myself because there was no good tracker or log at that time. That is what drove me to set up those systems and to talk to people to join in on reporting that information.

Regarding whether I think management attempted to gaslight me into questioning my conclusions: there is a lot of runaround, where it was obvious that there was just a fundamental problem with the Edison devices — the machine designed to execute the tests — and their performance, and that they should not have gone live. That was really what was going on, but people were like, "Well, maybe you should look at this quality-control material over here and test out these three different brands," or "Maybe it's the case that we didn't do the quality control of the machinery the right way," or "Oh, maybe you should talk to the statistician, and they need to look at some sort of algorithm that is being applied to the machine."

I was constantly getting the runaround, to a certain degree, about these devices, where everyone was trying to punt me to a different person to say, "This isn't my problem; this is this person's problem." It was good because then, again, it gave me more confidence in the sense that now I had a pretty big body of evidence to suggest and to show people, "Look, I've eliminated a lot of these variables and they all point to the same thing — that we shouldn't be using these devices. They're just not good enough, even by our internal standards."

Then, as I started to go up the chain, I heard a lot of "you're not trained well enough" or "you have no visibility in the company." When I had my conversation with Sunny Balwani, the COO, he did try and gaslight me by saying, "What makes you think that you're qualified to make these calls? Have you ever taken a statistics class? You need to do the job I pay you to do, which is to process patient samples without question." At that point, it turned from everyone giving me the runaround to Sunny directly attacking me and saying, "You don't know what you're talking about. You need to stay quiet and just obey orders."

The meeting with Sunny Balwani to discuss your concerns was not very productive and you got yelled at. You then talked to George Shultz, the former US Secretary of State and a Theranos director, almost immediately after the meeting with Balwani. After your conversation with Shultz, you put in your notice. Please tell us about that meeting.

After my conversation with the board and George Shultz — who wasn't receptive to what I was saying — there were a couple things going on in my mind. The first was the notion of processing patient samples without question. That did not sit right with me. There was no way I could do that, knowing that I would basically have to not take into consideration the impacts that these tests could have on human lives. Second, it was scary. I was very young and knew I was quite impressionable, and to push beyond the boundaries or the lines of what I found acceptable was a scary thought. I knew that it was a real possibility when you are saturated in a culture that tells you to violate the very basic principles of what you believe to be right and wrong. It can start to become a situation where you lose your own position on what is right and wrong. I think I was conscious of that, of the fact that I was too young to start making these types of sacrifices and messing with my ability to discern, "Is this okay or is this not okay?" It is a gut check. You just feel sick.

I really tried to push things internally. I was working, at that point, sixteen hours a day. I was very, very committed to seeing this thing through. Actually, within the organization, I was garnering good visibility. I was working with the vice-president, with all of the heads of the different departments, [and] had gotten promoted to a whole new team because I really wanted to see this product through and succeed. But it couldn't come at all costs, and I wasn't just going to do it because someone told me to. There is a right way to do business, there is a right way to do lab diagnostics, and I just couldn't reconcile what was happening in the lab. I had to go. In that type of situation, you can really start to feel like you are the crazy one, so you have to move yourself out of the environment and become grounded back in your own ability to trust your own judgment.

How did you get access to the board?

I was good friends with Tyler Shultz, a research engineer at Theranos. George Shultz was his grandfather. We knew there was a big issue with proficiency testing. Federal regulations require proficiency testing for clinical labs that do blood work like we did at Theranos. Basically, the testing compares a lab's results on a particular specimen to the results from other labs testing the same specimen. The purpose of proficiency testing is therefore to evaluate the accuracy and reliability of a lab's testing operations. I looked at the results and knew it was bad, really bad. The disparities between what was on the FDA-approved machines and the Edison devices were so stark that no one could deny [them], and Theranos was lying to regulators.

I had funneled a bunch of information to Tyler, saying, "You need to take a look at this. This is the implication of this information. It's no longer about you and me and all the people in research and development. This is in the clinical setting, this is how we're testing patients. This is not okay." Tyler then went on his own little journey with CEO Elizabeth Holmes, because I knew that he was close with her through his grandfather. So Tyler and I, after I had sent him these results, were operating in parallel — me going to Sunny and the vice-president, and him going to Elizabeth. After I had my conversation with Sunny, I talked to Tyler and he let me know he was going to dinner with his grandfather, so I asked if I could join. I thought there would be strength in numbers. That is how I ended up going to George Shultz's house.

How surprised and disappointed were you when you discovered that Theranos's lab results were not only faulty but that their practices were completely unethical?

It was awful. I was devastated. It was hard for me to reconcile the reality of what was going on in the company. I really thought I was going to work for a company that was going to make a real difference to millions of people's health and lives. There is so much suffering in the world, and I have always been oriented towards just wanting to alleviate it, to be someone who says, "Okay, I'm here, I'm ready." This is how I want to pay it forward in life, and how I want to carry myself going forward.

Elizabeth was a lauded young entrepreneur. She was being celebrated on the cover of every major magazine. You couldn't escape it. You would be going to the airport and you'd see Theranos banners up above the terminals and such. I went into a pretty bad and dark place. I think to go from a young

professional with ideals wanting to make a difference and then
descend so sharply — it was a huge deal for me. I questioned,
"What is the world that I live in now?" I felt very powerless,
because not only did I know all this stuff was going on, I didn't
know what to do about it. I also knew that there were people
who would be aggressors towards me if I did anything. It is a
very disempowering position to be in.

You were only twenty-three years old when you decided to speak to the
Wall Street Journal on the fraudulent practices at Theranos when so many
others did not say a thing — internally or externally — including scientists
with PhDs and medical doctors. What compelled you personally to make
this decision?

There were other people who came forward, but in terms of those
that spoke to the *Wall Street Journal*, there was a small group of
six people who were anonymous sources at the time. There were
other people who had come forward, or tried to, but because of
the culture of fear and secrecy, they got shut down. There are
many stories coming out of this recognizing that people tried to
do something and Elizabeth retaliated quite strongly to destroy
their careers. I think coming out of it, it makes me recognize even
more deeply how these are very difficult circumstances to be in,
especially against people who are going to try to be right at all
costs, and win at all costs, and are willing to do anything to keep
people quiet.

There are so many different reasons why people decide not to
come forward. It was very easy to see how those manifested in
Theranos, right? Nothing was going to be done. I tried to change
things internally but nothing was moving the needle. There
is also the social rejection and being ostracized. It's not fun
realizing you won't be invited to weddings or other gatherings,
even though everyone else is.

Also, there is the fear of retaliation and what it is going to do
to your career. Theranos employed a lot of people who were on

visas, who weren't from the US. You also have lots of people who have families, mortgages, lots of other commitments.

I think in terms of why I decided to do this was because every door and opportunity that I saw to get the truth out, I was going to take. I was going to take it because of how crucial and important I thought this was to stop them from processing patient samples. It was so clear to me the implications that could have on people's lives. It was so easy to build those stories in my head about who these people are, how it will affect them, what type of damage that it could cause to their lives. Also, these people are trusting you. They are trusting you with this very delicate moment in their health experience, in most cases. I think that's why every time I saw a door open, I took it. It is just identifying the right people and being able to take every opportunity that you get to reveal the truth. I was willing to take it to the length I needed to.

You were followed and stalked by professional investigators hired by Theranos. Such an experience can be intimidating and threatening for anyone, but especially a woman (and especially a woman who is a survivor of sexual assault). Did you ever feel your safety was in jeopardy? How did you handle that?

Yeah, I did. That was the hardest thing about this — the awareness that it could affect my personal safety and also the implications of that on my family. I knew very well this could be dangerous for me, which is probably why I didn't tell my parents. I didn't want them to worry. I also compulsively exercised, just because I needed to find a way to get my nerves in order and to stay vigilant, in the sense of being cautious and aware of your environment. It is important to have that spatial awareness of anything that could happen to you. The little bit of paranoia in a circumstance like this is actually very, very valuable because it just makes you more aware of your environment.

However, there is something about humans and uncertainty where we can become our own worst enemy. I think that is what they were attempting to do to me. It was as though they thought, "We're going to stalk you just enough to give you the fear [for] your personal safety, to rattle the cage enough to let you know we're here, and we are pursuing you, but we're going to edge in and out so you don't know what the severity will be." That's a very hard circumstance for someone to be in — to always have the threat of danger, when someone is following you, not knowing where that starts and where that ends. Is it happening outside of your house? Is it happening on the internet? Is it happening when you go on a flight? I don't think there are any good answers for how you manage a circumstance like that. Everyone is going to be different, but it's very, very stressful. It is like a form of torture.

You are young, well-educated, and have ambitions. Did you try to maintain your credibility among your immediate colleagues and stakeholders of the company in the midst of the events that unfolded after you rang the alarm bells?

I don't know if I was all that thoughtful around having any type of foresight about how to make sure I maintained my own reputation. When I worked at Theranos, I was very genuine — no one could deny that. Yes, I was identifying problems that were happening, but I was just as diligent about attempting to find solutions. I wasn't doing this to give people a hard time. I was doing it because I was invested in getting things to work, and making sure that the organization was on the right track. I wasn't saying things flippantly. I really tried to gather as much evidence as possible, to give to people and show them what was going on. In terms of the people that I immediately worked with, I think that was very obvious to them. My immediate bosses understood where I was coming from. They understood that this was my attempt to make the situation better.

In terms of post-Theranos, I think potential implications [for] my future career was a bit of a fear of mine and why I stayed anonymous for a long time. I just didn't know whether they were going to retaliate against me and what the professional impact would be. Because I remained anonymous and did not tell anyone what I did for many years, I was able to transition to new jobs and opportunities. I moved to Hong Kong, completely switched careers, and was determined to build a whole new life for myself. At this point, I wanted to honor, "You have done enough for other people; what do you want to do for yourself?" I had always wanted to live abroad.

I wish I had thought about speaking up a bit more, but I didn't until afterwards. Even now, as I have become more in the spotlight, I recognize that there are definitely going to be implications for my career. But, I have decided to lean into the identity of a whistleblower. For me, the value of being able to be an ally for other people in these kinds of circumstances is far greater than the potential consequence of someone deciding not to hire me. That was something I had to negotiate with myself and figure out — especially now having gone on the record and having to deal with all the unintended consequences which I wasn't originally perceptive to.

I only got on the public record because I was subpoenaed for a court case. However, the judge also decided to release all of the depositions and the media picked it up.

I woke up one day and my friends said, "Erika, you're in Bloomberg." They were misquoting me, and at that point people said, "Erika, if you don't control your story, other people will." That was a big eye-opener and when I started to think about the question of my credibility. But I believe the record speaks for itself — everything is in the public domain now — me reporting internally, all of my emails, the experiments that I had run. At this point, you can't fight the numbers. You can't fight the evidence. Hopefully that speaks for itself.

As one of the key whistleblowers that reported Theranos to health regulators, you provided one of several factors that led to a criminal trial where founder and CEO Elizabeth Holmes was found guilty of fraud and conspiracy. This was a high-profile public trial. What dimensions of character did you have to draw upon when you knew your character would come under attack?

First of all, what I was comfortable with was the fact that I knew that I told the truth, and it's very easy to keep telling the truth because you don't have to remember anything. You look at the emails and you answer the questions, and you don't have to be anything but yourself. Secondarily though, the experience was hard because whistleblowers are often seen as adversaries to an organization. But that is not it at all. Actually, whistleblowers tend to be one of the biggest champions of an organization. For me, I really wanted to see this thing through. I cared for my fellow employees, for the products that we were developing, for the patients that we were serving, for the commitments we made to different stakeholders — that care was so clear in all the work I had done. No one could deny that and I knew that going in. If you know this about yourself, you know that you went in with a genuine concern for all the people you worked for, then they can try to attack you, but at the end of the day, you know that you did everything to try to do right by people.

With the testimony, I wasn't going in there with an agenda. I had come to a place of forgiveness. I had to in order to move forward with my life. When I got subpoenaed, I knew I was in the hands of being accountable to the work I did. I had to show up in court and maintain the integrity of my testimony. I went in only with the purpose of answering the questions and fulfilling my duty. Don't get me wrong, it was stressful — it is a hard thing to do. I had to remember things that had happened eight years prior and make sure that I did right by everyone. It is never fun to be in a situation where you know people have every incentive to want to tear you down; when you have people telling you that you're wrong, or who want to hurt you or whatever else. You have to face them, realizing that you have made at least two enemies — maybe more! — and sit there, not having any control over the circumstance or anything else. You're just kind of at the mercy of everyone else. It's not a natural process.

As a normal, everyday person, nothing in life prepares you for a circumstance like that. You have to really keep up your own strength and your own sense of assertiveness. To answer your question, though, dimensions and elements of character that I relied on included but are not limited to integrity, compassion, empathy, resilience, tenaciousness, vigor, composure, and conscientiousness.

What may have been the lasting impact of Theranos on the industry?

Any cautionary tale has this remarkable ability to show people what failure can look like. There is a power in that. It makes people ask, "How do I prevent myself and prepare myself, if I am ever in a circumstance or an environment like this, to not fall into the same traps that these people have?" That has influenced the way in which healthcare companies have thought about shaping their culture, what types of systems that they have designed for their employees to reinforce behavior, and the types of governance structures they need to implement. I do think Theranos gave everyone a wake-up call. I'm sure that the story will carry on for a long time. One of the things that make me hopeful is when I talk to companies, especially biotech companies or regulated industries — whether that is finance or agriculture or healthcare — they'll have the book *Bad Blood* and give it to employees saying, "This is an example of the company we do not want to be, so read this." That is definitely worth something — to have people demand better, have higher standards, and make commitments to make sure these types of things don't happen again.

I have to admit, however, that there have been some unfortunate consequences from the Theranos events. For me,

I was very committed to point-of-care diagnostics — it was plausible, possible — but you have definitely seen a hit in that field. It might not be the full vision of what Theranos had promised, but elements or bits and pieces of it would have been conceivable. And I think it has also had a negative impact on female founders because the comparable standard now is "How do I know you're not the next Elizabeth Holmes?" This is really frustrating because if you look at all the other fraudsters, the large majority of them are men. Investors are not going into those meetings asking that question.

You became an advocate for ethics in the tech industry, launching a nonprofit called Ethics in Entrepreneurship. How are things going? Are you optimistic or pessimistic about seeing a change in the tech industry after all that has happened — with Theranos, Facebook, Google, and the like?

The nonprofit is going well. I have every confidence in a generation of entrepreneurs who will say, "We want to do the right thing," not only by organizations, but by society at large. We really need to see [an increase] in society of people who are committed to the public interest, who are committed to creating more equitable societies, and so forth. Even if that is a small community, I'm willing to work for that small community — and that's enough for me. We're going to start there. We're going to start with the people who are really in alignment between what they are saying, how they want to make change in the world, and actually putting that into action. I'm willing to work with and for those people.

I'm always optimistic. I think it is the best course to hold on to hope. I believe that if you have a true, authentic commitment to change, to saying, "We can make this better," I think if you are able to inspire enough people and you give people enough of that vision, you will start to move in that direction. I think I will perpetually be optimistic and hopeful about the future, because maybe I just don't see any other way.

The importance of developing clear leadership principles is articulated by former Harvard Business School professor Clayton Christensen. In an influential article, he bemoaned the fact that not enough students and executives have given serious thought to the purpose of their lives. He notes, "Without purpose, people just sail off without a rudder and get buffeted in the very rough seas of life."[1] This often leads smart, capable, and well-respected people to make serious mistakes. Do you agree? Have you come to discover your purpose? If so, what is it? Do you have any advice for others who are exploring their own purpose?

I have thought about purpose a lot in my life. What is the meaning of what I'm doing, how do I live in alignment with the things that I value, how do I do right by my family, how do I do right by myself? I'm going to die one day. When I get to that point, am I going to look back at my life and say, "Okay, I did this well" or "Ooh, I regret that. I wish I did that better"? I think I have always kept the end in mind. I know that may be a bit morbid for a lot of people, but I have thought this way for a very long time. I think it is important to live your life with intentionality — to understand who you are and have that self-awareness. To understand what types of relationships you want to have with the people around you.

I've been intentional about saying, "I think the purpose for me is to help other people." I thought that was going to be in the context of healthcare and to alleviate some of the suffering that I had seen in the world. It is about what makes you feel alive in certain ways. For me, I am an operator, usually. I love being behind the scenes. There is no better compliment than the fact that no one knows who I am, and then at that last moment, someone is like, "Wait, who did this?" and then they figure out that I was the person behind it. Or the compliment "because of Erika, I got the job that I wanted" or "because of Erika, I learned

---

1   Clayton M. Christensen, "How Will You Measure Your Life?" *Harvard Business Review*, July–August 2010, hbr.org/2010/07/how-will-you-measure-your-life.

how to do this thing." Those are the types of referrals that make me feel good — that I can raise other people up, that I can be an ally to those who are really trying to pursue their goals.

Purpose is definitely important — at least going through the process of trying to figure that out. Meaning and intentionality are important as well. And understanding your own value is helpful when you're finding a career, saying, "I can add value in so many different ways to society and to life, and it doesn't necessarily have to be what other people dictate." I think that's where people get trapped sometimes. They think that if they make a lot of money, they will be perceived as being valuable, so they take a job that they don't feel good about because it pays more than another job they feel more of a connection with. As a young person, I started to notice people fall into that. It is then hard when you start down a track to switch to a different one. It is possible — it's definitely possible — but it gets a little bit harder with time. It will take courage.

What is the last leadership-related lesson or insight you would like to share with readers — those whose ambition is to lead people and communities to a better world?

I believe whistleblowers in many ways are the gatekeepers of truth and perspective. They are really an effective mechanism for governance. One of the simplest mechanisms for governance is someone standing up and saying, "This is not okay. We need to do something about this." I work in the technology sector in the innovation space, where you have these technologies that have unintended consequences. We didn't recognize or realize that they are having these detrimental effects on society. You need people to be able to say, "This is not okay. Something needs to change here." You absolutely need people who are advocates for the public interest. They are ultimately champions of transparency. Thus I believe that whistleblowing can be a very crucial and important function of society. We've seen how it's created positive change.

The story of Cathy Harris, a former US Customs inspector and whistleblower, is one of my favorite ones. Her story is well documented. She stood up for the rights of international travelers, many of whom were African-American women, who had been assaulted and sexually abused by the US Customs and Border Protection employees and other federal agencies. Her work helped to address discriminatory racial profiling and create policies that are able to protect travelers who come to the United States and uphold their human rights.

Never underestimate the power of your own and other people's voices. Believe in your own and others' ability to say or contribute something truly remarkable, and never take that for granted.

CHAPTER 5

JOAN CHITTISTER, OSB

American Benedictine Nun, Theologian, Author, and Speaker

Sister Joan Chittister, OSB, of the Benedictine Sisters of Erie, Pennsylvania, is the author of over sixty books and eight hundred articles. She has spent her professional life sharing her ideas and philosophies on numerous contemporary subjects, primarily: the rights and place of women in church and society, issues of peace and justice, and spirituality topics within Christianity and in all belief systems. Her book *The Gift of Years: Growing Older Gracefully* has touched thousands of readers with her reflections on the journey through life, and *The Rule of Benedict: A Spirituality for the 21st Century* has introduced readers to the classic yet timeless spirituality of the early Christian centuries, along with applications and connections for people in today's world.

You have said that it is "in community that we come to see God in the other. It is in community that we see our own emptiness filled up. It is community that calls me beyond the pinched horizons of my own life, my own country, my own race, and gives me the gifts I do not have within me." What dimensions of yourself have been brought into awareness or strengthened due to living a vocational life within an intentional community?

That's a well-phrased question. I'm not sure that I've heard it worded that way before, and it should be, because community is what enables the rest of me. None of us are completely *full of fullness*. We are full of something — our gift, our desire, our

64

goal, or our purpose for functioning in society — but community completes us. Community teaches us (in business, we call it mentoring), and it provides us with an essential kind of friendship.

Friendship seems to be going out of style, but all the great writers and poets talked about it. Then it collapsed. Now we have "buddies" and "acquaintances," and even best friends from grade one. We may spend time with these people, and they are a necessary part of life, but so many of us no longer have the deep relations and connections that allow us to safely bare our souls and our vulnerabilities on a journey to self-growth. Real friendship is when you don't have to explain when and why things hurt, however they hurt. Friendship helps us to understand our burdens so that we can carry them ourselves. It gives us the confidence to be independent as well as vulnerable. Friendship, in the way I envision it, enables us to become more authentic and not a duplicate of someone else.

Today, perhaps more than ever, we find ourselves in a room full of people we have spent time with but do not know. We can spend time with them, and they will still be strangers — unless those people connect and learn from one another, where they become a community. In my experience, a community will carry me when I most need something. Community will not let me down.

My community gave me voice. They encouraged me to go out and teach, to share my experience as a young nun. My community fostered in me a commitment to the higher things of life, to something more than awards, money, or status. We are all just who we are, but community stretches us. It stretches us spiritually and socially, and it certainly stretches us psychologically.

Friendships across generations, place, and time are the foundation of strong communities. Those friendships bind us and hold us fast to one another when the world around us threatens chaos. When change in our health, our work, our very faith, and our spiritual lives threatens depression or loneliness, community keeps us moored and stable.

Community is about hearing one another and supporting each other as you draw wisdom from within yourself and take it out into the world. Every step you take is stronger, but taking them all is a burden. Community encourages you, champions you, telling you, "You did great this time! Do it again!"

You are one of the most influential religious and social leaders of our time, particularly when it comes to advocating for justice and equality for women in church and society. Several of your stances (e.g., on contraception, abortion, and the ordination of women) sharply contradict the official teachings of the Roman Catholic Church. In the past, the Church has banned you from speaking at leading education conferences. And yet you have a large following: you are a much sought-after international speaker and best-selling author of more than sixty books and hundreds of articles. What character-related lessons would you like to share to encourage people as they advocate for a more just and sustainable future?

I don't know how much influence I have had. That is irrelevant to me. What is not irrelevant to me is the moral commitment to engage in the question. You can learn a lot by listening to everybody else's side, but you must engage yourself. Far too many people sit in comfortable chairs, saying, "I don't pay any attention to climate change" (or whatever the issue is). People yawn; they deny the call of action. But you better give it a little thought and change the discussion to one of discernment. You better be open to grow in these difficult and now daily emerging issues, from climate change to racial tension, pandemics, voting rights, gun violence, and more. These are the stories that threaten all of us, whether we engage them or not.

You must enter into the question. You must be open to your own growth. I don't sell anything: I don't go on any stage to persuade anybody to do anything different than the moral, the compassionate, and the necessary. I do not set out to destroy any part of society, but I will call every inequality an inequality.

The people who need someone to advocate for them tend to have no voice.

I am searching for the ultimate truth in every serious question. I am deeply involved in wanting honest agreement over these honest concerns.

I look at what my country is calling a Congress today, and I weep. The personal profit that is being made there makes it impossible for one of the finest governments on the globe to collaborate. Instead, it destroys itself and us along with it as an increasing concentration of politicians seek to secure their seats for years ahead rather than secure the future of the country now.

We should have the most peaceful and mature country in the world. Instead, the two parties won't work together. For either side. We now have a Congress without a conscience that casts votes not for what's best for the country but for what's good for the power base of the party.

We have to ask ourselves what we can do about this. The answer is "Engage." Get into local groups. Bring the issues up at family gatherings. Talk to people. Ask them for their position. Change minds. Teach minds. We need to be voting for something — not a person and not even a piece of legislation, but for an outcome that changes the current state. If we don't, we are all going to be standing there when the institution comes tumbling down.

The current generation — high school and university students — are showing more life, more direction, more goals, and more acuity of pressure than anybody else. These kids know that it is their kids whose food security can become at risk. It's their kids whose property will be destroyed by extreme storms if somebody doesn't deal with the ruthlessness with which we live on this planet. What we are not fixing today is only getting worse. And if it doesn't undermine our own lives, it will affect the lives of the next generation. It will certainly affect the lives of our grandchildren.

You have referred to hope as being "what sits by the window and waits for one more dawn despite the fact that there isn't an ounce of proof in tonight's black, black sky that it can possibly come."[1] In this era of converging crises, it sometimes appears that many people are no longer sitting by the window, are no longer hopeful. How do you cultivate hope in your own life? Are you hopeful about humanity creating a better future?

First, you must understand that hope is neither magic nor naivete. Sometimes that kind of hope comes out of religion or superstition: rub the knee of a statue or say something three times. Rather, hope is a product of experience, of getting older and wiser. What do I mean by that?

I wrote in my book *Scarred by Struggle, Transformed by Hope* that hope is not a magic act. It is something that you experience through your life. It is the result of experiencing and surviving the necessary struggles of life: pain and sorrow, depression and darkness, stress and suffering. With every experience, you get stronger. Your hope gets deeper, and your ability to deal with difficult challenges grows.

President Biden has a tagline: "We're going to build back better." His plan sought the largest nationwide public investment in social, infrastructural, and environmental programs since the 1930s Great Depression–era policies. I believe Biden's plan is based on the right attitude of looking at what went wrong to begin with and using hope to set a path for where we might go.

We learn by growing, and we grow by learning. If we keep those two principles together, no matter what happens, we'll do better next time. Maturity has little to do with age, and wisdom is acquired more from experience than education. We experience feelings we could not have felt before the struggle began. Before we experience loss, someone else's grief is an enigma. We don't know how to console the grieving person, what to say to them.

---

1   Joan Chittister, *Scarred by Struggle, Transformed by Hope: The Nine Gifts of Struggle* (Grand Rapids, MI: William B. Eerdmans, 2005).

But once we have experienced that loss ourselves, we "learn" the feelings and our response changes. We learn from our experiences and subsequently make different decisions.

Struggle can also sour us, of course. But if we choose to reflect on the struggle and our experience in that struggle, we can emerge stronger and wiser than we were when it began.

As for hopefulness for humanity, it's easy to have hope for humanity. My concern is about those who are *designing* for humanity. Many of our cities do not support the way we ought to be living. Buildings are unsuitable, roads are too narrow, bridges are crumbling, and water systems are insufficient. We have the resources, but the right people are not doing what needs to be done with those resources. Again, it's about community: creating a community of people with unmet needs who have hope that things can be different, and enabling them with motivation and drive to exercise their voice for change. We don't need extremism or destruction of other people. We need a country working together to do good things.

You talk about hope as waiting for the light but note that "darkness deserves gratitude. It is the alleluia point at which we learn to understand that all growth does not take place in the sunlight."[2] We don't sit in that darkness very much, even when it is offered to us with the seasons. Winter, for example, is a season of darkness and introspection, not a season of growth in the sunlight. Broadening our lens, are we at an alleluia point — a moment of darkness harboring seeds under the soil, a time that will serve to grow human awareness and understanding so we can create a better world?

I have no doubt that's where we are at. Your metaphor of winter is very apt, very important. Without all that thick snow in Canada on the ground, the forest is not going to grow in May. But the wait requires patience and understanding.

---

2   Joan Chittister and Rowan Williams, *Uncommon Gratitude: Alleluia for All That Is* (Collegeville, MN: Liturgical Press, 2014).

We are on the cusp of change with this dark moment, and the change can go either way. We have to do more than what we have ever done in the past. We must do more with building our resources and sharing them, and importantly, questioning who we are creating prosperity for — the few or the many. Without keeping that question uppermost, what we are doing is building an underlying population of low-paid workers. We have already made it impossible for a large swath of the population to save. They are given the money they need to stay just where they are. What kind of growth does that sound like? The middle class in the United States is being eroded, and that is going to erode the whole country.

I feel there is currently a distortion in the mind, in the soul. It seems as though today's leaders feel that the question of whom they are serving is not worth answering. We lack leaders who will make change, move towards something, for everyone. That's the foundation of the tension between the Democrats and the Republicans. And that is immoral.

Do you think this darkness — the inequity — is also global?

That darkness has been growing layer upon layer upon layer, and we have been acquiescent, nodding our heads and mumbling, "Umm-hmm." We need to ask with every building we erect, every venture we start, "Who will be sustained by this? Who will be lifted by this?" I move through the major cities of the world and I see families struggling to meet their needs. Are we back in Dickensian days when people were begging for food and we didn't care?

We hear some people voice concerns and call for change — until they become elected leaders. Then their voices are squashed in the political battle for control. There is no reason that we can't provide proper living conditions. Too many people are unable to access basic human necessities..

You are critical of government. What role do you see for business in helping solve major societal challenges?

We aren't the blessed and blooming American culture that we pretend that we are. Business has to change society because politics, it seems, cannot.

Business has the potential to make change. Look, for example, at the film industry. Something like one-third of the American population has shifted with immigration and people are grappling with that. But American television and film is trying to be more diverse, showing all manner of lives, at every level of life. It's refreshing. For instance, previously you would never see a Black woman starring in a television drama (or the American vice-presidency!). Now, suddenly, representation is everywhere. The film industry is changing our view of society. It's uplifting.

However, that does not deal with the economic realities. The Economic Policy Institute reported in 2019 that compensation for America's CEOs increased 940 percent between 1978 and 2018. Employee wages — compensation for the workers who earned the CEOs their money — only increased by 12 percent during the same period.

I can't tell you how enheartened, how enlivened I am to know that a business school is examining these issues and asking these big moral questions about who drives value and profit. Is it profit for the few who are holding shares in the company or is it profit for all stakeholders, including the Earth?

We are people who work at a business school. Some of our readers may be surprised that we asked you to contribute to our book. In part, this is because you criticized capitalism in your book *Heart of Flesh: Feminist Spirituality for Women and Men*[3] (and in many other writings):

---

3   Joan Chittister, *Heart of Flesh: Feminist Spirituality for Women and Men* (Grand Rapids, MI: William B. Eerdmans Publishing, 1998).

> We have trained our children to go for jobs that bring the quickest corporate advancements at the highest financial levels. We have taught them careerism but not ministry and wonder why ministers are going out of fashion. We fear coddling the poor with food stamps while we call tax breaks for the rich business incentives. . . . What's worse, we have applauded it all — the militarism, the profiteering, and the sexism — in the name of patriotism, capitalism, and even religion.

What are your specific concerns with patriotism, capitalism, and religion? What do you see as an alternative to create a better, more compassionate world?

One approach to doing capitalism better is corporate payback. If I build a factory in Erie, Pennsylvania, say, the community will give me land (or tax breaks or other incentives) and will provide me with a population of workers. My company will earn a lot of money that I need to pay back to the community.

How would I do that? Well, I would see where the kids play sports, and build sports venues where parents can go with their kids and safely participate in sports. I would open a conservatory for musicians. I would do a lot of things that this little city could never have afforded for itself. We can take a percentage of profits and put it into paying back, building back, watching the city change in front of our eyes, because we are here enabling that growth. Then, when I tell you what a great company we have, I am certain that is what we have. That should be Corporate America.

If this is the way we have to get our country back, if the politicians won't, can't, or don't do it, then that is what I'm crying for. Stand up, speak out, and don't let anybody stop you. If we want to see change in our organizations or communities, we must not look for someone else to create it. You have been created with gifts and a purpose. We cannot sit quietly and allow our gifts to be dormant: we must be willing to step up to lead the change. The world is waiting on you.

Our readers may also be surprised that we are featuring you in this book because you are a religious figure, and readers may believe that business and faith have no connection, no relationship. However, you have shared in *An Evolving God, An Evolving Purpose, An Evolving World*:[4]

> A world without a sense of direction, a people without
> a conscious commitment to reason and rightness,
> to quality of life and character of purpose, shape both
> the culture of the nation and the ongoing dedication to
> life by the souls that guide it. Only then can we know if
> what we leave behind can possibly spur commitment to
> creation rather than commitment to the detritus of our
> so-called profit-making.

What role can a business school play in shifting towards a commitment to creation rather than the detritus of profit-making? Should spirituality play a role in a business school (or any secular educational institution)? And, how does spirituality serve leaders of any kind, particularly in business and organizations?

I think we have difficulty with the word *spirituality* because we misunderstand the word itself. We take spirituality and religion as synonyms. They are not. Religion, if done well, should build a person's spirit to the point suggested by your leader character framework.

You have managed to do something I have never seen come out of another business school — a visual representation, a postcard for me, with all the dimensions of character that are needed for *great* leadership. Something more than good

---

4   Joan Chittister, *An Evolving God, An Evolving Purpose, An Evolving World* (Minneapolis, MN: Fortress Press, 2022).

leadership and something more than the talents that keep the trains running on time.

I want leadership that builds things so that a number of other things can happen. So that the builders don't have to worry about their rent because tenants pay according to their means. So that their children don't have to worry about their schools. So that women don't have to worry about being overlooked in all their intelligence and gifts. We need corporate councils in every arena that say, "How can we help? How can we support change and equality? What can we do to make it even more than you think it is?"

It's a very spiritual work, business. But you can't make it a spiritual work if you yourself are not spiritual — if you do not have some sense, some notion, of a presence of a higher power. However you may conceive of that higher power, it is your reason to be alive. I believe everybody is born with a reason to be alive, but most people do not examine that reason until they are aged.

But it would be so much better if we come to know our reason to be alive, our purpose, when we are young. Or at least younger. Where we begin testing our steps by asking, "Is this a goal worth working for?" It's a basic question. It's a spiritual question.

Spirituality requires that you consider why you are doing what you are doing. In our culture, too often we work so that we can do something other than work as soon as possible. We routinely work at segmented tasks that have no overarching meaning to us. But spirituality requires that we work for the good of our community, the world, and the human race.

We need to work to leave the world in a better place than we found it. Work keeps us involved in every dimension of community. It enriches and develops our lives on all levels. Our work is our gift to the world, and it is a gift to ourselves. It leads to self-fulfillment by giving us a reason to exist that is larger than ourselves.

But, without a sense of purpose in life and a sense of obligation to leave the world a better place than when we found it, we can work in places that dump chemicals into lakes and rivers without a quiver of conscience.

I've been very negative about business, but we do have some wonderful businesses in this country. They haven't always claimed their own greatness though.

Do you think socially responsible companies contribute to what you call that commitment to creation? Instead of profit?

Yes, I think some organizations do. And some organizations have declared that they want to be that kind of company. But we must give employees jobs that are worth getting up for. We're going to have to bite into some of our profit. The federal minimum wage in the United States is $7.25 per hour. Two or three states have also maintained that rate, arguing that if it's good enough for a federal minimum wage, there's no reason to change it in their state. And we wonder why we're teetering.

Every single time we allow another insubstantial minimum wage to stand in place of a living wage and we fail to speak out for our neighbors or the people in the next town, we too become part of the violence. We can reshape the world by speaking up. It has happened throughout history with people like you and me doing just that. We must at least try and sustain the intention of true, positive change. Without it, things will continue to stay as they are.

In our book, we emphasize the importance of reflection to the development of character. You have said that today we need reflection in the midst of chaos more than ever, to get the most out of life. Can you please elaborate on the need for reflection for personal growth? How can it lead to us living our lives "fuller rather than faster"?

You're talking to a Benedictine, and any Benedictine will tell you that at our core is lectio. Lectio divina is what you teach every young woman or young man or possible monastic coming through the door. It means "think." It is about reading and reflecting on what you've read. We give them a sentence that says, "Oh great God, enable me to do in this world what you mean me to do, and give me the strength to do it." There's your reflection sentence. I want you to think about it. What is strength? What is your strength? What is going on in this world? Where would you put your strength? How much of a part do you have in what's going on? What can you do about it? That's reflection.

If I can't answer those questions, I am not a spiritual person. If I am going to work with people to do something that is highly moral, then I have to start with why we are doing this. I must ask what my work will do for the world and whether it is worth doing. Who will profit from my work? What will happen to the next generation if we do this work at this time?

Many businesspeople and the organizations they lead are doing big things. These people should have really adult, moral, mature values. The kind of values your parents wanted you to have: Don't lie. Be kind. Embrace learning. Be courageous. Those virtues and values never went away; the demand just got bigger, more complex, and more challenging.

We all bring some tradition with us. It could be a religion, a cultural teaching. We are all grounded in a moral foundation. We live in a secular state, meaning there is no single religion or faith in charge. We are all here together, trying to do something good together. So then, let's get together and do it!

Do you have any final thoughts on how character can lead our way to a better world, or anything that we haven't talked about yet that you want to add?

There is one thing, and I'm going to go back to being a Benedictine again. The Benedictine order has lasted over fifteen hundred years. We were founded in the year 480 and we are still using the same rule book. We have not edited anything out of it. It has stood the test of time because the rule is simple. There are twelve degrees, and the cornerstone is humility. The Benedictine rule says, "Here's what you have to do to be a really happy and strong person who contributes to society":

One, recognize that you are not God. God is God, and you are not it. Try to get over it.

Two, realize that what God has given, we are responsible for keeping. Therefore, do the will of God. That's where climate change comes in: The creator who created this world didn't create it to be messed [up] like we're doing.

Three, learn to take direction from somebody else. That's a community thing that you'll learn from. Don't walk in like you know everything when you know nothing. Take direction for a while.

Four, endure. Don't grow weary. Keep going after this thing. Don't give up.

Five, six, seven, and eight are where things start getting tough. Five requires that you get to know yourself. It's self-revelation: tell yourself what you will not tell anybody else. That's a deep, frank, honest assessment of you, by you.

Six, accept life. Just get used to what is. You don't have to have the best or the biggest in life. Try to accept the normal things in life. Deal with them well.

Seven, remember that there are limits. You have limits; everybody has limits. See those limits, and honor them. Don't push people and things out in your drive to have the corner office, the high-ranking position, or the big salary.

Eight, learn from the community, from the people around you. Recognize their value. See how good they are, how smart they are, how very noble they are, and how they stay.

The last four — nine to twelve — are listen, never ridicule anybody, speak kindly to everybody, and be simple. You don't have to wear the long black dress with the red lining and come swooshing into every room. A pair of slacks will probably do it.

When you take those twelve degrees of humility, then you're ready. Be very good and lead the people, the rest of the people, in your world. You're ready now.

CHAPTER 6

LYSE DOUCET

Chief International Correspondent, BBC

Lyse Doucet, a Canadian journalist, is the BBC's Chief International Correspondent. She is often deployed to anchor news coverage from the field and report across the BBC's national and global channels. Lyse spent fifteen years as a BBC foreign correspondent with postings in Jerusalem, Amman, Tehran, Islamabad, Kabul, and Abidjan.

Lyse received an OBE in the Queen's honours list in 2014 for her services to broadcasting and was invested in the Order of Canada in 2019 for her "empathetic coverage of world events." She has a master's degree from the University of Toronto, a BA Hons from Queen's University in Kingston, and honorary doctorates from leading British and Canadian universities. Her journalism has been recognized by major media and charity awards.

Lyse is a senior fellow of Massey College at the University of Toronto, an honorary patron of Canadian Crossroads International, a trustee of Friends of Aschiana UK, which supports working street children in Afghanistan, and a founding member of the Marie Colvin Journalists' Network, which supports Arab women journalists in the Middle East. As a journalist who often covers conflict, she closely follows the efforts of peacemakers.

What inspired you to become a journalist, and what is the role of journalism today in our complex world? How has the profession changed?

I grew up in a small town on the northern coast of New Brunswick. We were raised Roman Catholic in a community where families not that long before assumed that a son or daughter would join the religious life. I had thought for a time that I would become a missionary, but acquiring knowledge was my passion. As a youngster, I clamored to be in school. I remember the excitement of buying my school exercise book at the corner store: it had a blue cover with the crests of the Canadian provinces. I also remember lining up to be the first person to borrow a book from our new town library. The book was about trees. I ran into the park next to it and read it from start to finish; then I raced back to take out another. Years ago, I found a late slip for another book I borrowed — *How to Be a Journalist*. My first factual proof of my desire to be one.

University opened my world. I went first to Queen's University, which was the biggest culture shock of my entire life. I went from a small town to a posh university with a different language. I then went to the University of Toronto. At university I was always running up against deadlines for my essays — not because I was lazy but because I always wanted to read more. I was insatiable with curiosity.

I realized that one way for me to continue my education was to become a journalist. Now, my education is travel, meeting strangers, and making friends around the world. Every trip I make, my eyes become different. It's never-ending.

Everything and nothing have changed in journalism. First, technology has changed journalism beyond all recognition. I began when journalism was done with teletype. The telephone lines were of poor quality, so I would type up my report and it would be read by someone else in London. Our height of technology at the BBC was a "mutterbox," a small device that clipped onto telephone lines to improve their narrow frequency range. Now, with my smartphone, I can go anywhere and be totally functional. I can take pictures, record interviews, prepare notes, and send content wherever I need.

Alongside technology, the multiplication of platforms has also changed everything. I am no longer just a television and radio journalist; I am also an online journalist and a journalist who should be present on relevant social media platforms. There is a dizzying array of platforms, many of which I have not yet engaged.

It is a paradoxical time: never have we had so much information, but never have we had so much disinformation, misinformation, misunderstanding, and manipulation. While I was initially reluctant to join social media, it opened possibilities for me once I did join. It was so exciting, so positive, and so inspirational. But social media has transformed from opportunity to weapon. Facebook was the tool for democracy advocates in Egypt. Now it has become a weapon, a tool used with vengeance by anti-democratic or authoritarian rulers.

Journalism is in an existential crisis. We cannot take it for granted. In my profession, we say we are only as good as our next story. I start every day saying that I need to prove the importance of what I do. There was a moment at the start of the invasion in Ukraine when large, armored convoys were steadily approaching Kiev. My greatest fear every morning was not that I would be staring at a Russian soldier outside my window, but that I would be unable to find the right words to convey the moment. The whole world was watching and listening. I was acutely aware of getting the date right, getting the moment right, getting the feeling right. That was my role as a journalist in what I say was "the war of our time."

Ukraine has been the most recent to show us the importance of shining light in dark corners. That expression may be a cliché, but it's abundantly clear that things happen in darkness. We live in a time with so much possibility to do good, and also the possibility to do so much bad, [and] to do it with impunity and utter disregard for any of the norms and values of our society. Today, I think of Ukraine, but if we had talked last year, I would have talked about Afghanistan. In the worst of times, journalism has a role to play in peeling back and exposing what is happening and in asking the questions.

What differs from one journalist to the next is the questions we ask and don't ask. The questions can matter as much as the answers. We must keep asking the questions. If you were to ask me how to strengthen our journalists, I would say, check, check, check; ask, ask, ask; and never take for granted that our profession is intact. Media outlets are closing down, especially the local newspapers, and people believe they can choose not just their opinions but also their own facts. We are at a moment when journalism — the fifth estate — matters more than ever. I tell journalism students, "You are the generation that could make the difference between the survival or the success of journalism; it is under attack, and you must not take it for granted." I beg students to do something with the tools that they have, in whatever way possible, to make this world a better place.

You often report from places of conflict, where the risk of injury or death can be high. What compels you to take this risk? How do you mitigate the risk, and where does your courage come from?

I don't call myself a war correspondent, although I respect the many colleagues who do. I choose not to be defined by war because I don't just cover war. I don't choose my destinations because of war, but I become attached to places I've covered and return, often when there is conflict. For example, when I first went to Syria in 1994, it was under an authoritarian regime. People never expected a crack in the monolith that was the Assad regime. But I've lived a part of their history, so when conflict emerged with the Arab Spring protests, I returned to continue to tell their story.

War is a dark place that can exceed our imagination. It is unfathomable and very dark. Leonard Cohen talked about the cracks that let the light come in, and I suppose war is one of those dark places that reveals pinpricks of light. Ukraine is the most recent example. In the midst of what I find to be unimaginable cruelty and devastation, destruction, pain, and suffering, the Ukrainian people have exhibited extraordinary resilience, pride, strength, and hope.

The privilege of being a journalist is being among the pantheon of leaders, generals, politicians, aid workers, doctors, and activists and telling their story. I am not on the sidelines but smack in the middle of this history. I still have not lost that sense of "Wow!" How awesome is it to have this role, which of course also comes with responsibility.

You ask about courage? I don't want to say that I'm ordinary — no one is ordinary: we all have a story to tell — but my upbringing was unexceptional. I grew up on the north shore of New Brunswick in a modest family in a small community, and somehow, I found myself in the center of world events, working for one of the world's biggest broadcasting corporations. But I am no different than anyone else.

My bravery — and your bravery — come from a multitude of acts in our daily lives. I falter. I came home from Ukraine and asked my brother to deal with a contractor for me because I didn't feel up to the task. My sister is a principal in a primary school and exhibits acts of courage every day. I believe that people rise to the occasion. Sometimes — more often than not — we find within ourselves courage that we didn't know we had. Even a child plucks up their courage to go to the "big school" for the first time. A university student plucks up the courage to take a course or to speak in front of the class. I find strength and courage within myself because I am blanketed with support: the people I meet, the teams I work with, the strength of my background, and the courage of my conviction.

Obviously I'm honored when people say nice things about me. I don't take that for granted either. But I try to minimize the distance by emphasizing that I'm in one situation and the person is in another. I have found the courage to get up every day to do what I must do, and so does the other person. Perhaps that encouragement is a sense of leadership. Leaders should not be put on a pedestal. There is value in drawing inspiration from what others do. We can turn it around and consider how in different circumstances, we could do the same.

I am particularly struck by everyday courage. When I went to Syria, people would comment on how brave I was. But when I stood in the queue in the border office between Lebanon and Syria, I could see a little girl with her Hello Kitty backpack and a little boy with his football. I laughed to think of my bravery: What about that little girl with her knapsack, the boy wearing the number of his favorite football star, and the mother who is taking those kids into Syria and probably not coming out? That's courage. Everyday courage is, for me, the greatest courage of all. In understanding and appreciating it, we can find that courage within ourselves.

How do you keep your emotions in check in war zones — or do you keep your emotions in check? Which character dimensions do you activate to be at your personal and professional best?

My role as a journalist is to report the who, what, when, where, and why. That is what is taught in a journalism course. But I've added a sixth *w*: wow! Tell us why the issue matters.

The facts are what we know. Sometimes, the news is fast-breaking and fast-moving. We have to understand the story as best as we can. We have to step back a bit to explain what is happening and explain the context, which is different from a personal opinion. I work for a public broadcaster, but some media outlets want their journalists to give emotion. My story would be, "There's been a suicide bombing in a market in Jerusalem. The medical crews are on the ground, and we believe that there are many dead and injured." An emotion-driven story would be, "I was standing in the market when the bomb went off. I was frightened and I felt . . ." The emotion-driven story becomes about the journalist. For me, making yourself the story is a huge red line.

Once, when I was in Jerusalem, I was walking towards our office on the main road. A large market was behind me. There was a big explosion with people running, some shouting, "Suicide bomber!" I had a choice: make a five-minute run forward to the office or a five-minute run behind to the market. Where was the best place for me? I turned around. By the time I got to the market, the emergency teams were there. The doctors were trying to attend to the dead and injured. The body collectors — they have teams that pick up the dead bodies — were there. And there I was, the journalist. It was a vivid example of everyone having their job. My job was to convey what was happening. To be as professional as possible. I could get excited and emotional, but if a doctor did that, the patients would not get what they deserve. If the people collecting the fragments of the dead were lost in emotions of "Oh my god!" they would not be doing their job. People can say that anyone can be a journalist, but it is a profession with demands.

Another big red line for me is between emotion and empathy. I do get emotional. I had extraordinarily rare access to a camp just outside Damascus. It was a place besieged. Nobody got out, and no food or medicine got in. I've never seen such devastation, deprivation, and trauma in my life. When we came out, I cried. I broke down and cried. But when I reported, I did not cry. The emotion would have taken over the story. Emotion becomes the story, and people watching it will no longer be thinking about the victims of a suicide bombing in Jerusalem or the terrible plight of the people in Yarmouk. They will be thinking, "Oh, Lyse Doucet is crying."

That is not my job. Even though we are edging towards that, I don't subscribe to it — and most of my colleagues don't. But empathy is crucial. There is always more than one side. My job is to convey, to try to understand, to give voice to, or at least listen to the voices of all sides.

Now, I do have an exception to that. Especially in recent years, I have felt no hesitation in taking the side of the people, especially the children. In the Second World War, the adage was to save the women and children who were close to the front line. In wars now, women and children are not just close to the front line, they *are* the front line. They are being targeted, terrorized, and traumatized. I have no hesitation in trying to convey that tragic reality to people.

People are suffering — people who have nothing to do with the machinations of big geopolitics or the ambitions of one leader or another. Their lives are being shattered. I need to convey that to my mother in New Brunswick so that it is as understandable to her as it is to former ministers and prime ministers, who also watch the BBC. Empathy allows me to try to understand and convey what is happening.

It's not just a question of troops and trenches. Something is happening to people who are no different from you and me. If you drill down into any story, no matter how complex or consequential, you will get a story about mothers and fathers and children and homes and streets and neighborhoods and societies. They are human stories that all of us can recognize and see our lives in: the parents who worry if their children will return from school, the father who wants a job, the mother who worries about how she can care for her kids, the university students who have their dreams. They have them in Afghanistan; they have them in Ukraine; they have them in Syria. That is what I see and try to convey.

My job every morning is to determine the main story of the day and why it matters. During the war in Ukraine, I was part of the main story slot on *Today* on BBC Radio 4 for six weeks solid. Usually, that 8:10 spot is reserved for an interview with a prime minister or president — someone really important in a story. I was part of that segment to try to provide a combination of military analysis, because we must understand why this war is happening in this particular way, [and] what it means to the people.

That's how I see emotion and empathy, how I see my role and the role of journalists in what and how we tell stories.

The last thing I want to say about leadership is the importance of the team. Every member of the team I work with has their own fantastic story. The only reason I can stay where I am is because they stay. They are not looking to be on the front page, but without them, we can't tell the story. I have twice included a photograph of my team — the people behind the camera — with a story, and now, every time I do a live feed, the interview will end with something like, "Thanks, Lyse, and thanks to your team."

I'm not sharing this with you as a humblebrag. The people I work with make my job possible. If they didn't answer the phone in their little cubbyhole of an office in London at two minutes to eight every single morning from Kiev, I would not be able to be on the air at 8:10. If the satellite engineer left or the camera person couldn't go, it would be just me and my phone, and I would not be able to do the job.

Respect is like that precious china cup that your grandmother has in her glass cabinet and only takes out for special people at special times because heaven forbid that you should break it. You have to hold respect carefully because if it shatters, you may be able to put it all together again, but it will never be the same.

I remember being a naïve journalist, twenty-one or twenty-two years of age, going to West Africa and realizing that journalism is a profession that can bring out the worst in people. It's competitive, it's backstabbing, and it can be egotistical. I'm not saying I don't have any of those qualities because you do have to compete, but it is a lifelong struggle for journalists to stay with their better angels. Some people succumb to their egos. But at the end of the day, we are covering a war, people are dying, and I am not going to argue about who is doing the six o'clock news. In the end, we must understand the enormity of the moment that we're in and treat that moment with respect. We also need to do our part to behave responsibly and as honorably as we can, notwithstanding minor transgressions, weaknesses, and failures.

There is incredible power within the art of storytelling to connect people beyond borders, language, and cultures; to see ourselves in others; to cultivate empathy or action towards justice. Do you see yourself as a storyteller? Can you give us an example of a story you told that created an impact beyond what you anticipated, either on yourself or others?

Ukraine is top of mind right now for most people. One of the stories that sticks in my mind reinforces my point that the news is not just about trenches and troops and soldiers. It's about the mothers and fathers, the love and everyday courage. A grandmother had just finished doing her pickling, so the balcony of her flat was covered with tomatoes in pickle jars. She was on her balcony with the pickles when a Russian drone flew by. What does the grandmother do? She picks up a jar of pickles, throws it at the drone, and brings it down!

That's the kind of thing I mean when I talk about everyday courage. There are more. Ukraine is full of them: tractors hauling away the tanks, Ukrainians walking into the line of fire in some of the cities, villagers coming out en masse — little grannies with their babushkas on, pushing back a convoy of tanks, chastising the young Russian soldiers.

I told these stories to people as a way of saying stop looking at the war journals, which talk about Russia having fifteen times the combat power of Ukraine. Ukraine has reminded us that wars are about more than metal. It's about mettle as well as the metal.

Again, I remember being at Yarmouk, which was subject to the medieval tactic of laying siege to an area, and the worst tactic came down to bread. We get up in the morning, we toast our bread, we butter our bread. You don't think twice about it. But they had no bread in Yarmouk. We interviewed a little thirteen-year-old boy, and when I asked him, "How are you?" he broke down in tears. He was being a proud boy with his father standing near, showing his bravery, but the boy was just in tears. The next day in my broadcast, I talked about the bread, and it really drew a response. The message broke through; it was something that people could understand. I sometimes feel in these, the biggest of wars, it's the smallest of details that can help convey something enormous. Something very small, but very, very significant.

Syria taught me something else about courage and stories. Journalists have to really listen. It's not just looking and seeing; we also have to hear and listen. But not just with eyes and ears. We have to engage in deep listening; be fully open to seeing and hearing. Every time I left Syria, the incidents that clung to me were those involving children. Children often appeared in our reports, smiling or crying and sometimes just as decoration because we don't talk to them. We were getting criticized because the last picture was always the child or the first picture was an emaciated child. I realized that I really needed to listen to the children, so I did a documentary called *Children of Syria*. Two stories really stay with me to this day.

I went to a child-friendly space in northern Lebanon, run by an agency. I was interviewing a twelve-year-old girl with a long braid down her back. We didn't use her real name; we called her Randa. She spoke Arabic. She told me extraordinary stories about her and her twelve-year-old best friend, Khouloud. The two of them were playing in the yard when a piece of artillery — shrapnel or something — hit Khouloud. She died in front of Rhonda's eyes. The way that children do, Rhonda described things in great detail: how the shrapnel went into Khouloud's neck, came out her back, and left Khouloud in a pool of blood. She explained how Khouloud was her best friend and the same age, and how *khouloud* means eternity, but Khouloud died at the age of twelve.

Then Randa told a story about how another missile hit their own home. The wall collapsed and the roof came down. Everyone survived, but they all had to leave. It was too dangerous to stay. So they left to go to Lebanon. I replied, "You know, you're so brave already at twelve years old. What do you want to be when you grow up?" Without a moment's hesitation, she answered, "I want to be a lawyer and get people out of prison."

I went on to the next question, but in my head, I was still on Randa's last answer. Why would a twelve-year-old girl be so specific about what she wants to be when she grows up? I made it my last question: "Why do you want to be a lawyer to get people out of prison?" (It makes me cry even to remember.) She looked at me and answered, "My two brothers went to prison, and when they came out, they couldn't walk." In other words, they were tortured so badly that they lost their legs. But this twelve-year-old girl was not shrinking inside! All I could think was "Wow!"

Another time, we went to a checkpoint, to an area that had been under bombardment by the Syrian military warplanes. The soldiers said to us, "Nothing is happening here. Everything is fine." I was trying to determine how I could find out what was happening down the road when the loudspeaker of the mosque started announcing the names of the dead. The soldiers couldn't stop the mosque and the announcements. I had my microphone and wandered somewhat innocently down the road just a little bit. A mother and her little boy hurried by, looking worried. I asked the mother if everything was okay, and she replied that all was fine. But her boy, who couldn't have been more than ten or eleven years old, spoke in Arabic, saying, "Mama, Mama, tell her what is happening! Tell this journalist! The helicopters are in the air every night. They are bombing us. We are so scared. Mama, Mama!" This little boy had courage beyond his years. He saw his mother was terrified. He saw this woman — a journalist from overseas who possibly had the ability to tell the story — and he just seized the moment and told me that story. Then, of course, the soldiers — they couldn't hear what we were saying — called me to come back, so the boy and his mother scurried away.

I was a part of a surprise reunion in a park in Toronto one day. One of the six children that we featured in the documentary ended up in Toronto. At the time, I was back in Toronto and was doing a story on Canada's sponsorship program for refugees. I was in the middle of doing pieces for the camera when a boy came up to me and asked, "What is your name?" The children did this when they were practicing English, so I replied, "What is your name?" But he was insistent: "No, no, no! What is *your* name? What is *your* name?" When I replied that my name is Lyse, they shouted in reply, "Lyse!" Suddenly, there were six kids and a mother running. It was a reunion and crying in the park! We ended up helping to sponsor them.

That was a long-winded answer to your question, but my point is that the stories you tell change people's perception. How you tell stories can make people sit up and take notice. When I spoke in Fredericton once, a family approached me after to tell me that they had decided to sponsor a Syrian family, having been inspired by my story. I'm not sure if journalism changes events, but it does change minds, individual by individual. People will hear a story that resonates with them. It strikes a chord because the story reflects something within their own life and gives it even greater meaning. I think that is one of the great things about journalism.

The challenge in journalism is to maintain that intensity, that sense of connection. Sometimes I'm grateful that we only have to write about it. The politicians and other leaders have to *do* something about it. Although it's not easy to find the right words to convey the story. People are savvy: they can tell when you're just repeating a line, when it doesn't really matter to you. They know when your emotions are genuine or when you're trying to make yourself the story. Television doesn't lie. You must tell the stories in a way that conveys that this is someone's life, just like yours. Journalists bring everything that they've already lived — their emotions and lived experiences — to their own reporting. That leaks out in the story and raises the constant question of whether journalism is subjective or objective. But we must get as close to the truth as possible while bringing to bear the way you see and the way you listen.

You have a strong sense of service and justice. How did this emerge in you? What were the profound influences on your values, and how have these values guided you?

Aside from medics, journalists are the only people who run towards a blast or disaster when everyone else is running away from it. The drive and passion to be in places that matter is like a physical pang. Not every story you do captures your imagination in that way, but when it does, you want to be there. You have to be there. That's what this drive is about.

I mentioned that I grew up in a churchgoing family. I had an aunt who was a missionary and other more distant relatives who were missionaries. But even without that, I have been affected by the maxim, "Do unto others as you would like them to do unto you." That's where respect comes in. And kindness. I believe kindness, alongside empathy, is an essential quality for leadership. Of course, the guilty secret is that you feel better when you are kind, so being kind is actually a gift to yourself as well as to the people you are being kind to. When we do something good for someone and they thank you, you probably feel even better than them.

Journalism doesn't have a hierarchy. We don't have protocol. If you're a diplomat, the ambassador will see the ambassador. If you're the first secretary, you can only see the first secretary. But in journalism, we can speak to everyone: the person who drives the car, builds the car, pays for the car, owns the factory, or is the president of the company. We can talk to everyone. I think my comfort with that comes from growing up in a small town where everyone was treated with respect, whether that was the woman at the corner, my farmer grandmother, the Assafs who owned the corner store and sold me my first school notebook, the mayor of the town, or the school principal — treating all of them the same regardless of their title.

It is hard for me to be categorical or rigorous about it, but when people ask about my skills in journalism, I usually

say that if I have any skills at all, it is from growing up in
the warmth and humanity — and the humor — of a small
community. I'm not saying that my little town was perfect, but
in small towns, you have to live together in a small space. There
are not many of you.

I've always been fascinated by the belief that people can be
clustered by nationality. Canadians are expected to behave one
way, British another, and French yet another. But that may be too
simple. When I went to Queen's University, I realized that some
people had a narrow understanding of Canada and Canadians
although of course this has changed since I was at university. I
remember being told then that there were probably eight people
from New Brunswick at Queen's, and I was sometimes made
to feel somehow inferior because I was from New Brunswick.
Some students would joke, and it wasn't a joke, that they thought
Canada ended at Montreal. That understanding of Canada
missed the special character of the Maritimes. Even though that,
too, is a stereotype. The mix of geography and Irish, Scottish, and
French cultures creates a particular blend of influences. I like to
use novelist Robertson Davies's line, "what's bred in the bone." I
love this expression because we carry our family, our memories,
and our ancestry with us. Scientific evidence now tells us that
we carry trauma with us from generation to generation as well.
I grew up in an English-speaking family, but I have Acadian
names — both Lyse and Doucet. So I carry that within me too,
for better or for worse.

In one of the many interviews you gave, you shared an interesting quote by
Italian journalist Antonio Gramsci that resonates with you: "I'm a pessimist
because of intelligence but an optimist because of will." Could you
elaborate on that please? Why does that quote resonate with you? How
do you, considering the dark places you do visit, retain hope?

Every once in a while, I have to check the difference between
hope and optimism because they are different.

Looking at Ukraine as an example, you can make a cold analysis of the statistics and facts, and you reach a conclusion that leaves you feeling depressed. But as I said before, if you look at the mettle, not just the metal, and the fiber of people — their hearts, their love, and their courage — you reach a different conclusion that leaves you feeling hopeful. Journalism gives you the privilege of living in the experience. You're at the coalface meeting people with the guns — and with the passion.

Witnessing everyday courage gives you both hope and optimism. The difference between the two is that optimism is a belief. There is some confidence about a successful outcome, a choice to take a hopeful view. I am optimistic, for example, that the Canadian economy will recover. Hope is an emotion. It's an emotion that we sustain by individual agency, even when an outcome is less likely. Hope gives you the energy and courage to get up in the morning and strive for that better state because you are animated by a belief that the situation can and will get better. If you don't have that inner hope, you may not even get up in the morning. You are not fired up by that sense of "Yes!" Hope says not just that things can get better, but that I can make them better.

The South African Archbishop Desmond Tutu used to say that we are all prisoners of hope. That conveys the sense of not wanting to give up when everything else tells you the situation is absolutely dreadful — not wanting to admit to yourself, or to anyone else, that the situation is without hope. I want to be in this cage of hope because I don't want to lose hope. Then the Irish have an expression, "The situation is hopeless but not serious." Everyone has a different expression about hope.

I don't think I could do the job that I do without having some hope. My colleagues joke about how I am always looking for hope. When I was in Yemen, covering the world's worst humanitarian crisis, my colleagues found me a group of artists who were painting murals, saying they found me a hopeful story.

One of my colleagues tends to depict stories as dark and bleak, whereas I prefer to inject a little bit of hope into my stories. People tell me that they prefer to watch my stories. Trying to keep hope alive is an important thing. It may seem to be an outlandish way of approaching things, removed from the bare bones of reality, but I've learned, time and again, that things can turn out differently from what you might have expected or from what every analysis told you. I think you must keep that margin of opportunity open until, of course, all is lost. Sadly, some Afghan friends began to say last year, "We've lost our houses, we've lost our loved ones, and, worst of all, we've lost our hope." Hope is such a powerful ingredient.

Optimism and hope may be part of leadership, but you can't pretend. It has to be coursing through your veins. Once I was on a plane with two colleagues, flying from Kabul to the west of Afghanistan. The producer had never been there before, and the cameraman was clearly stressed. All of a sudden, there was knocking against the plane. I could see the other two looking at me, nervous. I was thinking that this is normal, it's Afghanistan, and something must be wrong with the plane. Later, they told me that they were thinking that someone had attacked the plane or was firing at the plane. It turned out to be a bird. There was a bird under the plane. My colleagues told me that they were watching me; they figured that I looked calm and that it wasn't possible that we would die. It's that sort of thing, leading by example.

My colleagues will make jokes about me being hopeful, but I think they pick up a little. Why do this job if it's all going to be doom and gloom? I find in war zones, people also want humor — the most wicked kind of humor. You cannot live dreading danger without laughing; otherwise, you cry. Of course, you do cry, but laughter brings out the humanity in a situation, and in situations where humanity is shattered, you do whatever you can to bring it back. Laughter and hope, at least for the moment, ease the pain.

There is the expression from the Sufi poet Rumi that when a door closes, a window opens. I prefer to say that if you miss your flight, there is a better flight to take. What can seem initially to be horrid can turn out to be better. August 15 was the day that Kabul fell to the Taliban, and it was, and still is, an absolutely devastating day of existential dread. So many Afghans, many of them friends, lost everything, including their sense of self and sense of purpose. Everything that defined them had been destroyed, including a country to which they may never return.

I was invited to speak at a meeting of the Journalists for Human Rights — a Canadian organization. There were a lot of people attending the event, including Afghans. I told the story about August 15 to them and reminded them that August 15 was also the date when the Acadian people turned Le Grande Arrangement [The Great Expulsion] from tragedy into triumph. In 1755, and for years after, the British ran the Acadians off their land, burning houses, putting people out to sea, chasing them into the forest — an event described by some lawyers as Britain's first ethnic cleansing. Britain tried to destroy the community, its independent spirit and way of life, but the Acadians came back.

If I could cover an event in history, it would be August 15, 1881, when the first national Acadian convention was held in Memramcook, New Brunswick. That was a day of Acadian renewal and identity. Over centuries, the British had let the Acadians come back, not to their original lands but at least to the area. They found a sense of self, purpose, and survival. Now the Acadian people have a flag, a national day, an anthem — everything short of statehood. It is a story of survival and maintaining independence in the midst of feuding great powers — the British and the French.

I respect most people having a sense of self, not wanting to be, in this case, British or French. I respect people who are themselves and proud of it. A sense of self leads to confidence and humor. You can't laugh at yourself unless you are confident about yourself. That's how we can draw on our own history to say that out of bad, something tragic, can come triumph. We don't want the correction to be so tragic or take centuries, but sometimes history has a way of being correct. We have lived the example of "bred in the bone." Generations before us have lived through the frailest of hopes and clung to the thinnest of threads because of their history and ancestry. We must hold fast to the stories.

I'm constantly talking about the power of words. A century after the Acadian debacle, Henry Wadsworth Longfellow wrote an epic poem, called *Evangeline*, about two lovers who are separated during the expulsion, and they meet at the very end. The story was popular in the United States and eventually crossed the border to Canada — a poem in English by an American who had never been to Acadia. The church spread the story and the schools began teaching it. Centuries later, the story is staged every year across Acadia and in Acadian communities around the world. This story about Evangeline and Gabriel has helped to give Acadians through the centuries their sense of self, their identity, and their sense of place and purpose. One of the great American poets found a way to give people who had lost almost everything a sense of self and hope. Words do not end wars, but they can help.

Words are an ingredient of leadership. The kind word, the word at the right time, the right tone, and sometimes no words at all. They make a difference in people's lives. Whether we use them in our profession — in this case, journalism — or as leaders, words are our magic wand. We can use them to make things good, or, conversely, they can be used to turn something very bad.

People tell me their stories because they want their story to be told, but I am still amazed. I can go around the world and approach strangers or friends and say, "Hello, I am Lyse Doucet. Can I ask you a question?" People open their hearts and homes and offer a cup of tea. We're often approaching people at their darkest hour, when they are sharing their last bit of bread. That's all they have, but they share it with you. With dignity. Respect and kindness are magical and powerful ingredients if you use them wisely and kindly. But you can't pretend; you must be genuine. People know the difference.

CHAPTER 7

TRACY EDWARDS, MBE

International Sailor and Founder, The Maiden Factor

Tracy Edwards was expelled from school at fifteen and began sailing as an on-board cook. She became a professional sailor in 1980 and, in 1985, was the first woman to embark on the Whitbread Round the World Race as a crew member of *Atlantic Privateer*.

In 1990, Tracy won international fame as the skipper of *Maiden* and the first all-female crew to race the Whitbread. *Maiden* won two legs and came second overall in her class, the best result for a British boat since 1977 and unbeaten to this day. Tracy was awarded an MBE (Member of the Most Excellent Order of the British Empire) and was the first woman to receive the Yachtsman of the Year trophy.

Following her success with *Maiden*, Tracy, with an all-female crew, entered the Jules Verne Trophy for the fastest circumnavigation of the world. During their attempt, Tracy and her team broke seven world records. She retired from sailing when pregnant with her daughter Mackenna, but later went on to manage other successful racing crews and broke many more records.

Today, Tracy is the founder of The Maiden Factor, a foundation committed to raising awareness and fundraising for the education of the 130 million girls worldwide who are currently denied this basic right.

What motivated you to put together an all-female crew to sail around the world in the 1990 Whitbread Round the World Race (now known as The Ocean Race), arguably the toughest test of a team in sport?

I initially put *Maiden* together for a quite selfish reason. In 1985–86, as the only female crew member of *Atlantic Privateer*, I was the first woman to ever race on an ocean maxi [a racing yacht over twenty-one meters in length] in the Whitbread. I was the cook, of course, because at that time a woman would never be given any other role. In fairness, I wasn't a great sailor, that's for sure, and I wouldn't pretend to be, but I *could* navigate, and that was where my passion lay. I took a huge interest in the navigation of the race (I think I drove the navigator absolutely nuts with all of my questions). But, I had this incredibly profound thought that, within my lifetime, likely no man would ever let me navigate on a boat in a round-the-world race. I was twenty-one at the time and that thought shocked me to my very core. It was the first time, really, that I understood the depth of misogyny and patriarchy in ocean racing and the overwhelming maritime history which prevented any change.

But, I had a deep desire to navigate. I knew the only way I was going to be able to do that was to put my own project together: to get my own boat, to raise my own money, to put my own team together, and then I'd pick myself as navigator. That was my first thought. My second thought was "Maybe there are other women that want to prove that they can race around the world." So, ultimately, *Maiden* became an all-female crew through an organic process. At the time, it wasn't, "Oh my god! I'm a feminist, and I've got to put together an all-female crew!" Although, later on, obviously, I did become a very committed feminist. But, to answer your question, it was originally a selfish reason that ended up becoming an overwhelming drive and need to change everything in ocean racing.

You were twenty-four years of age when you started the planning process for the grueling race. You had (and continue to have) a deep love for ocean racing. How did you make sure your youth did not lead to overconfidence or reckless behavior that put you and the crew in danger because, as you said in the movie *Maiden*, "the ocean is trying to kill you"?

Well, at the time, I had no self-confidence. It would have been unfathomable to me to have overconfidence to such a degree that it would lead to reckless endangerment. That said, what I did have confidence in was us as a team. I had confidence in the project. Also, by participating in the 1985–86 Round the World Race, I learned so much about how to put the project together. I had actually been such an integral part of the '85–'86 project without realizing it. It's typical: you throw a woman in amongst a team of men and she will end up organizing everything, and that's the way it ended up.

So, practically, I knew I had the skill level to do everything I needed to do to build a successful project. What I didn't have confidence in was myself as a skipper. I knew I could probably organize this, raise the money, and get us to the start line (although there were moments when I didn't think that would happen either). But, I wasn't overconfident in a way that would risk our lives. Having said that, we obviously did risk our lives, but I felt that all the risks we took were calculated.

In a TED Talk that has over 2.5 million views you share the following quote: "Stop being a bystander in your own life, and start taking part."[1] Can you please give that quote some more color and describe how that has guided your ocean racing career?

I was doing my second transatlantic trip from Antigua over to Portugal. We were probably about five or six days into the trip and the skipper, Julian, asked me if I could navigate. I said, "Of course I can't navigate. I was expelled from school before long division! I've always been told I'm useless at maths." His response was "Well, don't you think that's a bit irresponsible?" When I asked him why, he asked me, "What happens if I fall

---

1   Tracy Edwards, "Stop Being a Bystander in Your Own Life," Ted, posted June 2020, www.ted .com/speakers/tracy_edwards. Tracy explains how she went from school dropout to skipper of the first all-female crew in the toughest race on the oceans.

over the side? What would you do?" When I told him that I didn't know what I would do, he then asked me, "Why are you being a bystander in your own life? Why aren't you actually taking part?" This was the second most profound thing I had ever heard in my life, and I just thought, "Bloody hell! Why don't I know how to navigate? Why am I just playing around at this?" I told him that numbers look like hieroglyphics to me, but "If you can teach me to navigate, please fill your boots!" In two days, he taught me to navigate. I remember thinking at the time that if my math teacher's response to me asking him why I needed to learn maths was "If you learn math, you can be a pirate," it could have changed everything! It was just such a celebratory lesson.

Navigation then became my passion. It was like someone had showed me magic. I couldn't believe that with just the sun, a horizon, a book of tables, pencil, and paper chart, I could find out wherever I was in the entire world. That, to me, was power. It was the first time in my life that I'd ever felt that I have power. I've never gotten over that. So, you know, not being a bystander in my own life, I do admit that I have taken it to a slightly extreme degree, but I kind of get what Julian meant.

In your response just now, you said it was the second most profound thing you had ever heard in your life. What was the first most profound thing?

When my mom said to me, "Every human being on Earth is good at at least one thing." I think she had her fingers crossed behind her back.

From the start of the race, and throughout the race, the *Maiden* crew had to fight the notion that women had no business competing in what was seen as a man's game. How did you deal with the many nasty, derogatory, sexist, and misogynistic comments as well as the outward anger directed at the crew and you? Have things changed since your monumental achievements in ocean racing?

I think that in a way it was very helpful — that sheer anger and disbelief that we women were stepping out of our roles — the utter gall of us! How dare we think we could take on the male preserve? This space supposedly belonged to them, remember. I do actually think back to then; I was only twenty-three when I started raising the money for that race and telling everyone I was going to put together an all-female crew to race around the world. So I do kind of understand the "What!?" And, I often wonder if we hadn't had such huge pushback, would that have made us a little bit more relaxed about the race? I think the reason we were so successful, not just in getting to the start line, but in the race itself, was how hard we had to fight for it. By the time we crossed the start line, we were battle-hardened warriors because we had already been through so much. And, importantly, we were so utterly focused on the battle ahead. I think that maybe if we hadn't had all those things to deal with — with men telling us you can't do that, and you're too weak, and you're too pathetic, and you're not intelligent enough — would we have had that anger and that passion that gave us the drive?

What's changed? Not enough has changed. We have now had 102 young women through the Maiden program, and through apprenticeships, and we hear the same stories now from young women as we were telling thirty-five or forty years ago. Which is shocking!

Today's women sailors are so much better than we were. They are just amazing and it is great to see those numbers climbing. There are not only many more women sailors, but there are many more skippers and many more navigators. They all have extensive experience under their belts, which we didn't have in my time. *But*, they are still not getting on the big boats with big money. They are still having to do all-female crews. The point of doing Maiden was not the all-female crew in and of itself but to prove that women could race around the world. Ocean racing is one of the very few level playing fields for men and women in sport. What we are still hearing from the girls who are trying out for Maiden is "We can't get on the big boats with the big money because we don't have the miles. We don't have the miles because we can't get on the big boats." It's this never-ending cycle, which is why we would give them the miles on *Maiden*, and give them certifications and everything that goes with that. I think this is really important to point out.

But to be clear, this isn't about individual men stopping women getting onto boats. This is the patriarchy. Almost every male sailor I know says, "Of course we should have women on boats. Why wouldn't we? There are all these amazing women sailors, absolutely!" Many of them do have one or two women on the boat. But, in the end, it's about breaking the patriarchy, breaking this maritime tradition that exists in England and likely elsewhere.

You had to build a team from the ground up. Ocean racing skills are a key ingredient for success. However, in presentations, you noted that the character component cannot be discounted. What were you looking for character-wise in your crew? And how did you assess which women had what it takes to operate together in an elite team?

I think this is quite a difficult question. We had the luxury of taking two years to find our crew and test them out and try them out in different combinations and situations. This question makes me think of Ernest Shackleton, who is my absolute hero. The legend of the advert he put in the newspaper when he took his trip down to the Antarctic for the expedition there was as follows: "Men wanted for hazardous journey. Low wages, bitter cold, long hours of complete darkness. Safe return doubtful. Honour and recognition in event of success." I just thought, "Great advert!" And, Shackleton did receive a deluge of applications. So for Maiden, this was the messaging I gave out: "Nothing is easy about the race. Nothing at all." I had young women literally turning up on my doorstep and I would have to say to them, "I can't pay you. There is a crew house, but you'll have to get a job to buy your own food. Then you'll have to work restoring the boat . . ." That was quite a defining moment with some realizing this really wasn't for them, and others saying, "Okay, I'm in." So that was the first little signal to indicate this might be one of the crew we were looking for.

So then, we turned the numerous disadvantages or obstacles we faced in leading up to the start of the race into an advantage, because by the time we had all gotten through the process of restoring the boat, we knew each other inside out. I could look into their souls. I knew their very being. I had seen them at their worst moments. I had seen them angry, upset, tired, exhausted, and frustrated. And how you behave in those moments is what makes you who you are. It doesn't matter that you have those moments or you get downhearted or you want to give up, because it would be superhuman if you didn't experience those emotions sometimes. But, it's what you do with those feelings to overcome them. It's like the expression, "You're a fool if you're not afraid of the ocean, but it's what you do with that fear that counts." That's the indefinable thing that I was looking for — that character, that backbone. And to me that was essential because it almost doesn't matter how much experience you've got or what you know or how many qualifications you've got or how much you've studied, or how many miles you've got under your belt — it's your character that's the most important thing.

How did you empower one another amid all the highs and lows? We ask this because we understand that patriarchy can be internalized by women, and women are often socialized to pit themselves against one another, or be mistrustful of each other, and so forth. We can imagine there would be no room for that on a boat, especially one where you are risking your life. So what lessons did you learn about how women can support and empower each other?

I think that is such an interesting question because I must be one of the very few people on the planet, if not the only person, that has ever raced around the world on a boat with either seventeen men or twelve women. I have seen characteristics of both genders and it is absolutely fascinating. One is not better or worse, but they are just very different. Men tend to externalize their frustrations and their anger, and so it radiates outwards. For example, they will just shout at one another. In a way, although that can be quite intimidating as a female in that male environment, it's also . . . I don't want to say healthy, but it's out, it's done, it's gone, and then they move on to the next thing. Women, however, tend to internalize. They will harm themselves. I often find when women are anxious or depressed or worried, we go inwards. Men go outwards and attack outwards, and we attack inwards. Once I understood that difference, it was really important for the crew members of the *Maiden* to verbalize and really articulate our support for each other. With men, it seems they tend to leave each other alone, or they grunt at each other or just give a pat on the back. We need more than that. We needed to actively encourage talking and externalizing any anxieties we were feeling. Also, I found that we were very noncompetitive with each other. There were very few egos on the boat. Actually, I don't think there were any egos. Very different with men — lots of competing, lots of egos. Not in a detrimental way, it was just my experience of how they function, and it worked for them. But it wouldn't work with us. So, it was as though we had to build each other up, because we wouldn't build ourselves up. We can be our own worst enemies.

Can you share with us a defining moment — either in the lead-up to the race, or the actual race — that helped to shape your leadership and character? What was the situation? What did you learn from working through that defining moment?

I think the time that I finally became the skipper of the boat — even though I actually didn't want to be the skipper. I was going to be the navigator. I didn't in my wildest dreams think I could skip *Maiden*. I brought Marie-Claude Kieffer on the boat as the skipper. There was a total breakdown in communication, which was absolutely my fault. I had suddenly realized that I was a control freak and didn't want to give any control or power away. This is something I learned about myself which I hadn't realized before! Unfortunately, she was on the receiving end of that. I handled it really badly. I didn't communicate properly, I didn't give her a chance, and we ended up in a battle against each other, which was horrendous for everyone else. When I did finally sack her — because at that point I had no choice, I had been pushed into a corner — I had to step up to the plate.[2] But something within me kicked in, something that I also didn't previously know I had. It was the first time in my life that I had ever marched myself into a situation and completely dealt with it. I suddenly had no fear, no qualms. I thought, "Can I skip this boat? Well, I have to now. I've left myself with no choice!" I had to make sure that the crew, who were threatening to leave, stayed. I had to restructure the team. I didn't miss a stride. When I look back on it, I am really proud of how I stepped up after the incident with Marie-Claude. I dealt with that situation, I think, very well.

How did you stay mentally strong during the nine-month race with more than 59,000 often grueling kilometers? People have said that everything is unpleasant about the ocean.

Human beings are extraordinary. Until we are put in certain situations, I don't think we have any idea what we are capable of. When you're at sea, you are truly fighting for survival. And you are so focused on survival, and so focused on living through to the next day that you don't really need to consciously motivate yourself. Staying alive is a really good motivation! You may have

---

2   Tracy Edwards fired Marie-Claude Heys (formerly Kieffer) just before the Whitbread Round the World Race. However, as the saying goes, time heals all wounds. Heys is now deeply involved with The Maiden Factor and serves as a skipper; see www.themaidenfactor.org/meet-the-crew.

times where there is quietness or a lull in all of that where you need to remind yourself that you're racing, and you need to race fast and everything else.

I feel like in our world today, many of us are in a weird dynamic where we are living in this false sense of fight or flight. It can be an almost constant state within us now. What I mean by that is that it seems like every morning I turn on the news, the anchor is saying, "And here's your thing to worry about today! You can add to your list of worries — which already includes global warming, that Vladimir Putin's going to nuke us all, the rising cost of everything — and this morning, AI! Add that to your list of things to worry about." We are so deluged by crises all the time! I often feel that there isn't any more room in my brain left for anything else to worry about. It is a constant and negative relationship with the responses of fight or flight. Whereas, on the ocean, when you are physically up against the immediate crisis of survival, those responses actually help.

I did a lot of talks during the COVID pandemic and I thought it was interesting how little people understand about resilience. We all build up resilience all the time, every day. I have found that it is often seen as an unattainable thing and [something] that only strong people have, which I think is rubbish. I remember doing a talk at a school over Zoom and one of the kids said, "Miss, it's easy to understand that you have resilience because you're old." I said, "Yes, I am. But, you can learn how to have resilience. You can build it up every single day. Just be aware of your surroundings, and the lessons you learn in a day. Store them, remember them, to learn to build your resilience." I think there are so many things that we don't understand about ourselves. Human beings can be ridiculously inept at using what we've been given — the power in our mental and physical states.

We can only imagine that on *Maiden*, the flight option wasn't really there. There's nowhere to go! So, you have to fight. You have to build up that resilience. Perhaps that is a lesson and reality we need to take to heart amid our current crises like global warming or conflict and so forth. There is no getting off this boat. We have to choose to fight to create the change necessary for a better future.

That's a very good point. There's no Planet B.

Most of the time you were on a small boat with eleven other sailors, dealing with personal and racing issues under sometimes extremely challenging circumstances, yet at the same time felt a need to perform at peak level. What is your advice on creating a workplace culture that enables individuals to be their very best?

This may be obvious, but it is the way we treat each other, and by having respect for each other that makes a profound difference. I also think that giving each other space to grow is critical. None of this is rocket science, but it is hard to do sometimes. Thankfully, I have sailed with great skippers and had many awesome mentors. One of the things they helped me realize was the importance of the manner in which you speak to people. For example, as a leader you could bluntly say, "Don't do it like that." Rather, I have learned that a better approach is to say, "Have you thought about doing it like this?" The use of language, when you're speaking to people within a team, is really important. We want to create a positive learning experience and provide that environment within which people can truly learn. I think creating a positive environment and [using] that positive speak, rather than negative speak, is a good start to enable people to be their very best.

You talked about mentorship. The late King Hussein played a significant role in the success of *Maiden*. He became a mentor to you. How did that happen? And what was the most valuable lesson he shared with you?

I was stewardessing on a charter yacht when I was twenty-one years old in Newport, Rhode Island. King Hussein had just been to Prince Abdullah's graduation ceremony at Georgetown, and then they chartered that boat for the day.[3]

He was a collector of people from all walks of life. He loved humans. He was one of the most extraordinary, if not *the* most extraordinary, human I have ever met in my life. He had this incredible ability to listen and make you feel like you were literally the only person in the world. He was absolutely fascinated with what you were saying. We had a conversation about navigation and radios and taking things apart and mechanics and that was our thing that we each loved. We had tons to talk about. Before he left the yacht, he said, "This is my number in the Royal Palace in Jordan. Give me a call when you get back to the UK." It was like, "Yeah, right. Okay! That was surreal." So I did call, and we formed a great friendship, which lasted for the rest of his life.

He would persuade me that I could do things I had never dreamed of and be someone I could never have imagined. He was always on the end of the phone if I needed him. What I learned from him more than anything else was patience and process. So, related to process, we can metaphorically think, "Yes, I know that the top of the mountain is there, and I should look at it because I need to remember where I'm going, but right now I need to look here [*Tracy points down*]. Right here." So it's the understanding that we are not going to get up there until we have got this bit here right. At the time, he was negotiating the Middle East peace process. The example that he would give would be having patience in order to see it through,

---

3   A detailed write-up about the initial (and remarkable) meeting between Tracy Edwards and King Hussein can be viewed here: themaidenfactor.org/tracys-story/#:~:text=If%20I%20 had%20not%20met,can%20all%20do%2C%20was%20unquestioning. Tracy ends the article: "If I had not met HM King Hussein I of Jordan and if he had not stepped in, Maiden would not have happened. It is as simple as that. His vision for his country and for the world was limitless. His treatment of his fellow beings was legendary and his belief in what we can all do, was unquestioning. I often think of the King and I wish my daughter could have met him. He was and will always be one of the most remarkable human beings to ever walk this planet and I miss him so much, as do so many."

and engaging in the process of bringing the different parties together. If he didn't get that part of the process right, he'd never get to the end piece.

You did participate in the 1990 Whitbread Round the World Race. (King Hussein helped secure *Maiden*'s sole sponsorship — Royal Jordanian Airlines — when no one else would take a chance on the all-female crew.) In the end, you and the crew won two of the six legs and finished the race in second place in your class. Yet you were heartbroken with the outcome and felt, initially, that you had achieved nothing. How so?

I was angry with myself more than anything else. I believe we could have won that race, and I blew it because of some navigation mistakes. I still look back at it and go, "Bloody hell! What were you thinking?" I think saying that we had achieved nothing was maybe the wrong thing to say. I knew we had achieved a lot. But I think I said that because my goals were so high and my own expectation was to win. Really, there is no point in getting that wet, cold, miserable if you're not thinking about winning. It wasn't really that I thought we hadn't achieved anything, I was just frustrated that we should have achieved so much more, and we should have won.

Upon deeper reflection, though, what was the legacy that you and the *Maiden* crew created during the race?

I think we disrupted the patriarchy of the maritime world. We shook it to its very core. Mind you, at the time we didn't really think that. We just thought we had annoyed a few people — which gave us huge pleasure, and still gives me great pleasure today — but I don't think we had any idea of just how much we had shaken the very foundations of what everyone believed to be the absolute truth of the matter. We were disruptors. Just the shock that we hadn't died in the Southern Ocean — and not only that we hadn't died, but we had won the bloody leg! It's hard for me to remember how shocking that was.

But, I had a nervous breakdown at the end of [crewing] *Maiden*, and I disappeared for two years. I couldn't deal with what was being asked of me and everyone wanting a piece of me. I became a recluse. I thought I was never going to go back to sailing. It is a shame that we didn't realize what we had done at the time. We did not have any structure behind us: the management of people and an understanding of how you use press and agents. We didn't have any of that. We did what we did, and then it went quiet.

So, once we had the initial impact, unfortunately, there wasn't the follow-through. What I didn't quite realize, and what the film completely changed my mind about, was that we'd had an impact on lots of young girls all over the world. And now, thirty-three years later, I am meeting them! Some of them are on my boat now. We have women on *Maiden* who were inspired to start sailing by the film. The film really opened our eyes as to what we'd achieved. Even though I know we have all felt proud of *Maiden* through the years, but I don't think we've really, really understood.

For six months, my daughter and I followed the film around from premiere to premiere. It felt like a rock star on the road! It was surreal seeing people like Whoopi Goldberg or Jamie Lee Curtis or Alec Baldwin attending the premieres. And so many people are queueing up to see the film. The best part, though, was all the young girls coming up to me afterward and saying, "I think you're so amazing, and *Maiden* is so amazing." That's what we didn't get then, that understanding of impact.

I remember the premiere in the UK, when our whole *Maiden* crew came back together again for the first time in twenty-seven years. Of course, we'd been in touch and would have mini-reunions, but it was amazing to have all of us together and with our children, the majority of which are daughters! And they are looking at us in a whole different light. I remember Jenny's two sons looking up at her, saying, "Mum! You're cool!" Yes, we did have a life before we became mothers. A whole life! It's

extraordinary. I understand the impact much more now than I
did then.

How did the movie *Maiden*[4] come into being, twenty-seven years after the
actual race?

During the race, most of the other boats didn't have or want
cameras on board because they thought they were just far too
busy racing. But we chose to have a camera because we knew
something special was happening here. Some of the other boats
did have cameras, but we practiced with ours and read the
instructions. One of our sailors, Jo, actually went to the BBC
and learned how to film. She's only four-feet-eleven, and the
camera back then was absolutely bloody massive. I don't know
how she carried it around the boat. One of the things we found
out as we were practicing with the camera was when we needed
all hands on deck, she would pick up the camera. I said to her,
"Whoa, you can't do that. We need you as a sailor." But then we
realized we were going to miss filming the best bits, because the
best bits are the emergency bits. So, what we decided to do —
and we were the only boat that did this — was to fix a second
camera to the radar mast. If you are watching the film and you
see those shots that make you feel a bit queasy because the frame
is rocking back and forth, that is from the camera on the mast.
The last person out in an emergency situation would hit the
panic button and it would start filming.

   Years later I met Alex Holmes, a film director. I did a
presentation at his daughter's school. He came up to me and
said, "I'm a film-maker and I'd love to make the story of *Maiden*
a film." When I told him we had all this footage from the entire
race, he nearly died with happiness. Over the next two years

---

4   *Maiden* is a documentary film by Alex Holmes about Tracy Edwards and the crew of the
    Maiden as they compete as the first all-woman crew in the 1989–1990 Whitbread Round the
    World Race. The film debuted at the 2018 Toronto International Film Festival. The trailer of
    Maiden can be viewed here: www.sonyclassics.com/maiden/#4thPage.

while we were rescuing *Maiden* and restoring her, he was finding the footage, piecing it together and editing it with other race footage, and supplementing it with crew interviews.

Please share with us the work you currently do with The Maiden Factor.[5] The webpage says:

> At twenty-six years old I captained the yacht *Maiden*, with the first all-female crew to ever sail around the world.
>
> We were told we couldn't do it, but we showed how sailing is a level playing field. Now, I'm making it my mission to advocate for girls' education around the world.

How are you changing the lives of girls? Why is education — particularly for girls in the developing world — so important to you?

We found *Maiden* rotting in the Seychelles in 2014. I had to rescue her. We raised the money to do so. King Hussein's daughter Princess Haya actually called me up one night and said, "I hear you've rescued Dad's boat. How can I help?" I met with Princess Haya and I admitted that I didn't know what we were going to do with *Maiden* once she was restored. But when my daughter suggested we sail *Maiden* on a lap of honor around the world, it made me think that maybe we could use that as an opportunity to inspire and empower the next generation of girls. Then, when Princess Haya shared that her passion was for girls' education, I became interested in raising money for girls' educational charities.

This all came about as *Maiden* was being restored. By the time she was launched, we had established The Maiden Factor

5 The Maiden Factor is a global ambassador for the empowerment of girls' education: www .themaidenfactor.org. Edwards's personal webpage, featuring articles and events which highlight and celebrate the empowerment of women and the need for increased opportunities for the education of girls can be viewed at www.tracyedwards.com.

Foundation, our charity. To be clear about how this works is that *Maiden* is a working girl; she has always been a sporting entity sponsored by companies. What that sponsorship does, is it allows us to use the yacht to raise funds for girls' educational charities all over the world. We focus on STEM. The reason I'm so passionate about girls' education is because I read a United Nations report, which, to paraphrase, says, "If every girl had twelve years of quality education, we could solve every problem the world has right now." That's a pretty powerful statement. When you really start to understand that if you educate a girl, you educate her family, her community, her village, her town, her city, her country. You raise the socioeconomic status of everyone around her. You provide girls with opportunities and hopefully a better life. So once I realized that I could do something really small on the ground level, working with all these amazing girls' educational charities, we could be helpful in something that can have such powerful end results.

In 2000, Nelson Mandela said, "Sport has the power to change the world. Sport has the power to inspire. It has the power to unite people in a way that little else does. It speaks to youth in a language they understand."[6] Has Maiden lived up to this idea? How?

When we were first thinking about what we could do when we sailed *Maiden* into a port, a destination, or a country, my thought was that in addition to giving talks and screening the film, we would have loads of schoolgirls down to the boat. We have one man on our team. He said, "I think you need to invite girls *and* boys down to the boat." I resisted this because I wasn't focused on inspiring boys, but inspiring girls. But he told me, "You are missing the point. You should be educating boys to show them

---

6   Nelson Mandela's iconic speech, "Sport Has the Power to Change the World," at the Laureus World Sports Awards 2000 in Monaco, can be viewed here: www.youtube.com/watch?v=y1-7w-bJCtY.

that girls are equal." It was a lightning bolt moment and I said, "Oh my god, you're right. I totally missed that point!"

There are two things I love about the power of *Maiden*. First, *Maiden* isn't a teacher, or any adult, just saying to a teenager, "You can do it if you put your mind to it." *Maiden* is a solid, physical representation of the proof of what a girl can do when just one person believes in her. It's actually there! Look, you can touch it, you can get on board. You don't need any words. Second, *Maiden* encourages boys to look at girls in a whole different light. I love that awakening, that awareness of their peers. My favorite conversation ever on the entire *Maiden* tour was one I overheard when we were in Los Angeles. I was just walking past, and there were two young kids sitting in the wheel well of the boat holding on to the wheel. The little boy looked at the little girl and he said to her, "So, is it only girls that can sail around the world?" And she looked at him and she said, with a bit of a huff and an eyeroll, "I *suppose* boys can do it as well." Yes! This is what we're aiming for!

The power of sport for young people is immeasurable, which is why we are so desperate to keep girls in sport. Unfortunately, girls often leave sport around the age of fifteen. But, sport is such a visual example to them of what they can achieve. There is no guile, there is no pretend. I love that. I do think that sport can change the world, and I think sport has the ability to build bridges instead of walls. It can shine a light into dark corners. It can open things up. I know *Maiden* is playing a part in that process.

Is there anything that we haven't asked you that you would love to see in this chapter?

I talked about Ernest Shackleton briefly earlier, and I think what you might find interesting about Shackleton is that when he went to Antarctica in 1914 and lost his ship, he managed to rescue all of his men. Frank Worsley, who served as captain of the *Endurance*, captured the tale in the book *Endurance: An Epic of Polar Adventure*.[7] His description of Shackleton is really interesting, considering it was a time when "men were made of steel and ships were made of wood," and no one talked about their feelings. Worsley writes about Shackleton that his best qualities as a leader were his feminine qualities.

---

7   Frank A. Worsley, *Endurance: An Epic of Polar Adventure* (New York: W.W. Norton & Company, 2000).

CHAPTER 8

LADY BRENDA HALE

**Baroness Hale of Richmond, President (Retired) of the
Supreme Court of the United Kingdom, Dame Commander of the Most
Excellent Order of the British Empire**

AND JULIA HOGGETT

CEO of the London Stock Exchange

Lady Brenda Hale retired as President of the Supreme Court of the UK, the most senior judge in the country, in January 2020. Before becoming a judge, she had a varied career: she was an academic lawyer at the University of Manchester (also qualifying and practicing for a while as a barrister in Manchester) and the first woman member of the Law Commission, where she led successful projects in Family Law and Mental Capacity Law. She was appointed a High Court Judge in 1994, was promoted to the Court of Appeal in 1999, and in 2004 became the first and only woman "Law Lord" in the House of Lords, then the apex court in the UK. In 2009, the Law Lords became the judges of the newly established Supreme Court; she became the court's Deputy President in 2013 and its first woman President in 2017.

In retirement she has spent her time in good works, events, and writing — her memoir, *Spider Woman: A Life*, was published in 2021. She holds a number of honorary or visiting academic appointments and is visitor of her alma mater, Girton College, Cambridge.

Julia Hoggett joined the London Stock Exchange as CEO in April 2021. Previously, Julia was Director of Market Oversight at the Financial Conduct Authority (FCA), overseeing the conduct of market participants. Julia joined the FCA in 2014 as Head of Wholesale Banking Supervision, responsible for the conduct supervision of the investment banks operating in the UK. Prior to this, she was a Managing Director at Bank of America Merrill Lynch, running various fixed-income origination businesses in Europe, the Middle East, and Africa. Julia was previously a board member and CEO of DEPFA ACS Bank in Ireland. She began her career at JPMorgan.

Julia holds a degree in Social and Political Sciences from Newnham College, Cambridge, and undertook a research scholarship at King's College, Cambridge, on public policy in East Africa. She has been an active speaker on diversity and inclusion in London for two decades. Julia is the daughter of Lady Brenda Hale.

Lady Hale, you retired as president of the Supreme Court of the United Kingdom in 2020. You then wrote a memoir titled *Spider Woman.*[1] What new insights about yourself did you gain from that process?

LBH: That's a very interesting question. I was recently interviewed by a very skilled journalist at a literary festival, and he said that he noticed several, what he called "grenades," at various points. The grenades were things that I had written about early on in my personal life that unintentionally pointed to what was going to happen later. These were things like my childhood in a small Yorkshire village, where I was exposed to my parents being interested in social justice. They recognized the social stratification in the village — the great British class structure, in other words — and, to some extent, challenged it. So that was one of the grenades. Then there were grenades from when I was studying at the University of Cambridge, related to the unfairness of the quotas which were restricting women's opportunities. [Lady Hale graduated at the top of her class in 1966 as one of six women in a year of well over a hundred men, according to a September 20, 2019, *British Vogue* article.] Then, when I went to the University of Manchester to become

---

1 Lady Brenda Hale, *Spider Woman: A Life* (London, England: Bodley Head, 2021).

an academic and a barrister, I wrote about the significant amount of lawful gender discrimination taking place, so there was that grenade. Manchester is also where I began teaching constitutional law. It never occurred to me that in the future, I might be the author of a rather important and significant constitutional law judgment.[2]

Throughout my life, there have been many episodes that were leading to other things but without my consciously knowing it at the time. But, I think that's the point. Things come your way, you do your best with them, and then you find out that it has a resonance later on.

Julia, when your mother was telling that story, I saw you nodding. What was it like for you as your mum worked on her memoir? Was there any conversation and reflection between you?

JH: There were bits and pieces of conversations, but the one thing that was interesting was reading the galley copy of the book. On one level, I experienced the same story from the inside. So, having the opportunity to read my mother's observations from a perspective where she is standing back to describe them provided a really interesting insight into my own world, as well as my mother's world. For example, my grandmother — her name was Marjorie Godfrey and then later Marjorie Hale after she married my grandfather Cecil Hale — is still as powerful a part of my sense of who I am, even though she died when I was only eight, as she is for my mother. I got to see some of the same maternal lineage or through-lines in a sense by being able to hear my mother's telling of the story of my grandmother, and to come to learn and know more about her. My mother and I

---

2   *Miller v. Prime Minister* and *Cherry and others v. Lord Advocate*, holding that the prime minister's attempt to shut down Parliament for five weeks just before the United Kingdom was due to leave the European Union was unlawful and of no effect.

hadn't previously had those conversations about Grandma and Grandpa Hale's history in the way it was outlined in the book.

There are lots of ways in which my through-line is just a continuation of the one that my mum has described. It was very useful for me to reflect on, and made me think about my own daughter much more, who is the fourth generation of that lineage. I recognize that, because of the book, I was given the ability to deeply reflect — in a way most people aren't offered the chance — not only on their parents, but on themselves.

Julia, you mentioned that your grandmother impacted you in a powerful way. What dimension of her leader character are you now trying to pass on to your daughter?

JH: There are two facets for me. Firstly, even though my memory of her as a human being is from the perspective of a young child, she still taught me that you need to dust yourself off, get on with it, and apply yourself. Her resilience really exemplified her. Secondly, she never lost her kindheartedness and her real care and consideration for others. She taught me that you can be tough as well as kind and open-hearted at the same time. She summed that up to me as a young child.

LBH: My mother was a qualified teacher who had to give up teaching in the 1930s when she married my father because of the marriage bar. [The marriage bar required single women to resign from their job upon marrying and disqualified married women from applying for vacancies.] But then my father died very suddenly, and so she had to pick herself up, dust off her teaching qualifications, and find herself a job — which she managed to do. That was a hugely beneficial lesson to her daughters, or at least her two younger daughters, one of whom was me. It taught us that we should always have qualifications, always have something to dust off, and never be completely dependent upon somebody else. You also need to have such spirit to be able to pick yourself up. She had not had a salaried position for over twenty years and yet had to go back into the job market — but that was part of her toughness. My father was headmaster of a boarding school for boys, and she ran the boarding house. Everyone used to say that although she was small in stature, the boys were more frightened of her than they were of my father. But at the same time, Julia is completely right about her kindness, because apart from being resilient, tough, clever, and scary, she was also very, very kind. It was all of these qualities that we could observe, and that I think both of us have wanted to emulate, if we possibly could.

JH: I think it is noteworthy that we have both pointed to a primary school headmistress in a small Yorkshire village as our reference point for leader character. For me, I think one of the things that's important is for people to find their reference points in their own circumstances. I think that too often people feel that for someone to be a powerful leadership role model, they must occupy a vaulted position or tick certain boxes. Rather it is the character, the resilience, or the approach that someone takes within their life's circumstances that is really the powerful role-modeling exercise. I wonder whether, reflecting on it just now, the fact that my grandmother had that impact on both of us is maybe the biggest lesson to learn.

Lady Hale, we see you smiling.

LBH: I have never thought about that before, but I think Julia is right. For me, this may also be partly because in the 1960s when I was starting off in my career, there were not a lot of female role models available, professionally speaking. There were hardly any women judges, very few women legal academics, and only a few women barristers whom I could say were role models. But even though there were very few of them, I did get something from each of them. At the time, a woman had to make her own path for dealing with personal or professional challenges. I think Julia is right that a lot of that came from my early upbringing as much as from senior people.

Lady Hale, your life has often been described as a life of firsts. You have long been a trailblazer: the first woman to be a Law Commissioner, the first female Law Lord and, in 2017, the first woman president of the Supreme Court. What is it about your character that helped you achieve that? And what is the lesson for all of us — in particular, for women and members of equity-deserving groups?

LBH: One of the things I should add to that question is that there are as many seconds as there are firsts. I was the second full-time woman academic at the University of Manchester law faculty. I was the second woman in the barristers chambers that I joined. I was the second woman in the Court of Appeal of England and Wales. Being second is sometimes harder than being first, but of course, that all depends on who the first was. We were talking about role models earlier, and I wouldn't say that the firsts were role models to me necessarily, but they certainly were not the sort of first women who would pull up the drawbridge and make life difficult. A lot of women leaders owe a great deal of thanks to the women immediately before them.

I'm not very reflective about my character, but I think a certain amount of sheer bloody-mindedness contributed to my career path. Would you consider that a Canadian academic expression? [*smiling*] I simply refused to notice or accept that there were reasons not to do something. The best example of that is from the days when judicial appointments were essentially conducted by a tap on the shoulder. I was asked to go and see a very senior official — the head of judicial appointments — in the Law Chancellors department. This department, among many things, was charged with appointing and advising on the appointment of judges. He discussed the idea with me, and then I went back to Manchester and discussed the meeting with my professors. Two of them said, "You'd better not do that. It will stand in the way of your academic progress." The other two said, "Of course! Go for it, girl!" But, I didn't need their encouragement. I was always going to go for it. It was an off-the-wall idea that seemed scary but exciting, and so I did it. I think that's where the bloody-mindedness comes in. And just not noticing, when a lot of the time there might have been things going on behind the scenes that would have been disparaging.

Julia, how has that bloody-mindedness worked out for you?

JH: I would observe that the outcome is the same as Mum's, although I think that sort of bloody-mindedness is actually about what you pay attention to and what you don't. There are two facets to it. The first is deciding that something is interesting to do, and deciding that the thing is more interesting than the fear of the unknown, as it were. There is a certain willfulness in that decision to leap. The other is that if you are the only woman in a room, or the first woman in a room, you may experience other people's discomfort with the strangeness of it, but you must plow on regardless. Well, not regardless, but rather conscious of it but not acceding to it because to do so would be to concede their discomfort as being something worthy of not changing rather than something needing to be changed. So, in part, you are being a change agent. That piece of the bloody-mindedness I completely identify with.

Lady Hale, somewhat surprising is your admission to suffering from impostor syndrome. In your memoir, you describe situations where you felt like you didn't belong. Can you comment on that? Where did such feelings of doubt come from — that you are not as competent as others perceive you to be? And, importantly, how did you deal with it?

LBH: We didn't, of course, call it impostor syndrome in those days. What I was talking about though — and I remember the occasions very clearly — was when I found myself in a new situation, or a new-ish situation, I would ask myself . . . not necessarily if I shouldn't be there, but am I able to cope? That was true when I first went to the senior school, it was true especially when I first went to Cambridge, when I went to the Law Commission, and when I first became a judge. Those would be the four times when I was particularly conscious of questioning my ability to cope.

I think it's completely sensible when you are starting something new to ask yourself, "Can I do this? What do I need in order to be able to do this?" The other thing that, in retrospect, I would say to myself was "Well, somebody else thinks I should be here!" They admitted me to the high school, they admitted me to Cambridge, they appointed me a Law Commissioner, they appointed me a baby judge — so somebody else thinks I can do it. Therefore, it is my job to prove them right, if I can.

The last thing I tend to say, but I probably dreamt it up quite recently because I think it is encouraging to others is, "If, having given my best, it turns out that I should not be in this particular position, well, it is their fault, not mine." That tends to go down quite well with people. I've only just begun to think that, but I think it's a good counterbalance to impostor syndrome because obviously you wouldn't be there unless somebody else thought you should be.

Obviously, you give it your best. But if it turns out that you are a square peg in a round hole, that's on the judgment of the people who put you there, not yours. I think people should not feel overly discouraged if they find themselves in a place that happens not to be the right one for them.

Julia, what concrete learnings did you pick up from your mother — dimensions of character, if you wish — that helped you to become your own person and be a trailblazer and highly successful executive?

JH: Very few people get the privilege of the ringside seat that I have had because of my parents, and from which they can learn. Many years ago, my mother gave a speech at the Financial Conduct Authority in London not long after I had joined and somebody asked her whether she had a plan to get to where she did in her career. Her answer was "I have never had a plan. I have had a very simple philosophy: do what I'm doing to the absolute best of my ability and trust that opportunities will come as a consequence to me, *and* don't close myself off to those opportunities when they present themselves."

I almost started laughing because when I have been asked that question myself, I answered it in exactly the same way, almost word for word. But the fact is that my mum and I had never discussed it. So, I suspect there is a parental osmosis effect that has supported every single step of my career!

LBH: I think mothers can learn something from daughters as well, can't they? Because Julia's resilience, hard work, and drive have also been a source of great inspiration and encouragement, probably to both her parents, but certainly to me.

Julia, we want to return to exploring the question of what dimensions of leader character helped you to become the successful executive that you are today.

JH: I actually had the Ivey Leader Character Framework stuck to my computer screen for years when I was at the Financial Conduct Authority. I use it as a reference point. Courage and humility are the two dimensions that resonate strongest with me. The dimension of courage is really important for me, because every single day I feel that there will be something scary that you need to do that you have never done before. It is possible that there are more moments in a day when I have to be consciously courageous than any other dimension in the framework. The need to have frank conversations with people about either themselves or the team not hitting the mark is just one example. Courage gives you the ability to say, "Right, I'm going to do this. I'm going to give it my best," whatever it may be. But, it is also important that when you succeed you don't get cocky about it. The way I approach things, and I feel I have gotten this from my mother, is I try to take what I do incredibly seriously, but try to take myself absolutely no more seriously than is necessary. What I do is really important, but I'm not any more important than anyone else. This is the humility piece.

Having said that, all the components of the framework make absolute sense and are central to how I think and act, or try to. The dimensions are comforts rather than challenges, you know? It is always easier to do the right thing, even if it seems hard. You learn this with the more crises you have had to manage. Even if it is difficult in the moment, the comfort and the confidence that it is the right thing to do is much more sustaining than having done the convenient thing in the short term. You learn that over time, you learn that forged in the fire of experience rather than in theory, I believe.

Ultimately, I am a risk manager for a living. I've spent my entire career managing risk. I have learnt that the biggest problem with risk is that a great number of the risks that ultimately blow up organizations started out as very small issues that got put in a drawer, usually because the culture didn't make it possible to surface them. People felt the consequence of raising the problem was greater and more negative for them than the nature of the risk at the time. Then, when it got too big, they absolutely couldn't say anything. As such, I have a very particular leadership approach, which is *to undertake a brutally honest mark-to-market of where we are*. If I think we haven't done something well enough, I will say so. But, for my own part, if I think I have made a mistake I will say so too — and I will try to be the first to say so. The purpose of doing this is so we can all move forward collectively and be better tomorrow. It is not about wanting names and numbers.

As a leader, you need to create a sense of safety for people where they feel that you have got their back. When you first admit your part in something that has gone wrong before asking them to have to do so, it shows you are trusting them with that information. Then, you can ratchet up the honesty in the feedback you are providing and people will take it as fair. But, you need to build this trust up over time. So again, when I have seen risks that blow up an organization, it is often the culture that caused the problem. As a leader, I feel absolutely bound to make sure I'm not creating that kind of environment. It requires an element of bravery, but also humility, in the way you deal with people. You need to own your part of it *and* you need to hold people accountable, all the while doing it in a constructive fashion.

Lady Hale, on appointment to the Lords, in 2004, you created a coat of arms bearing the motto *Omnia Feminae Aequissimae*, translated as "women are equal to everything." What was your inspiration to do so? And how has this motto guided you throughout your personal and professional lives?

LBH: It just has! My philosophy is that women are equal to everything, and that of course includes being equal to every man. We can discuss the wide range of meaning behind that for ages because it is a big subject, but ultimately the motto sums up what I have always believed. I say "always" because I was brought up to believe that. My parents believed that women were the equals of men — their capacities and ambitions, and so on. That is what my parents believed, it is certainly what I believe, and I think it is something that we transmitted to you, Julia. Now, Julia can do things that I couldn't possibly do. I have no idea what sort of a judge she would make, but I have always known that the things she has done in her life are completely different from the things that I have done in my life. But even though we have had different lives, I think our approach to our lives has been very, very similar. Obviously, our approach to women's equality has been identical, which is believing that there is nothing that a woman cannot do, provided, of course, that she is inclined or chooses to do so. In fairness, this is also true of men. There is nothing that a man can't do, provided that it is the sort of thing that he wishes to do. These things are so obvious, and yet they need to be said.

Lady Hale, the title of our book is *Character: What Contemporary Leaders Can Teach Us about Building a More Just, Prosperous, and Sustainable Future*. How do you see the law as facilitating a more just and sustainable future? And also, what dimensions of leader character would you elevate to being critically important in achieving that objective?

LBH: We have two sorts of law. We have the law made by parliaments, and we have the law made by judges. Some of the judicial decisions that judges make are in applying the law made by parliaments. I think that the law made by parliaments — and I'm including constitutional law and things like your Canadian Charter of Rights and Freedoms in that — that is the way of actually driving things forward for a sustainable future. On the whole, the judges are only implementing, interpreting, applying the laws that parliaments have made, which is the right way for it to be. That is how I see the law. Of course, the law can help create a more sustainable future. But that depends on parliamentarians. Parliamentarians are, of course, driven by all sorts of influences — which are different from the influences that drive judges. So, leader character would obviously drive or influence political leadership, it seems to me, more than it would judicial leadership. I'm afraid it's political leadership which is the way to a sustainable future; that is, it is the law made by parliamentarians that is going to drive change much more than the law made by judges.

Julia, would you want to venture into that direction — a key dimension that you believe helps to facilitate a more just and sustainable future?

JH: For me, it would be transcendence, actually. One of the biggest challenges I think I've observed — and this debate happened at COP26 in Glasgow, and I had the utter privilege of being there — is that previously most COPs [United Nations Climate Change Conferences] were held as a public government-to-government discussion. At COP26, the UK government inserted the private sector and developed a huge financing and private sector agenda, which led people to say, "COP has gone corporate." My response to that was "That's a good thing!" To create a sustainable future, you actually want every single corporation that can mobilize trillions of dollars — with often far more agility than governments around the world — to be fundamentally embedded in this agenda. One of the things COP26 was doing was creating accountability between investors and companies about the climate transition. If you are the CEO of a listed company and you make commitments about the climate transition, then shareholders will hold you accountable. Not for the next five years or the next parliamentary cycle, but for much, much longer. Actually, I spoke to a number of politicians who realized that the thing that really elongated the impact cycle on climate change was moving it out of the shorter time frames of the political agenda and into the ironically longer time frames of the private sector. Unfortunately, this is not how some people perceive things, as they view the private sector or the markets as being driven by quarterly results.

But, taking a long-term approach as well as a focus on your business today is critical. I describe my job as a "five-year, five-year forward job" (taking a term from the derivatives markets). I need to spend a third of my time on securing the venue — ensuring its resilience so that we open on time, close on time, and do everything we need to do in between. The second third of my time is spent on running the venue with the business model it has today. The final third of my time focuses on growing the venue — on building the conditions for the venue to exist, to succeed and to thrive, long after I've stopped being in the role. That is a part of my job and a privilege to be able to think that way.

But politicians are often constrained by the next election cycle. That ability to project forward, to me, is what actually creates good policy. Most of the most significant "change agent" policies that have happened in most countries have not been short term. They have been genuinely long term, and they have transcended the political cycle. For politicians, that is really hard to do because the construct doesn't reward them for doing it, especially if short-term pain is going to lead to long-term gain. That's the price that politicians understandably find very difficult to pay, whereas ironically I think a lot of businesses understand it more, I think.

Julia, you are a trailblazer yourself. For example, you are the first openly gay person to serve as head of the stock exchange and have been a pioneer for women and the LGBTQ+ community in financial services for many years. Can you comment on that experience?

JH: To go back to some of the conversation before, whichever bucket you stick the sheer bloody-mindedness in, that probably fits. But, I have never seen my identity as an obstacle: I know it sounds weird. Most people presume it is an obstacle, but honestly, for me, I actually think it has been an advantage. Now, let me be clear, I have been very particular about deliberately choosing institutions that were supportive of LGBTQ+ people throughout my career journey, and therefore I knew I was going into a safer space than I might have been in had I gone elsewhere.

Also, when I started in investment banking, there were not that many women on trading floors and there was still a host of stereotyping attitudes. To be blunt, I believe there were some men who, when viewing a young, straight female colleague, couldn't decide whether to think of them as a colleague, a friend, or someone they might ultimately marry. The great benefit that I experienced in being an openly gay woman on a trading floor of predominantly straight men is they didn't think of me that way — they thought of me as a mate. They thought of me in many ways the same way they thought of their male colleagues.

There was a very funny story once when I moved from my first to my second team at JPMorgan. The boss of the new team phoned up my old boss and said, "Look, we know about Julia. She is one of the most visible openly gay people we have in London. She is going to be moving into the middle of the trading floor with a host of traders who are 'the real bee's knees.' What do we need to know?" My old boss said, "Nothing. Just know whether Manchester United won at the weekend or not." It summed up the institutional attitude I experienced at JPMorgan, which was "Actually, she's just the same as anyone else." It is true that I could be "one of the boys" in a stereotypical regard. I could talk about cricket, I could talk about football, and they were used to me doing it. In their head, I sort of occupied this third space between men and women, as it were. And it meant I was able to go into a room and take command of a situation if necessary.

I think they gave me the benefit of some of what are perceived to be the more male attributes, whereas a straight woman doing the same thing might, unfortunately, still have been seen as a bit pushy or a bit shrill. I think that gave me the space to develop a style of leadership which is now entirely my own.

I believe I was actually fortunate enough to have it easier than quite a lot of my straight, female colleagues. However, I do need to add that I have two kids who are now teenagers. I took two weeks off after the birth of my son and two weeks after the birth of my daughter. My career continued to progress during the time they were zero to six [years old], which is not what happens to most women in the workplace in the same situation. So, when I came back into investment banking in London, I was put up as a poster child: "She's a senior managing director, she's female, she's openly gay, and she's a mother." The first thing I did was stand up and say, "I'm evidence of why we haven't fixed it yet, not why we have. My life looks more like my male colleagues than my female colleagues. I have architecture around me that is more akin to what my male colleagues would have than my female colleagues. We haven't got this right yet." I feel very strongly that I have a duty to advocate for that, to be the one who stands up and says what needs to be said for those who don't have my circumstances, rather than "just" taking advantage of my situation. So, I have never seen my identity as an obstacle. I have often seen it as an advantage and a bit of a privilege rather than something I have had to overcome, but I fully recognize that is not the case for many women and many LGBTQ+ people.

LBH: I'd like to add something. Most women in my era, when they entered into roles that had been traditionally held by men, had a choice to make: whether they are going to act or behave as much like men as possible, or whether they are going to make no secret of their womanhood. The first two women who were High Court judges in England and Wales exemplified each of those choices. The first one looked, sounded, and acted very much like a man or with stereotypically masculine behavior. The second was a woman of great beauty, charm, and femininity and made absolutely no secret of her womanhood. If you choose the first of those options, you could be accused of being bossy and strident (or worse). If you chose the second, you are quite likely to be accused of being flirtatious or trading on your femininity in order to get what you want. It was really difficult for women to decide which of those two models to adopt, because you really had no choice but to adopt one or the other.

JH: I believe the world is changing and that we have moved the diversity and inclusion agenda from "women can do anything that men can do, but masculinity is the benchmark" to a realization that actually women and men can bring different things to the table, and both are equally valuable. So, I hope that a young woman starting out in financial services today wouldn't think that she needed to be anything other than herself. Certainly, when I started my career, that evolution was taking place but, let's face it, it is not fully baked in yet.

Julia, as you are a strong advocate of improving diversity, do young professionals come to you for mentorship?

JH: I don't solely get people coming to me for mentorship because they are gay and because I am as well. It tends to be a much broader range of people than that. But, I do a lot of speaking on subjects related to diversity. I feel I have a duty to make it easier for the next generation in whichever way I can. This has meant that I actually need to get comfortable talking about my story, in a way that certainly initially was uncomfortable. For instance, when I went back into investment banking and they rolled me out as a "full strike" diversity candidate, I realized that my life didn't look like the lives of the young women who were up-and-coming analysts and associates and who wanted to get married, have kids, and keep progressing in their career. I jokingly say (which is true) that I haven't worn a skirt to the office since 1998!

At first glance, I am not a great role model for young, straight women coming up through the industry. So, I realized that my duty was to talk about my experience, and that was actually really uncomfortable at first, even though it has now become normal, so that they could find something that resonated for them. So they could connect to something about my experience and my story to feel that this path was possible for them as well. But that required me to acknowledge and articulate where it was different and to frame that. I think it is really critical to try to reflect on the privileges you have had and to use the privilege to support the next generation. It's like that Madeleine Albright quote, isn't it? — "There's a special place in hell for women who don't help other women."

As CEO at the London Stock Exchange, you have been given a platform for advocacy and change. At a recent event you said that the UK's capital markets need to change their image from being something that "enables bankers to drive Lamborghinis"[3] to something that helps companies grow. In the same vein, you consistently articulate a more transcendent and holistic vision of the markets and its capital flows than is usually considered. Why do you feel it is important at this point in time to change the narrative surrounding capital markets?

JH: It comes back to purpose. I always say that I am accidentally in finance. Essentially, I have spent my entire career answering exam questions. Meaning, I went into investment banking in the first place in order to answer the exam question I had set for myself in my postgraduate research, which was: How do the least developed countries in the world operate in the global economy? I knew I was not going to figure it out by sitting in the university library, so my father said, "Why don't you go and work for an investment bank that does emerging markets? You'll probably learn more there in two years than you ever would in the stacks in Cambridge."

He was right. I began my career at JPMorgan as an investment banker in debt capital markets. The first question I got asked at the interview for JPMorgan was "With your academic background, what is to say you're not going to take everything you can from a few years of working here and then go back and finish your PhD?" I thought, "That's a really good question, because that's my plan!" My answer was "I have two parents who do really difficult jobs that evolve and change every single day. I don't want a job where I learn how to make widgets and then make widgets every day for the rest of my career. If it's challenging, difficult, and evolves, then I will stick at it as long as

---

3   Paul Clarke, "LSE Boss Julia Hoggett: Capital Markets Are Seen as Something That 'Enables Bankers to Drive Lamborghinis,'" *Financial News London*, April 28, 2022, www.fnlondon.com /articles/lse-boss-julia-hoggett-capital-markets-seen-as-something-that-enables-bankers-to -drive-lamborghinis-20220428.

it is challenging, difficult, and evolving." That was my answer at the time. I still remember the answer — and the answer is still right for me to this day.

For me, capital markets are not about basis points and bid cover ratios and a lot of technical jargon that most people outside finance don't understand. Fundamentally, the job of the capital markets is to drive financing into the real economy; to create the jobs, the products, the innovation and the productivity that drives economies, changes lives, creates tax revenue, and also creates the assets for our pensioners, our investors, and our policy holders so that they have enough money for a wealthy old age, or at least a secure old age. That is what capital markets do.

However, so many people who are working on capital markets never describe them that way. They describe them through the lens of a particular policy statement, or the lens of "I got to do this deal!" The deal is only interesting not because you did it, but because of what the deal actually involves. For example, it is a fee event for the banker who makes an IPO happen, but that IPO might be for Oxford Nanopore Technologies Limited. Oxford Nanopore creates a technology that sequences the genome on the ground in west Africa in the middle of an Ebola outbreak and isolates ground zero quicker. To me, that's what the IPO did. It raised £895 million so that the company could do that better and save more lives. So yes, incidentally, the investment banker got a fee, but that's not the market's core purpose — that is its secondary purpose. We need to be able to talk about that primary purpose much, much more.

It should matter to everybody in this country, in any country, that there is an effective capital market. If everybody cares, we might actually mobilize the momentum to reform it and make capital markets what they need to be. So, to me, purpose is critical to being able to frame and communicate what you do and why.

I'll leave you with a final thought. Purpose actually transformed the strategy of the London Stock Exchange (LSE).

I describe the purpose of the LSE as a convener of capital: Our job is to bring together those who have capital with those who need capital, in service of an objective. Today, one of the most important objectives is the just transition to net zero [emissions]. But, fundamentally, if you think of our job as a convener of capital, there is no reason why we should only do that in the listed securities market. We can actually convene capital in every space where it is useful and necessary across an ecosystem. We have transformed the LSE business model over the last year from one that is purely focused on the publicly listed market to now having a mission to be the first global exchange group in the world that is genuinely indifferent as to whether a company is public or private. Our job is to create the venues to facilitate the flow of capital across companies' lifecycles. That is a purpose-led business model. It is not fluffy at all, but that logic fundamentally changes the way you think about our job. That is why I get to do my hobby for a living, because I have to the privilege of trying to transform what I often describe as a three-hundred-year-old fintech. My job is to make sure that it is just as viable, just as vibrant, and just as effective in another three hundred years as it is today. That isn't going to happen by doing the same thing, but by changing it. Purpose is utterly critical in this. It isn't a soft or soppy concept in my head.

Lady Hale, what is the last leadership-related lesson or insight you would like to share with the readers — those whose ambition is to lead people and communities to a better world?

LBH: The only thing that I would say is what has been apparent from our conversation — that the style of leadership and the qualities that you need to lead depend on what it is you are leading. Julia has been leading very different organizations from the ones that I have been leading. The skills, the talents, and qualities that Julia needs are different from the ones that I needed. But, there is character underneath that which, I think, is common. So, what you do and how you think about things may be very different, but the character that you need in order to lead, to set an example, to produce forward movement, are the same.

JH: My reflection would be one that you posit — that it isn't any one of those dimensions, but all of them. It is how you find that sense of yourself within them. Leader character matters. People need a sense of who they are as a human being, and one can never lose that in trying to be all the things that a good leader can be. You can learn layers and layers and layers of management techniques, but the best leaders I've ever worked with have always been fundamentally themselves.

CHAPTER 9

ALAN JOPE

Former CEO, Unilever

Alan Jope was Chief Executive Officer of Unilever from January 2019 to June 2023. As CEO, Alan was responsible for leading one of the world's largest and most geographically diverse consumer goods businesses, with presence in 190 countries, serving 3.4 billion people every day.

Alan joined Unilever in the UK in 1985. Before being appointed as CEO, he served as President of the Beauty & Personal Care Division. He also worked in leadership roles in North America for fourteen years and Asia for thirteen years. When leading Unilever's business in China, Alan doubled its size and laid important foundations for future success.

Alan is currently Chair of the Board of UNICEF's Generation Unlimited, served as vice-chair of the World Business Council for Sustainable Development's executive committee, and was appointed to the World Economic Forum's International Business Council executive committee during his time as CEO of Unilever. He was appointed to the Board of Directors of Accenture in April 2023.

Alan holds a BA Hons in commerce from the University of Edinburgh and graduated from Harvard Business School's General Management Program in 2001. In 2021 he was appointed Visiting Fellow at the University of Oxford. This interview was conducted in September 2022, prior to Alan's retirement from Unilever.

Unilever is a global company whose products are used by 3.4 billion people every day. Consequently, the organization has the potential to make a monumental impact on the world, in both good and bad ways. How do you and your leadership team deal with such an enormous sphere of influence and the responsibility of being a good corporate citizen?

There are a lot of problems in the world right now. We view most of these problems as derivatives of three overlapping, superordinate global challenges. The first is the climate emergency; the second is the long-term destruction of nature; and the third is social inequality. None of these challenges make for a good place to sell soap and ice cream! When COVID hit, even though our hygiene business boomed, our out-of-home food business collapsed and people's consumption of personal care products dropped significantly. It was a net-negative for us. People have naïvely said, "Oh you must be happy with climate change because people are eating more ice cream!" But we are not at all — our factories are getting flooded and adverse weather events are shutting down our supply chains. It is a disaster.

These are huge problems that no one sector can solve on its own. The climate emergency is not going to be solved by government, it's not going to be solved by academia, it's not going to be solved by NGOs, and it's not going to be solved by the private sector. It will require a multi-sector effort across all these parties. As part of that, at Unilever, we profoundly believe in business as a force for good. Business has a role to play in solving these problems, not only for the common good but also out of enlightened self-interest. It is in our interest that nature is preserved, that the climate emergency is addressed, and that we deal with rampant inequality. You can imagine the derivative arguments for each of those points.

It is in Unilever's DNA to see business as an opportunity to address problems like public health or social imbalance. William Lever founded the business in the 1870s — at least the soap side of the business — and, at the time, he described the purpose of the firm as to make cleanliness commonplace and lessen the load for women. Imagine that! He was expressing what we would now clearly recognize as a purpose back then. I don't know if he was an early feminist, but he certainly recognized that women were burdened with an unfair share of the unpaid work in the home. So, you see, this goes a long way back in Unilever's DNA, and it survives to this day.

You often talk about building a new economic system: a multi-stakeholder approach; measures to ensure environmental and social externalities are priced in; mandatory ESG (environmental, social, governance) reporting for large businesses; and a shift from linear models of production and consumption to a circular economy. In addition the leadership at Unilever initiated (and made significant investments in) actual programs that focused on a multi-stakeholder approach — that is, the belief that organizations should serve not only their shareholders, but also deliver value to their customers, invest in employees, deal fairly with suppliers, and support the communities in which they operate. What does this commitment mean for you professionally?

I do think that when you're appointed as the CEO of an organization, your focus suddenly becomes much more external and you realize just how much governance matters. Even though I was a member of Unilever's executive team for several years before I took this role, I had very little visibility to the board and limited experience with shareholders. I also had hardly any engagement with civil society or with academia. Then suddenly, when you're put in the role of CEO, that changes. You see the roles of multiple stakeholders with new clarity — of course, the success of the company depends on how strong your talent bench is and how able that bench is to address the needs of your consumers and your customers. You also realize that you're being watched carefully for your impact on society and on the planet, and you realize that, at the end of the day, the shareholder must be rewarded appropriately.

It took me quite some time to sort through my logic on how it all works together. I came to firmly believe that if we take good care of our people — and I mean that by a broad definition, not just that they have good pay and benefits, but that they are working in a healthy culture, that they have clear direction, that they are well led, that they are able to express their opinions, and they can take action in a psychologically safe environment — then they will do a fantastic job of looking after our consumers and our customers. If we set guardrails that mean that we conduct ourselves properly with regard to our business partners and society, obey the rule of law, and treat the planet and communities where we do business with respect, then the shareholder will be very well rewarded.

I don't believe that one stakeholder is more important than another, but I do believe that there is a sequence to it [that starts] with looking after your people and encouraging them to look after consumers and customers . . . Admittedly, we have not yet proven the link between a multi-stakeholder model and superior shareholder returns, but as you well know, there is a growing body of work that shows that companies with strong ESG scores have generally yielded higher returns than the average within their broader market. That's the logic that I've come to believe in since coming into this role. You do get a different perspective as CEO versus other roles in the company.

In a recent interview you said, "The discussion we find ourselves at the center of at the moment is the very future of capitalism. . . . Certainly, there's a lot of good that has come from capitalism. It has been the economic system that has lifted hundreds of millions of people out of poverty. The innovation drive and the competitive spirit of capitalism are very important. . . . However, the single-minded pursuit of profit is damaging. It has many unanticipated negative consequences."[1] What have been the defining moments for you personally that made you so

---

1   Louise Prance-Miles, "The Green Recovery — Who Is Setting the Standard for Sustainability?" *Global Cosmetics News*, October 16, 2020, www.globalcosmeticsnews.com/the-green-recovery -who-is-setting-the-standard-for-sustainability.

strongly believe in this statement? What has been the evolution in your thoughts around sustainable or responsible capitalism?

I think big business is intrinsically not trusted. The default position, I find, of citizens, of civil society, is that there is a very suspicious attitude towards big business. It really bothers me, because 99.99 percent of the people who work in our wonderful company are outstanding, high-character individuals who want to do the right thing and be part of an organization with high integrity. Yet, business — and big business in particular — is seen as this malevolent force. It is easy to understand why. I have seen how some businesses manipulate things to avoid paying their fair share of taxes, and I've sat across the table from petrochemical company leaders and heard climate change denial. I've seen the waste and litter on the beaches of Southeast Asia, where I have spent a lot of my career and which is still one of my favorite parts of the world. We own our share of the waste problem.

The reason why big business is distrusted is there are bad actors — like the climate change deniers or the people who don't pay their taxes. We've set up a capitalist system that treats air, water, and nature as free goods, which get destroyed in our ordinary course of doing business because there is no price on carbon to speak of. Capitalism is failing in its redistributive power. If economics should be about anything, it's fair distribution. We make the statement that hundreds of millions have been lifted out of poverty, and it's true. But 75 percent of the world's population still lives in countries where the national Gini coefficient — a measure of statistical dispersion to represent the wealth inequality within a nation — has widened over the last five years. The rich are getting richer, and the poor are getting poorer. It's not surprising then that big business is seen as contributing to these problems despite the fact that I'm surrounded by the most magnificent, wonderfully principled people working in our company.

We made a commitment to broaden our thinking on the future of capitalism, with the help of thought leaders in the space. Our early thinking is that the next evolution of capitalism will formally embrace a multi-stakeholder model. It will put a price on things like carbon and clean water. It will be more redistributive in how it spreads the creation of prosperity, and where non-financial outcomes from companies will be measured with the same discipline and comparability as the financial outcomes. So, yes, I believe that as a global company it is impossible for us to do our fiduciary duty without considering climate change, the destruction of nature, and social inequality.

In December 2020, the Unilever board announced its intention to put a Climate Transition Action Plan before the shareholders and seek a non-binding advisory vote on the company's ambitious emissions-reduction targets and the plan to achieve them. The action plan sets out the steps Unilever will take to reduce emissions to zero within its own operations by 2030 and to net zero across its value chain by 2039. Was asking for a shareholder vote largely symbolic given that it was a non-binding advisory vote? Or an example of authentic leadership?

In this case, I think there were two things that came together at the same time to make this happen. The first was that we noticed how a Spanish airport operator had been forced by an activist to develop and publish a plan to decarbonize. The second was a growing debate in the sustainability community about climate pledges and goals versus actually having a plan to deliver on that pledge. So when we viewed these two things together, we said, "Wait a minute! We don't want to get forced to publish a plan. We want to have a plan!"

Thomas Lingard, our global climate and environment director, was given about three months to take our existing climate goals and augment them as well as capture our current best plan to deliver those goals. Specifically, we didn't want just one goal; we wanted a series of milestones along the way so we could judge if we were on track or not. Thomas led a team from the company which worked around the clock for those three months, coming up with the plan. In parallel, I went to the board and told them how we thought it was important for Unilever to have a plan for carbon so we could move forward on it with the shareholders' endorsement. The reason shareholder endorsement is important is because it gives us a mandate to get on with it.

There was some anxiety in the board. Some members thought that shareholders would think we were going too far and were not going to like it. Others thought the opposite — that we've got shareholders on the register who are pretty active in this space, and they may say we're not going far enough. Could we end up with an embarrassing level of support — with some of those supporters saying we're not going far enough, and conversely others saying we are going too far? In the end, it went through with 99.6 percent shareholder approval. That is a clear mandate!

I can tell you this kind of stereotype of shareholders not caring about sustainability is absolute nonsense. BlackRock, an asset management firm providing investment and risk management and advisory services to institutional and retail clients worldwide, has spent many hours meeting with us on our carbon reduction plans.

We wanted to build something that was a plan and not just a set of targets. The board endorsed and supported it. Shareholders overwhelmingly want to see companies raise their game in this. My one caveat was to say that we're not going to refresh it every year. We're going to report against it every year, but we're going to refresh it every three years. We've now started working on version 2.0.

You have stated that companies should get used to "crisis being more or less the new normal"[2] and have labeled the COVID-19 pandemic child's

---

2   Reuters, "Unilever CEO Sees Crisis as New Normal for Industry," June 21, 2022, www.reuters .com/business/retail-consumer/unilever-ceo-sees-crisis-new-normal-industry-2022-06-21.

play compared to the impact of climate and inequality. Can you please elaborate on that? And what are the implications for leaders in the public, private, and not-for-profit sectors?

I must admit that I'm fed up living in "unprecedented" times. I'd quite like some "precedented" times in the remaining fifteen months in this job, and for the world. However, I am not optimistic. Take the climate emergency alone. We are passing tipping point after tipping point. Crossing multiple planetary boundaries.

If we could snap our fingers and tomorrow 100 percent of the Earth's energy came from renewable sources and not fossil fuels, we still would not hit the 1.5 degree limit set by the Paris Agreement. It is going to require massive regeneration of nature to suck in the carbon and probably substantial investment in new carbon sequestration technology for us to stay on track for 1.5 degrees. The picture is pretty gloomy. I think we've all actually got our heads in the sand. There is little chance we're going to hit the Paris limits.

And Jonathon Porritt wrote a book recently about this, *Hope in Hell*[3], arguing that we're really teetering on the edge of runaway climate change with events like the loss of the Antarctic ice shelf, the methane that is escaping from the thawing of the tundra, and various other tipping points. We're getting into self-reinforcing mode. There are no easy answers on the climate emergency. There are no easy answers on restoring nature. There are no easy answers on inequality. So, by contrast, a COVID emergency, I think, is really quite manageable compared with these systemic changes. It's going to require massive collaboration across the world, across sectors. But we don't yet have powerful mechanisms to do that.

I'm getting onto a bit of a philosophical tone here, but I was struck recently by Plato's *Republic*, which I had never read

---

3   Jonathon Porritt, *Hope in Hell: How We Can Confront the Climate Crisis & Save the Earth* (New York: Simon and Schuster, 2021).

before. It's really interesting what it says, and I apologize for the oversimplification. Namely, that the republic needs to be led by educated governors and that those governors should be educated in morals, in strategy, and actually in war. The other half of their education should be in gymnastics, on the belief that a healthy body and a healthy mind go together. And, that those intellectual and physical education opportunities should be made equally available to women and men. Interesting! Remember, this was written in 350 BC.

It goes on to warn, however, that if that doesn't happen, the republic will go into a slide and descend into democracy. The danger with democracy is that the governors can decide just to do what is popular, not what is right. It will then erode further to an oligarchy, where power will be increasingly concentrated to fewer and fewer hands; and it will ultimately end in tyranny, where power is concentrated in one person's hands before completely collapsing. What an allegory of what is happening across the world at the moment! . . . It's not in great shape from a governance, from an environmental, and from a social perspective.

What are some of the implications of having a world in [such] poor shape? Well, first of all, business has to see itself as part of the problem *and* part of the solution. Secondly, business needs to think about resilience. This is the reason why Unilever now has two hundred water projects. Projects that are trying to build water stewardship around our key places of manufacturing in water-scarce areas. We need to play a role in securing water resilience. Fixing in on one view of the future is a foolish thing to do because things are so unpredictable. What we should do is build multiple scenarios and create organizational adaptability and flexibility.

Some CEOs — including you — have been criticized by shareholders for allegedly "obsessing" about sustainability while, their critics claim, neglecting share performance and growth. How do you deal with such sharp criticism from shareholders?

I think your question is based on a false paradigm, and I tried to answer it earlier in our discussion. We must avoid the belief that there has to be a choice between sustainable business and strong financial performance. I believe just the opposite to be true and the vast majority of our shareholders are extremely supportive of our sustainability agenda and of putting a multi-stakeholder, responsible business model at the heart of what we do. We get virtually no pushback on that.

Now, having said that, our share price didn't do very well last year [2021]. One of the top ten shareholders of Unilever is Fundsmith, and Terry Smith of Fundsmith said, "Unilever has lost the plot. Jope is too woke, and why on Earth would Hellmann's have a purpose? Isn't it obvious that the purpose of Hellmann's is to make sandwiches tasty?" Of course, that is catnip for newspapers. It's absolute gold. So it got blown out of all proportion.

What Terry was really saying was "I'm not happy with your share price performance." Unfortunately, he picked the wrong root cause, because right now, Hellmann's is one of our best-performing brands and the recent success is being driven by Hellmann's brand campaign on the platform of "Make taste, not waste." It is our effort to help tackle the issue of food waste because if food waste was a country, it would be the third biggest carbon emitter in the world. We know that if one night a week a household says, "I'm going to eat what's left in the fridge" instead of going to buy new stuff, it cuts their food waste by 40 percent. Just from that one change.

Of course, eating what otherwise would become food waste saves people money, but it also drives sales of mayonnaise. Mayonnaise goes very well with lots of food that would otherwise be chucked out. Unilever has fourteen brands in the company with sales of more than €1 billion — and through the first half of this year [2022], which is the only data I can give at the moment, the pattern continues. Hellmann's grew 19 percent and remains the fastest-growing of those billionaire brands. Terry is right to be critical of our total shareholder return in 2021, but he is in a tiny minority of investors who feel that the cause is an excessive focus on sustainability or brand purpose.

We don't generally suffer shareholder criticism on our sustainability efforts. It's random and occasional, and I don't get tired making the case that when we take care of our employees and they take care of consumers and customers, the shareholder will be rewarded for us doing business the right way. I just wish we were doing a better job of contributing to the empirical evidence that that is the case. I will go to my grave slightly frustrated that in my five years I didn't nail the argument with Unilever's own performance, but I deeply believe it will come.

It seems clear that Unilever approaches sustainability through a justice lens. Please share with us your view as to why business leaders and business itself are key players in the movement towards greater social justice?

There is quite a strong sense of fair play or fairness in our values and our culture, and it extends into our business. Let's be clear: unequal societies are not a good place to sell the kind of mass products that 3.4 billion people use every day. We're not in the private jet business. We're not even in the luxury clothing business. We're in the business of everyday necessities. We do well when societies prosper. I think the reason why Unilever is a fantastic bet in your long-term portfolio is because of the almost immutable law that shows that as socioeconomics improve in the emerging markets, increases take place in the consumption of hair care products, high-quality food ingredients, homecare products, and so on. Market penetration increases, per-capita consumption increases, and average unit price increases. So, the market grows. Prosperous societies are really, really good for Unilever's business. I think concepts such as fairness and equality permeate our values, our culture, *and* our business model.

When my executive team formed four years ago, we said we wanted the company to be famous for three things. We wanted to be famous for an envied and beautiful portfolio of purposeful brands — brands that stand for more than just whiter clothes or tastier food or shinier hair, but that make a positive impact in the world. The second thing we wanted to be famous for was proving the link between a sustainable business — a multi-stakeholder sustainable business model — and better financial outcomes. The third thing we wanted to be famous for was to have Unilever be a beacon for equity, diversity, and inclusion.

When we talk about these issues, we have a theory on creating change. Let's take EDI and opportunities for women. Here's our theory of change. The first is to get our own house in order. So, eight years ago, 38 percent of our management level and above were women. It's now at 52 percent; our non–executive board is six men, six women. But we've still got pockets. My executive team is still imbalanced towards men. We've got work to do there. So, number one, get your own house in order.

The second layer or ring of concentric circles is our value chain. We want to make sure that women are represented in our suppliers. For instance, that women are well represented in the smallholder farmers that we buy from or in our distribution systems. We've got 150,000 women in India who we have set up as micro-entrepreneurs and who distribute our products into the most rural of rural villages. By the way, these women generate €500 million of revenue for us from that system, so it's no small thing. And it's creating opportunities for women in our value chain.

The third circle is our brands. And what do I mean by that? What can our brands do? The best example is what Dove is doing. Dove is trying to break these ridiculous representations and stereotypes of beauty that turn beauty into a source of anxiety for women instead of a source of pleasure. The work that we've done on campaigning for real expressions of beauty through Dove is an example of what our brands can do to try changing societal norms.

The fourth and final circle is our advocacy. We work with all kinds of organizations that are trying to drive change for women. One that I'm particularly proud of works towards un-stereotyping advertising. I believe we are now well down the road of changing the whole advertising industry. Five years ago, if there was a leadership position being depicted in advertising, it would be cast as a white man; there was no representation of the LGBTQ+ community, and Black characters were almost entirely missing. But now, the whole industry is changing, where if there is someone doing household chores, it's now much more likely to be a man that's cast in that role than it would have been a few years ago. The reason why? Again, it is not just a moral case. We now have unequivocal data that progressive, un-stereotyped advertising is more effective advertising. It isn't detached from business but connected to it.

So, our model of change is built around these four rings of influence, and I can use exactly the same model for carbon, the same model for nature as I did with gender. Get your own house in order, leverage your value chain, use your brands as a force for good, and change the system through effective advocacy.

You have stated, "You build your credibility by what you do, not what you say."[4] How do you ensure that when Unilever (or one of your brands) takes a stand on an issue it is viewed as credible and authentic rather than opportunistic?

I don't understand why more companies haven't figured this out. The idea is simple: action has to precede rhetoric. What I mean by that is, the reason Dove can authentically talk about campaigning for real beauty is because we've worked one-on-one with 60 million young people — mainly girls — on what

---

4 Marc de Swaan Arons, "Humanizing Growth Series | Alan Jope on Brand Purpose," April 15, 2021, www.linkedin.com/pulse/humanizing-growth-series-alan-jope-brand-purpose-marc-de -swaan-arons.

real beauty is and means. Respected scholars have done studies that show that it changes perceptions; it changes the girls' attitudes towards beauty and self-esteem.

The reason why Domestos [a bathroom disinfectant] can talk about tackling the scourge of open defecation in emerging nations is because we've worked with various NGOs to put 30 million toilets in homes so that women don't have to go out and defecate in the field, which creates vulnerabilities to disease, all kinds of sexual violence, and so on. The reason why Hellmann's can talk about food waste is because they are taking action on United Nations Sustainable Development Goal 12.3 to fight food waste. The reason why Knorr can talk about regenerative agriculture is we're making real progress on converting whole industries from destructive agricultural practices to healthy ones. I think your authenticity comes from your actions, not your words. Our brands are engaged in these multi-year, impactful programs that underpin what they then talk about.

This book is about developing, supporting, and promoting leaders with strength of character to tackle boundary-crossing grand challenges in society. Do you have any final thoughts on leadership, leader character, and business as we are trying to create a better world?

I love the dimensions and elements in your leader character framework. I think they are indeed some of the characteristics required of good leaders.

When I look at, let's say, the CEO portion of the leadership cadre, there is a whole generation of CEOs coming through who are low-ego; they are humble and see themselves in service of the organizations that they work for. They understand that they are nothing without their people. They see that the world is too complex now to imagine that one leader has all the answers . . . it needs the wisdom of the team, of the organization. CEOs still get paid a lot, but I think the days of chauffeured limousines and rose petals being thrown around in front of every step that the CEO takes are disappearing — thank goodness. That new breed of CEO, for me, jibes very well with some of the character dimensions that you're calling out in your model.

Over the years, Unilever has used every competency model that you could imagine — some very simple, some very complex. My empirical learning has been there are three characteristics of people who tend to do quite well in our company. The first characteristic is that they are bright. You need a certain level of intellectual and emotional horsepower to succeed in business. It's quite intellectually demanding. The second is they are driven. They have evidence in their lives of overcoming setbacks or driving things through to resolution without falling over, not backing off at the first sense of failure or difficulty. Because business is difficult. The third is they are people who other people want to be around. They are great collaborators, they take blame and share credit, and they are sources of energy.

I've always said people who are smart, driven, and good human beings tend to do quite well. At one time, Unilever developed a leadership model which was built around judgment, drive, and influencing. I said, "Wait a minute! That validates my own experience!" So the only concern I would have about your model is it's so multi-factorial that it is hard to internalize and remember. But those three things I just mentioned I do think sort of capture a lot of what you're describing.

Good leaders remember the moments and people that shaped them. What moment or people truly helped shape your leadership, and in which ways?

I have been asked this quite a few times about role models or big influences, and I really struggle with it. I think I am a kleptomaniac; I steal little bits from lots and lots and lots of people. I had lunch recently with Leena Nair, who is our former chief human resources officer. Leena left about six months ago to become the global CEO of Chanel. She is a force of nature and I am so happy that she is in the Chanel role. She is a role model for so many people. I learned so much from Leena on the importance of mentorship and really progressive people practices.

Also, very early in my career — I was thirty-five years old — I was put into a gigantic job running our North American Home and Personal Care business. I was not fully prepared to do it, and in early July one year we realized we had a massive problem. We were going to undershoot our financials. My reflex was to get my team in the room and say, "We're in trouble. What can we do about it?" We spent two days together working through and recasting the business plan, and well, we delivered the numbers. The minute I've got a problem, my reflex is to bring the team in because someone in the team or the team collectively will know how to solve it. I can still remember those two days. It was really a formative moment for me. It gave me a lasting belief that none of us are as smart as all of us.

CHAPTER 10

ADAM KAHANE
Director of Reos Partners

AND BRUCE LOURIE
President of Ivey Foundation

Adam Kahane is a director of Reos Partners, an international social enterprise that helps people move forward together on their most important and intractable issues.

Adam is a leading organizer, designer, and facilitator of processes through which business, government, and civil society leaders can work together to address such challenges. He has worked in more than fifty countries, in every part of the world, with executives and politicians, generals and guerrillas, civil servants and trade unionists, community activists and United Nations officials, clergy and artists.

Adam is the author of *Solving Tough Problems*, about which Nelson Mandela said: "This breakthrough book addresses the central challenge of our time: finding a way to work together to solve the problems we have created." He is also the author of *Power and Love*, *Transformative Scenario Planning*, *Collaborating with the Enemy*, and *Facilitating Breakthrough*.

Adam is a member of the Order of Canada. In 2022 he was named a Schwab Foundation Social Innovation Thought Leader of the Year at the World Economic Forum in Davos.

Dr. Bruce Lourie is a best-selling author, policy expert, social entrepreneur, and award-winning global sustainability leader. In addition to serving as president of the Ivey Foundation, he is a scholar-in-residence at McGill University's Trottier Institute for Sustainability in Engineering and Design and a guest lecturer at the Saïd Business School's Social Finance Programme at the University of Oxford. He is active on many boards of directors and advisory boards including at the Transition Accelerator and Canadian Climate Institute.

Bruce is one of Canada's most influential leaders and experts on climate change and has been instrumental in creating more than a dozen organizations that play critical roles in Canada's transition to a net-zero economy, including Canadian Climate Institute, Institute for Sustainable Finance, Farmers for Climate Solutions, Efficiency Canada, and the Transition Accelerator.

He initiated the largest climate action in North America, the phasing-out of coal-fired electricity in Ontario, and helped establish the Ontario Greenbelt. He is also the co-author of two books, including the international bestseller *Slow Death by Rubber Duck*. Bruce holds a PhD in environmental studies, examining the intersection of risk, science, and policy.

Take us back to 1991–1992 in post-apartheid South Africa and describe the backdrop to the initiative that became known as the Mont Fleur Scenario Exercise. Nelson Mandela had been released from prison, and the negotiations to end apartheid had begun. A multi-stakeholder team of South African leaders — including the opposition and the establishment, left and right, Black and white; businesspeople, politicians, academics, trade unionists, and community workers — wanted to use the Shell scenario methodology to work together to create a successful transition to democracy, and they invited you to facilitate their workshops.

AK: My experience in South Africa in 1991 and 1992 was transformative and inspirational. It was, in every respect, a turning point in my life. I was only thirty years old, but I had worked in several institutions — academic, governmental, and corporate, including Shell. What struck me about this experience was the nature of the group. There were deep political, social, cultural, and economic differences among them, and a long history of violent conflict. I knew that. Everybody in the world knew it. At the same time, the group was more relaxed and surprisingly more open and creative than any I had encountered before. That contrast was striking to me.

To aid in South Africa's transition, the team of leaders who gathered for the exercise constructed a number of scenarios describing possible futures for the country. While the exercise may not have had a large impact on the transition from apartheid to democracy, it did affect the economic policy of the soon-to-be-elected Mandela government. Nobody was paying much attention to economics at the time: attention was largely on constitutional, political, and military matters. But the Mont Fleur scenario exercise included economists and businesspeople, and their scenarios had a big influence on the economic thinking of the new government.

Mont Fleur revealed a way of working that I had never seen or even heard of before. The exercise wasn't as much about creating the scenarios as it was about bringing together a diverse group of leaders from across a given social system who didn't agree with or like or trust each other, yet need to and were able to work together to influence the evolution of that system. The exercise taught me that such collaboration is possible. It's not easy or straightforward or guaranteed, but it can be done.

I also learned what conditions were required to make the exercise possible. First is the context: enough people think that things need to change, and they understand that they can't change them unilaterally. Second, the participants: the people in the room need to have the capacity to change the situation if they act together. The third consideration is what I would call the space. I'm using the word *space* in the way [management scholar] Ikujiro Nonaka uses it, meaning the political, social, or physical space in which people are meeting. A boardroom is different from a cafeteria; the House of Commons is different from a small hotel in the mountains. Those elements — context, participants, and space — come together in what I call *facilitation*.

You said participants were "surprisingly open and creative." Could you please elaborate on why it was surprising?

AK: I had never been in such a meeting before, but I expected, given the degree of difference and conflict, that participants would be rigid and doctrinaire. I had experienced such rigidity, even in much less conflictual contexts. My experience in corporations, government, and research institutes is that people often have perspectives and positions that they hold on to tightly. I was expecting more of that, and what I witnessed was less. The difference was the participants, the space, and the process.

An explicit goal of co-creating different scenarios is to challenge the mindsets of the participants — to open their minds to possible futures beyond the single possible future that they are focusing on. In scenario planning, the question is "What could happen?" rather than "What will happen?" or "What should happen?" That disarms people.

In my most recent book, *Facilitating Breakthrough*,[1] I give the example of Trevor Manuel, a South African politician who served for twenty years as a minister in the cabinets of President Mandela and his successors. He was an activist and worked for political equality as well as social and economic equality. And, at the time of the Mont Fleur scenario exercise, he was the head of the African National Congress's Department of Economic Policy. Manuel highlighted the importance of openness and learning in processes like the Mont Fleur exercise. You weren't coming with a manifesto; you were trying to engage in discussion.

After your experience in South Africa, you left Shell to work full-time on collaborative efforts to address what you call "transforming complex social systems." A major example is the work you did in Colombia. In 2016, Juan

---

1   Adam Kahane, *Facilitating Breakthrough: How to Remove Obstacles, Bridge Differences, and Move Forward Together* (Oakland, CA: Berrett-Koehler Publishers, 2021).

Manuel Santos, the president of Colombia, was awarded the Nobel Peace Prize "for his resolute efforts to bring the country's more than fifty-year-long civil war to an end, a war that has cost the lives of at least 220,000 Colombians and displaced close to 6 million people." In his acceptance speech, he said, "Allow me to tell you, from my own experience, that it is much harder to make peace than to wage war." President Santos also credited you for making peace possible. He said, "Adam Kahane is a friend of Colombia." What was a key lesson unique to the Colombian experience that you learned?

AK: It has been thrilling to have President Santos praise my work. Santos is a brilliant politician, and one of the things that politicians do well is to make other people feel special.

As you said, Santos won the Nobel Peace Prize in 2016, which was twenty years after the work we had done together. He initiated the process and then, because he understood that he was too partisan to be able to convene such a trans-partisan process, he stepped aside to allow a broader and lower-profile organizing committee to continue the work.

The committee's objective was to build a scenario team that would represent the whole conflicted society and, especially, enable the combatants to talk with one another directly. To do this, the committee had to decide who they considered to be legitimate players with plausible commitments to the future of the country, and who was too criminal or corrupt. The committee elected to include guerrillas and paramilitaries on the team, as well as academics, activists, businesspeople, journalists, military officers, peasants, politicians, trade unionists, and young people.[2]

In 2016, the day Santos was awarded the Nobel Peace Prize, his office issued a statement acknowledging the prize and saying, among many other things, that the Destino Colombia scenario project had been a significant step on the road to

---

2   An extensive blog written by Adam Kahane on the Destino Colombia scenario project can be found here: thesystemsthinker.com/%EF%BB%BFnew-stories-can-generate-new-realities.

peace. Of course, I was thrilled and immediately retweeted. I also genuinely didn't understand why Santos had highlighted this project in particular, because many bigger things had happened in the twenty years since. There had been millions of dollars of US military aid, five years of negotiations in Havana, innumerable UN missions, and so on. Why did Santos even remember the Destino Colombia scenario project, let alone mention it? In fact, he mentioned it often in speeches and books.

A few months later, I was in Bogota and interviewing Santos. My first question was to ask him, "Why do you remember Destino Colombia?" Santos replied, "The reason I so often refer to Destino Colombia is because that's where I learned, contrary to all my political and cultural upbringing, that it is possible to work with people that you do not agree with and will never agree with."

Most people think that you get together, have a workshop, share a meal and a drink, and realize it was all a terrible misunderstanding. Santos is saying something that is more challenging. He is saying, "No, we don't agree and will actually never agree, and yet we still have to work together." That, for me, is the big lesson of Destino Colombia. It was like Mont Fleur, except the parties were even more senior and diverse. Destino included all the armed actors, representatives of democratic governments, business leaders, and members of an active civil society, et cetera. In fact, the most remarkable feature of the Destino project was the participation of two then-illegal, armed, left-wing guerrilla groups: the FARC [Revolutionary Armed Forces of Colombia] and the ELN [National Liberation Army].

We succeeded in dialogue by respecting the rules we formulated at the outset. The team members agreed to speak frankly; to express their differences without irony; to assume the good faith of others; to be tolerant, disciplined, and punctual; to be concrete and concise; and to keep confidences. They were proud of these ground rules, which, in the midst of so much lawlessness and violence, helped them to construct a strong and safe container. Within this container, the team members were gradually able to open up and deepen their relationships.

The Destino Colombia scenario exercise is also where I began to understand the importance of human connections. This was not at all in my mind, and I can't recall any stories about that from South Africa. The culture in Colombia, the people in Colombia, and the drama of the moment — and the fact that half of the participants in Destino Colombia had lost an immediate member of their family to the violence — meant that there was an extraordinary open-heartedness. I've come to believe that the capacity to connect at a human level is often the route to break through conflict. Destino Colombia was a dramatic example of that.

You have helped resolve many conflicts around the world — across most or all continents — and you have written five books about your experiences. In your 2017 book, *Collaborating with the Enemy*,[3] you explore what you see as a growing and troublesome trend, "enemyfying." You write:

> Enemyfying means thinking and acting as if the people we are dealing with are our enemies — people who are the cause of our problems and are hurting us. In different contexts we use different words with subtly different connotations for the people from whom we differentiate ourselves: others, rivals, competitors, opponents, adversaries, enemies. We use these characterizations often, in both ordinary and extraordinary contexts, sometimes thoughtfully and sometimes casually, even habitually. But the enemies are always the others: those people. It's like the jokes about the conjugation

---

3   Adam Kahane, *Collaborating with the Enemy: How to Work with People You Don't Agree with or Like or Trust* (Oakland, CA: Berrett-Koehler Publishers, 2017).

of irregular verbs, such as "I am firm, you are obstinate, he is a pig-headed fool." The enemyfying equivalent is "I see things differently, you are wrong, she is the enemy."

We see enemyfying all around us. It dominates the media every day: people identifying others not just as opponents to be defeated but as enemies to be destroyed. These others are variously labeled as nationalists and cosmopolitans, immigrants and racists, corporations and environmentalists, terrorists and infidels. Enemyfying, vilifying, and demonizing pervade political discourse around the world. And we enact this enemyfying syndrome not only in politics but also at work and at home.

Enemyfying is a way to understand and deal with real differences. It simplifies into black and white our overwhelmingly complex and multihued reality, and thereby enables us to clarify what is going on and mobilize energies to deal with it. But, as journalist H.L. Mencken said, "There is always an easy solution to every human problem — neat, plausible, and wrong." Our enemyfying, which feels exciting and satisfying, even righteous and heroic, usually obscures rather than clarifies the reality of the challenges we face. It amplifies conflicts; it narrows the space for problem solving and creativity; and it distracts us, with unrealizable dreams of decisive victory, from the real work we need to do.

You have also written about increasing polarization — and that it is growing almost everywhere — and that polarization is not just that "you're wrong" but "you're the devil." How do we get past enemyfying and polarization and work on solving conflicts? How do you even get entrenched enemies to talk?

BL: I guess this was the point Adam raised, which was establishing whether there is an actual interest in collectively solving a problem. I think if there is absolutely no interest and things are so polarized, it would be difficult for anyone to lead that to some kind of successful conclusion.

Some people will come to a collaboration believing that they are there to put a stake in the ground and defend their position. This could be any stakeholder on any side of an issue. Others with a different opinion will also join the collaboration and want to represent their own position. We can start a collaboration with this. We don't say that you must leave your positions with your organization, but we are trying to develop a collective new position and a shared understanding of where we want to get to.

There are people who will not participate in that exercise, and you can't include them if you want to solve the problem. It is a challenge to choose who can be included, but it is important to select people who, while legitimately representing an opposing view, won't hold fast to that position. I think that open-mindedness or flexibility is what is often missing in government processes and large, inclusive, collaborative processes where everyone is invited to participate. And, I think that's a recipe for disaster. The line I use is "There is probably a room for you, but it's not this room." There is another conversation somewhere, with someone trying to solve another problem in a different way.

This is what made South Africa and Colombia so interesting: very, very different people who probably would find themselves enemies, but they all accepted that they were trying to make a change.

Participating in change is difficult for someone who has a current position that they understand and benefit from when they cannot see the value in an alternate proposition. It is difficult, but not impossible. We have managed this situation successfully by getting everyone to agree on the facts behind the need for change. This is a more of an empirical and analytical approach than a "love and humanity" approach.

Often, people will offer what they see as the facts, but their facts will contradict what another also identifies as facts.

Somehow, you have to bring those people together so that they at least share a common understanding of the problem. One tactic we've used is to create an independent, fact-based analytical capacity for the collaborative. Instead of people arguing about their different understandings of the situation, you get them to agree on who they will accept as an independent arbiter of the truth, and then stick with that. Resolving one of the biggest complicating factors can have an amazing effect on the process.

Another strategy is to help people realize that not only can they sit in a room with people whom they may not trust or like, but also to understand those people are needed in the room to get where you're trying to go. Suddenly, it's a different calculation. We have no choice: if we want to work through this together, we must be in the room together.

Some questions require that everyone be together in one room; other questions require a different breakdown. It depends on what we're trying to work on. For example, if working on climate change and the question is how to phase out nuclear power, you don't want nuclear power companies as part of the process. If the question is how to get lower CO_2 energy systems, then maybe you do want the nuclear power companies there. It depends on the question.

In a call earlier today, we were looking at bringing together the mining industry with electric vehicle manufacturers, parts manufacturers, industry people from government, and an environmental group that want to see more electric cars on the road. They all realize that they need each other to overcome a lack of coordination and alignment across policy, government, activist groups, and the mining industry. It was pretty clear that they will all benefit by working collectively on this vision. I was happy I didn't say it, but someone else on the call said, "It sounds like what we all need is a shared vision of the future!" Bingo! It's the group collectively building out the scenario that gets them to that new future. They see where they fit in and why they are part of this bigger group. They need everyone else at the table and they want to make sure that they are included too. Together, they are helping to create this vision. That, I think, is the best, most successful way to build.

AK: As a facilitator, I don't try to get anybody to *do* anything. The starting point for collaboration is the self-realization that "I need things to change and I can't change them on my own. I must and will work with others, including people I may not agree with or like or trust because that cooperation provides a new opportunity to get where I'm trying to go."

I remember this well-known joke: How many people does it take to change a lightbulb? It only takes one, but the lightbulb has to want to change! People have to want things to be different and realize that they need to work with others to make it so. The way to get beyond polarization and enemyfying or demonization is by realizing that maybe we need to work together, even though we may wish we didn't have to, and by connecting as humans.

It has always interested me that in our workshops, far and away the most popular activity is the simplest activity: a paired walk. You look around the room, pick someone different than you, and go for a walk with them for forty-five minutes. It couldn't be any simpler, yet people always say, "That was the best module of the workshop — much better than all the scenario planning or discussion or committee meetings" or whatever.

For a long time, I tried to figure out what is so powerful about the paired walk. I used to think it was the mechanics of the walk. Two people who want to connect move forward side by side, look at the world together, and talk casually, without any papers or other distractions. The walk offers people an opportunity to connect on a human level, as equals, and to share their perspectives. This experience can produce profound changes. Almost everyone who has gone on these walks over the years says that they were surprised and affected to see the world through the eyes of their partners, with whom they expected to have nothing in common.

Lucila Servitje, a Catholic theologian who participated in this activity at another workshop I facilitated, offers a deeper explanation for why the paired walk is effective. She said, "The real reason is when I go for a walk with someone, I am firstly a human being, and secondly, as a result of that, I may be willing to change my relationship, or my thinking, or my actions." She suggests that the walk and the informal sharing of stories has impact because they involve mutual acceptance, and this feeling of being accepted is what enables us to change our thinking and actions. The sequence here — first, we are accepted, and then we reconsider our position — is the opposite of the traditional Catholic confession, where, first, we confess (we reconsider), and then we're forgiven (we're accepted). The walk, she says, is like God's grace: love we receive that we don't have to earn.[4]

As Santos said, we may not agree with each other, we may never agree with each other, but we are both in this situation. How do we deal with it? In English, the word for that phenomenon is *coexistence*, but in Spanish, the word is *convivencia* — living together, which has the same connotation as cohabiting as a couple. For me, this is an interesting difference. We don't say, "I'm coexisting with my partner." Living together doesn't mean that you necessarily agree, but it does mean that you're making a life together and you're working it out as you go along. That's my approach to this work.

You also write in your book, *Collaborating with the Enemy*, that most people believe they "are right and others are wrong; they are innocent and others are guilty; and if only the others would listen to and agree with them, then the situation would be rectified." The belief that "I am right and you are wrong" can easily turn into an "I deserve to be superior and

---

4   A fuller description of the paired walk concept is provided by Adam Kahane in an article for *Strategy+Business*: www.strategy-business.com/blog/Walk-your-way-to-transformation.

you to be inferior" mindset. As you explained, for many people, feelings of superiority are a condition of being and become integral to their identity. How do we break this dichotomous and injurious belief?

AK: I come back to the reason why connecting as human beings is so central. The Peruvian psychoanalyst Max Hernandez was in one of my workshops and he said, "The important thing is when I realize that your dreams may not be my dreams, but nor are they my nightmares." In other words, we are different and we may want different things, but there is a place where we can live together. That is the opposite of "I've never met you, I don't agree with you, I think you're inferior, and I think you may not even be really human." And the extreme of that is "you are a vermin and should be crushed."

When I worked at Shell, I got to know the founder of the scenario department, Frenchman Pierre Wack. He was the first to use scenario planning in the private sector, which resulted in a 1972 report outlining the impending energy crisis. Wack had an unusual upbringing, and during the Second World War he lived in Paris in the home of G.I. Gurdjieff, a famous Greek-Armenian spiritual teacher. Gurdjieff wrote an odd book called *Meetings with Remarkable Men.*[5] I say it's odd because these "remarkable men" were subversive — unknown individuals with unconventional ideas — not famous erudite people. Wack brought an element of that to the Shell scenario practice with his insight that you don't change the minds of successful people by sending them photocopies of articles from the *Economist*. You change the minds of successful executives — Wack's clients — by having them encounter firsthand somebody they respect who sees the world differently from them. I think that was a Gurdjieff idea.

That is what happens in these workshops, people coming to understand: "I'm encountering people with different positions and perspectives who I recognize are fellow human beings. I

5   G.I. Gurdjieff, *Meetings with Remarkable Men* (London, England: Penguin Books, 2015).

may not agree, and may never agree, with them, but I've become interested in them. What are they seeing that is different from what I'm seeing?"

It has always interested me that the people whose views are most changed in the encounters I facilitate are the elite. This is because the people at the top don't understand what is going on as well as people on the bottom. When the elite meet the others and get a glimpse of how things really work, then they change how they think.

I used to have a colleague in South Africa who would say, "When you find yourself pounding the table saying, 'The truth is,' try putting at the front of the sentence 'In my opinion.' And if that doesn't work, try 'In my humble opinion.'" The point is to create some space between yourself and the opinion you have, in order to create room to interrogate that opinion. You may still have the same opinion after examining it, but by suspending your judgment about the "rightness" of your opinion, you may think about it differently. Without suspending judgment, we end up simply projecting our own stream of thoughts, ideas, and concerns onto a situation we encounter rather than shining a light on it.

Achieving the breakthroughs despite the acrimony of participants takes humility and humanity. It's hard to imagine that these elements of character are present to any degree in the settings you describe. Can you comment?

AK: I relate humanity and humility to power and love, and in my most recent book, *Facilitating Breakthrough*, I've added the question of justice. In many social systems, the drive for power dominates. I don't think we should abandon power for love, but we need to do them both. What often happens, though, is that humility and connection are "specialized" by placing them with the HR department. Assertion and ambition are expected of other people.

I added a third driver, justice, to the power–love configuration, and in my writings, I have explored what this combination might mean for those of us who navigate social change. My colleague Rebecca Freeth who works in South Africa captured it as follows:[6]

> Injustice stymies social change in several ways; I am particularly aware of two. Those with relatively more privilege than others often — not always — have a particular set of blind spots regarding the impact of their privilege on others. And those with relatively less privilege than others often — not always — bear resentment and anger, exacerbated by acts of privileged blindness. When social challenges affect us all and require us to collaborate with each other across divides of privilege, we may collapse under the weight of our deep mistrust and fear of each other. Unless we can openly discuss the injustices that make it difficult to work together and unless we aspire towards greater justice and equality, our social change efforts may prove to be inherently unsustainable. And if we who dream up, lead, convene, or facilitate these processes are unaware of the privilege we and other collaborators carry, our efforts may unwittingly perpetuate the injustices embedded in our social systems.

I'm trying to enable all three things at the same time — power, love, and justice — and recognize that all three of them are present in almost everybody and in almost every group, but what's required is to remove the obstacles to their expression. I call love "the drive to reconnect the separated." I think that is what you are associating with humility and humanity. That

---

6   This quote is from an article written by Rebecca Freeth, an associate in the Johannesburg office of Reos Partners. She a dialogue facilitator, organizational development practitioner, and writer. She specializes in designing and facilitating multi-stakeholder dialogues, scenarios exercises, and Social Labs on issues that matter to South Africans. Rebecca teaches systems thinking, scenarios planning, and facilitation skills in South Africa and globally.

drive is always there, and if things are set up well, that can be unblocked. People experience joy when they recognize that they are connected to and are a part of the same larger whole as people whom they thought of as their opponents or enemies. Relationships and interdependence — that's the expression of love. Not instead of power, but as a complement.

The joy at reconnecting, which I have seen in my work and have experienced myself, is one of the most powerful experiences people ever have. We had a workshop between native Hawaiians and other residents of Hawaii — two groups that are severely alienated from one another. Today, the participants are still speaking of the workshop experience with awe, and it was the awe of realizing that they were part of a larger whole from which they had become disconnected.

For better or worse, I've chosen these simple and resonant words of power, love, and justice. The words also have other connotations, which may seem counterintuitive. Power relates to the *wholeness* of an entity, such as my company's health and profitability and vision. Love relates to the *partness*: my company is part of an ecosystem of other companies and regulators, societal norms, and the natural environment. I need to reconcile the ambitions and health and power of my organization with the fact that my organization is part of a larger whole. That's what I'm talking about. When people say, "I don't want to work with this other person or entity, but I need to because we are part of the same larger whole and we share a vision about what we're trying to do as a larger whole," they are exhibiting the phenomenon that I'm labeling love: the drive to reunite the separated. It has nothing to do with romance.

Conversations about climate change fit this scenario. The conversations are difficult for reasons everybody knows, but there is an effort to understand how the parts and the whole can be healthy. That is the power versus love, or the power *and* love, dynamic. The good news about climate change, if I can say that there is good news, is that we are increasingly and widely recognizing that the whole we are part of is failing, and therefore, we all are going to have to change what we're doing. This helps. If I think back to my experience with Canadian political scenarios twenty-five years ago and reflect on why the project failed, I would say it was because the elites in the room said, "What's the problem? Things are fine the way they are." Nobody is saying that now about climate. Nobody thinks things are fine the way they are.

In relation to the wholeness and partness that you speak about, can that philosophy apply not just to organizations but to social dynamics — say gender dynamics, for example? If love is about reunification, do you think that can work on our collective consciousness? I [Milani] am asking this because, for over fifteen years, I was a part of organizing an event in London, Ontario, that commemorated the Montreal Massacre. We called it the Ritual of Re-Membering, because we sought to re-member what had been dis-membered through gender-based violence, which manifests as the ultimate separation of male and female, woman and man into an eons-old abusive power dynamic. At that time, gender was understood in more binary terms, but now, it is more fluid and identified along a spectrum — it is less separated. If love drives the unification of the separated, how can we apply that philosophy to humanity as a whole?

AK: That question makes important connections. If love is the drive that unites the separated, then one of the separated — a primary separated — in many societies is between men and women or between the masculine and feminine. Or between people and the Earth, or the economy and the environment, or the Indigenous and the settler. The physicist David Bohm said that we look at the world as if in a cracked mirror: it is whole but seems fragmented.

I come back to the definition I'm using of love, which is the drive to reunite the separated. That particular separation or fragmentation or polarization is very important. Maybe, as you referenced, the softening of the binary (as we are seeing with gender) will help with that. I notice my grandchildren are more comfortable with, or more familiar with, the ideas beyond the gender binary. I think that may help in a way.

Another consideration is how we listen. I repeatedly use a model of four different ways of talking and listening. In this model, *downloading* is different from *debating*, which is different from *dialoguing*, and is different from *presencing*. The key to shifting from one way of talking to the other is to change the way that you listen. We know there is more than one way to talk, but we fail to recognize that there is more than one way to listen — just as you noted that there is more than one way to define gender. I think it's very rich, the area you've mentioned.

An important stage in fostering collaboration involves making our way forward amid uncertainty and contestation. You quote Deng Xiaoping: "We are crossing the river by feeling for stones." Does this mean people need to feel, more than plan, their way forward? What are our present-day stones?

AK: With most complex issues — like racism, reconciliation, climate, and health — we have some idea of where we need to go and roughly how to get there, but we don't know the details of what is going to work. Crossing the river feeling for stones just means that we have to advance by trying things out, learning as we take one step at a time. In a way, COVID has offered an example: we have had to, and are still, feeling our way. People had strong opinions in March 2020 about what they believed was right and would work, but it's been a learning process with lots of changes and adjustments along the way. The same with the climate crisis: we have a lot of ideas about how to address the crisis, and we have lots of pathways and calculations and hypotheses and proposals, but we're only going to figure it out by doing it one step at a time. Deng Xiaoping's quotation is not saying anything more complicated than that.

There appears to be so much conflict embedded in social systems around the world. If a major global pandemic cannot unite people, what can? Are you optimistic or pessimistic about working our way to a better future where we can learn to live together in such a way that love, power, and justice enhance and support one another?

BL: I'm optimistic. If you remember my suggestion that there is another room for someone who may not agree with you, I would say the response to the global pandemic was largely successful. There were issues around equality of access that were problematic — and are always problematic for everything. The anti-vaccine element is fringe and those are the people who can find their own room somewhere.

The pandemic response in the Western world was successful and there seemed to be considerable global cooperation. We are seeing something similar now with climate change. There are always some people on either edge of an issue — either trying to prevent any action or pushing extraordinarily hard for action. The necessity of action is found in a simple framework of urgency and doability: once you get to the point where something is believed by many people to be urgent and believed by many to be doable, you get real action.

It's taken many years to reach the point of action with climate change — it takes many years with most things — but I think we're there. I think enough people recognize not only that we must address this issue, but also that it is doable. We already see electric cars on the road. I recognize that I'm again speaking from a Western perspective, but I think there is almost too much emphasis placed on polarization and negativity. If 80 or 90 percent of the population is on board with climate change initiatives, I think it becomes quite easy to move forward.

What makes you believe we're there in terms of doability and urgency?

BL: The nature of the conversation has shifted so dramatically over the twenty-five years I've been working on climate change. We are no longer trying to figure out how to manufacture electric cars or manufacture as many as we need or get the needed electricity. We are no longer thinking about how to get the policies. Electric cars are well on their way, to the point where our primary concern in Canada is how not to fall behind a rapid global shift. Now the question is, How can we benefit economically from a rapidly building snowball when Canada is such a small player in a global market? We need to be at the table, even if it means picking up the biggest crumbs we can. We're not leading global battery supply chains — China and the United States are. There is a sense now that if this is happening, we need to be part of it, and we need to make the most of it for our economic future. We're seeing that with hydrogen. The single biggest challenge we have, quite frankly, is still the oil industry. Their lobbying efforts are what's stopping us from moving forward more quickly. That's happening globally — in every single country and very much so in Canada.

AK: I want to agree with Bruce and add something different. I've come to understand in the last few months that the contribution Bruce and I have been making is telling hopeful stories. Someone pointed out that I've been doing that in all my books, but I didn't understand that my function was to say, "This is possible." Whether it's about electric cars or a dialogue among enemies — and however difficult it might be — my function has been to say that it can be done.

A Norwegian government official once told me that he visited the Czech Republic at the time of the Bosnian war. He was meeting with Vaclav Havel, the former president of the Czech Republic. They were on the steps of the presidential palace when Havel was besieged by reporters who asked him, "Mr. Havel, are you optimistic or pessimistic about Bosnia?" Havel had a dramatic way of answering questions, and he said, and I am paraphrasing here, "I'm not optimistic because I don't believe everything will turn out well. I am not pessimistic because I don't believe everything will turn out badly. I have hope."

My answer to your question is that I am not optimistic or pessimistic. That's not how I think about things. The way I look at it is I know what I need to do. What I need to do is not dependent on my mood or my sentiment about being optimistic or pessimistic. What I need to do is the stuff we've been talking about for the last hour and a half, including telling hopeful stories.

CHAPTER 11

DAVID KIPPING

Associate Professor of Astronomy, and Principal Investigator of the Cool Worlds Lab, Columbia University

Fascinated by the solar system since childhood, David Kipping, Associate Professor of Astronomy at Columbia University, is widely known for his research on planets and moons outside our solar system, including their impact on the origins of our solar system and beyond. "I seek to understand our home's uniqueness in the universe," says David. "Our parent star, solar system, home planet, and companion moon have all played a role in the story of how we came to be. My passion is to follow the trail of cosmic breadcrumbs left behind to reveal whether this story played out elsewhere across the ocean of stars."

At Columbia, he leads the Cool Worlds Lab, where he and his team study extrasolar planetary systems with a particular focus on the detection and analysis of worlds found at longer orbital periods. He is also active in science outreach, including operating a YouTube channel called Cool Worlds, which, with more than 750,000 subscribers, serves as an international platform to discuss his group's research and related science.

David earned his bachelor's and master's degrees at the University of Cambridge and received his PhD in astrophysics from University College London. He spent time doing postdoctoral work at Harvard University before joining Columbia University in 2015 and has authored more than one hundred scientific publications.

You study exoplanets, moons, rings, and stellar hosts. Please tell us briefly about the questions you pursue and how the science of astronomy has the potential to contribute to the betterment of the daily lives of people.

Astronomy is the oldest science. It is a huge topic because its subject matter is, itself, the universe; so really, it's the study of everything. In contrast, there are not that many professional astronomers — there are only about ten thousand of us on the planet — so we are dwarfed by the number of objects we have to study in the universe.

There are many reasons to study astronomy and to learn about the universe. In a way, astronomers are akin to mapmakers — especially the current generation of us like myself — that are looking for planets and moons. I think there is a nice analogy in thinking about how many centuries ago we were exploring our own planet and discovering new continents. There were large regions of the map where we just didn't know what was there. It wasn't obvious at all what the benefit of that exploration was at the time necessarily, but it seems fundamental to human nature that we are driven to explore and want to know what is beyond the horizon. But it starts just with drawing a map, then eventually taking steps and actually going out into the universe — I think in a very long-game sense of what we are doing. A part of our job is to figure out where we are in the real estate of the entire universe.

I think in the modern world, what astronomy can do for humankind is to give us a sense of awe or wonder about who we are or where we came from. We are trying to fill in the story of our origins to some extent. As well, astronomy seeks to understand questions such as, where did the Earth come from? How did it acquire an atmosphere? Where did life begin? These are all fundamental questions about our origins. Every time we look at another star, we are, in effect, looking back in time, both literally and figuratively: literally, because of the length of the light travel time in some cases, meaning that the light that is now being perceived by our eyes was actually generated potentially light-years ago but is only now reaching us; and figuratively, because sometimes you are looking at stars that are very similar to our sun but that were born only recently. We get opportunities to see ourselves in a mirror, providing analogies of ourselves at different points in our planet's journey and our solar system's journey. Perhaps even the human journey as well.

Some of my work also looks for evidence of life itself in the universe, as well as technology in the universe and intelligent life. That's something that I think the public really understands the appeal of, but to try to quantify the value of that is very difficult. What is the value of making contact with an alien civilization, for instance? It's difficult to put a dollar value on such an enterprise, but I think we all understand that it would be transformative to our place in the universe, and the benefits would be completely unpredictable. I think a lot of what we are doing speaks to the human condition — about who we are.

Of course, I actually think in an educational sense that all of the reasons that I just spoke of are appealing to many people, and that's why so many people are drawn to astronomy and maybe watch my YouTube channel and others. And I think as public educators we try to use that appeal as a vehicle to get people interested in the science. When we talk about astronomy, we try to use it as a way of bringing people into the scientific discussion, understanding how science works and the scientific method, and how scientists determine things as well. I think in today's society, that is crucial.

What got you interested in astronomy? There must have been a spark, that something that said, "That's the field!" What was it for you?

Since I was a child, I have always been fascinated by space. I'd stay up at night looking up at the stars, lying out on the grass. I was always just fascinated about what was out there. I wanted to understand how things work. For me, it's felt intrinsic to my life.

You enjoy publicizing science and run a YouTube channel discussing your research and that of your colleagues at the Cool Worlds Lab.[1] You shared in one of the Cool Worlds videos some mind-boggling numbers. For example, there are more stars in our universe than there are grains of sand on all the beaches on Earth put together. You said, "It's an absurd number that defies human comprehension." How has your research in astronomy impacted you personally?

Being an astronomer changes your way of thinking just by being aware of the vast scale of things. I think there is kind of a paradox here, because that vastness can make your problems feel insignificant and you don't need to worry about them. You're having a bad day and you think, "What does this bad day matter in the grand scheme of things?" But I also think we often grapple with "Does this make my life insignificant?," which can feed into a sense of despair for some people. We can ask, "What's the point in all this? There's no greater power; we're all just an accident." And that is indeed what astronomy teaches us — that we are just here by fluke. There is no reason for anything. We are just dirt and mud that happened to come together in the right way. This can lead to thinking very deeply about what then, exactly, is this thing we call "being a human" all about?

The way I have tried to make sense of that is, yes, a collection of atoms is not an unusual phenomenon at all in the universe — you can find them everywhere. *But*, a collection of atoms that is alive is quite rare! In our solar system, that is clearly true, but it also seems to be true in the greater expanse — in the solar neighborhood around us as well. A collection of atoms that can think, that can talk, that can feel, that can dream, that can have abstract thoughts — that is an extremely rare phenomenon as far as we can tell. I think it is important for us to realize and understand that this experience we are in — of possessing a conscious sense of

---

1   Watch the YouTube channel at www.youtube.com/c/coolworldslab.

awareness — is certainly an extremely rare phenomenon. Therefore, so are you and so is each and every one of us.

You can travel a billion light-years in any direction and you will not come across another human being or likely any being that could understand you, could understand your thoughts or your feelings about anything. That makes me think how each of us is very precious; that each human being is a rare phenomenon in the universe. As such, we should treat each other with kindness and respect, because that's probably all that there really is that is real in the end, in the grand scheme of things. Each of us is precious. If we are aware of that, it can encourage us to listen a bit more and try to understand; to be more empathetic with each other. That is the paradox that the vast scale of things elicits and how I try to come to terms with it.

In a *Cool Worlds* episode called "Watching the End of the World" (which has close to six million views and garnered many emotional comments), you explore what we would see if we could journey through time, from Earth's birth up to its death. Towards the end of the episode, you state:

> Earth finally rests, returning to its maker. In Earth's twelve-billion-year-old story, life blossomed for just over half of its age, and multicellular life makes up just one-fifth of that story. And humanity? Well, we may be just the blink of an eye. We recognize that *where* we live is special but so too is *when*. For we live in Earth's glory days, a world of temperate conditions, stabilized obliquity, active geology, and diverse flourishing of life. An era where not just multicellular life is possible, but animals, agriculture, and even civilizations. Ultimately, the fate of ourselves is up to us. We can choose to accelerate our demise, or we can look after our world, its life, and each other. The candle doesn't have to go out here — new stars, new worlds are forming right now. The universe offers infinite potential to those who

> dare and so where we go from here is a choice that I
> leave to you.[2]

This segment of the video is touching and evocative. It offers perspective. It challenges us to be and do better. It speaks to interconnectedness — connections with other human beings as well as the space around us. What messages did *you* want to convey?

I love thinking about the timeline of the Earth, because I believe a lot of people tend to operate under the assumption that the Earth has, more or less, been the way it is for a long time, and that life as we know it has been on this planet since almost the beginning. It just isn't true. The Earth is 4.5 billion years old now, but multicellular life has only been here for about 800 million years. [For] the vast majority of time, there was only single-cell life on earth. There were no plants on the surface; there were no animals. The Earth looked like a desolate world for the vast majority of time.

That is also true in the future. Multicellular life will probably persist for only another 800 million years or so, which means we are about halfway through the multicellular life story. Biodiversity is expected or predicted to diminish because of the warming of the sun over a timescale of billions of years. Therefore, we are living in a very unique moment, at this apex of bio-productivity. Earth is probably the most beautiful it will ever be. Well, maybe rewind the clock two hundred years, before we started screwing things up. I think that is an important thing to emphasize, because we are obviously damaging the planet with our activity, and right when it is in the most pristine and beautiful state it will ever be in. It urges me, when I think about that, to want to work harder to protect the Earth and to preserve this wonderful state our planet is in. I think that is also something I wanted to emphasize in the video.

------

2   The episode can be accessed at www.youtube.com/watch?v=p9e8qNNe3Lo.

The other thing I was trying to get across, and certainly I think about a lot in my own life, is urgency — how precious time is; how the clock is ticking and time is running out. On a cosmological scale, whether we are trying to preserve Earth or not, eventually time will run out on the planet just because of the sun. But on a human scale, all we have are about one hundred years, if we're lucky, to live on this planet. Your time is finite. There is a finite amount of time to engage in the things you want to accomplish. You should wake up with a sense of urgency, a sense of how every moment is important and you have to live it. Otherwise, it will slip by and you can't get it back. We are all on the same kind of decline, in a sense, as the planet is, so we should try to get the most out of each of those moments. I think about that a lot, in terms of an analogy of my own life and what is happening to the planet.

You mentioned that we must take action against climate change. What other big topics are on your mind?

I think the scientific process is something I'm also very keen to get deeper into. I am thinking a lot about anti-trust of science. In the post-fact world that we live in, I think a lot of people are confused about what science is, how it works, and why it is valuable. Carl Sagan wrote a fantastic book called *The Demon-Haunted World: Science as a Candle in the Dark*.[3] It is tragic that so many of his predictions about the direction and loss of scientific literacy have come true. I think scientists — all of us — have an obligation to highlight the importance of the scientific process and why it is so powerful. It was born and developed during the Renaissance to be able to cut cleanly through the noise of what was going on in the world — a time when the world was very mysterious and demon-haunted. Now,

---

3   Carl Sagan, *The Demon-Haunted World: Science as a Candle in the Dark* (New York: Ballantine Books, 2011).

today, I feel like that cloud of confusion is with us heavier than it has ever been. That is a way I would like to use our channel to make a positive impact.

You often conclude your videos with the expression "stay thoughtful and stay curious." Is there a special meaning behind that expression?

I think at the very simplest level, it is just to keep your head up and keep your head out of the ground. We all get caught up in the swipe culture on our phones. Unfortunately, that awareness and ability to just observe the world around you, and to ask questions about why things are the way they are, is almost hammered out of us because of the ease of access to information. For example, sometimes you can ask a question like, "Why is the sky blue?" and then you don't even look it up and seek the answer. Instead, you think, "I'm sure someone has figured it out and I'm sure there is an answer if I look it up, so I'm not even going to bother."

We have become intellectually lazy with the way we ask questions, but the actual process of thinking about that is really important. That is curiosity — it's wondering why things are the way they are, and diving in and learning about them. That is why I like to remind the audience to stay thoughtful and curious every time. It's important. The viewers have obviously been curious enough about the topic to watch the video, so I want to encourage them to continue that. Even if it is just half an hour a day — just take some time out of your day to really ponder deep questions.

May we please ask you to share your thoughts about how anthropocentric bias may cloud our decision-making, and how you try not to fall victim to that bias?

Bias is something I think about a lot, especially because my other hat is an astro-statistician's. My videos and my research are strongly themed around bias. There are all sorts of biases that cloud what we would call inference — our ability to learn about what is really happening in the world. With anthropocentric bias, certainly one place that it has a huge impact in my work is the search for extraterrestrial intelligence. We are on a quest to try to make contact, but I think we often have the idea that they will be a humanoid — someone who will have two hands, two feet, and walk out and do the Star Trek or Vulcan salute. It will almost be like talking to a long-lost cousin or something — that first contact. That is anthropocentric bias in action. It is like putting ourselves out there in the universe and imagining that is what we're going to see. Really, the greatest challenge that we face in this search is how to look for that which we do not know.

In terms of my everyday life, I don't worry too much about anthropocentric bias as an individual. The bias I worry about is what you want to be true, about objectivity. For instance, I am an astronomer who looks for moons. I am very aware of the fact that if I find a confirmed Earth-like moon, it will be beneficial to my career. The moment you realize that, you realize you are biased. Every time I am looking for moons, I am biased because I want to find moons. And so, I have to consciously and actively push myself back. I think this is a really important lesson that I use in the videos sometimes as well when I talk about the scientific method. If we have some evidence for something, then our job is to find as many reasons as we can — any reason we can — to reject that hypothesis or challenge that hypothesis, and to be internally very skeptical. I am probably the biggest skeptic. When I see a moon, I immediately think, "I want that to be true, so I have to be extra skeptical about the validity of that claim." I think that has a lot of value in how we think about everything and navigate the world around us.

If you don't want climate change to be true, because it's going to mean you can't drive your truck around anymore, you are biased. You are going to be affected by that way of thinking when you interpret some plot [behind] how the planet's temperature is changing. Therefore, it is important to be extra skeptical of yourself, to be aware that "Oh, I actually want climate change to not be true, therefore I should be extra cognizant of that and try to correct for it." That is the bias I worry about more in everyday life. In my opinion, it is clearly ever-present in society right now. It is all over the place, and we need to be careful.

It seems, at least in Western culture, that we are losing our sense of humility and openness to learning. Would you agree that this is a significant challenge and why?

Yes, and especially in science. I'd love to write a book about it one day, but I think there is a very interesting relationship between ego and science. When I graduated, I was approached by hedge fund companies who were offering me ten times the salary of an academic. I chose to do science, because it was my passion. All scientists have made this choice, but there is something else that science offers besides money, and that is ego. We are all inspired by these scientific leaders in the past, such as Albert Einstein, Richard Feynman — these giants in the field whose names are immortalized because of the things they discovered. Isaac Newton — everyone knows his name. I think one of the egotistical appeals of science is the promise of being immortalized in some way that you could never achieve working for a finance company.

I don't think anyone will have the same immortality that Isaac Newton had. Some of us, at some level, we have to be aware that we are motivated by ego. It's a problem because when you are chasing a Nobel Prize and you're driven by that peer acknowledgment, it can be a dark force. We have seen it many times in science. In planets, for example, where people claimed a planet was detected, but then new data came out and said it was not real; they refused to back down even though the evidence was overwhelming. They lost their objectivity because they were desperately hoping it was true and their name could be immortalized. They were clinging to that. A good scientist should be looking at the data and saying, "Yes, there is a challenge to this and we should revisit this." I think there is an interesting relationship between our egos and our quest in life, certainly in academia, of trying to make impact in the world. We want to make impact, but at the same time, we are partially driven by that allure of being remembered.

We hear what you're saying and that makes us a bit wary of the future because if our great scientific minds — those who know the depth and rigor that go into scientific investigation — still refute the truth when it is presented to them, how do we have hope that non-scientific people will not do that? What advice do you have for us to park our egos and be able to really look at truth in a much more objective way in order to avoid consequential ignorance?

That's a great question. I'm not sure I have all the answers to that, but one thing that comes to mind is celebrating those who admit they were wrong. I know a really nice story related to this. A paper in my field came out claiming the discovery of the very first exoplanet, but it turned out that the authors were wrong. There was a small effect because of the Earth's orbit around the sun, which they hadn't quite corrected for, and so they arrived at the wrong conclusion. Now, these scientists were attending a conference at which their findings were to be presented. One of them stood up and said, "We were wrong. The planet is not there." They received a standing ovation after the talk for their admission.

It just so happened that the next speakers were also to announce the discovery of a planet. Now, they thought theirs would be the second planet, but because of the retraction of the other group of scientists, theirs became the first planet. But they didn't get a standing ovation. People were skeptical because of what they'd just seen. I really like that, and I really admire and respect scientists, and any of us, who can admit we were wrong and show why. They followed the data.

We have become so dogmatic these days that once we've made up our mind on something — especially if we've voiced it publicly — we feel wedded to it and can't consider changing our mind. That's just crazy. That is not how learning happens at all; it is the antithesis of learning. One thing we can do is try to celebrate those who admit they were wrong or who change their mind.

I feel badly for politicians because so often, they are caged-in the most. They absolutely cannot admit they were wrong because we have these pundits who will just hammer them. I actually really admire it when someone says, "New information came to light, and it is worth it in the face of that new evidence to change our view." Trying to celebrate those people is one possible way.

Of the eleven dimensions of leader character, which one is underdeveloped for you? You could work on it, so to speak — your Achilles's heel? And how might that manifest itself?

I think there are two I clearly need to work on and that are underdeveloped — collaboration and justice. For collaboration — this is just my research style and it is somewhat true of my outreach style — I've always been sort of averse to teams or at least large teams. In some cases, this has been a detriment to my career, and at other times, it has been a kind of peculiar driver for me.

To relate a little story about this, I first arrived at Harvard for a predoctoral position they had while I was still doing my PhD, and was hired by a research scientist who didn't really have a big team. Most of the other scientists didn't know who I was, as I wasn't part of any of their collaborations. I remembered feeling very intimidated as I walked down the corridor, seeing the names of these famous scientists whose papers I'd been reading and thinking, "I can't believe I'm in the same corridor as these people and I get to have coffee with them every day!"

I was nervous about those interactions and what they would be like. Obviously I got to know [the scientists] quite well, but during the beginning times especially, I always felt like they all looked down at me because I was not at their level. So, I worked extra hard. I felt like I had to prove myself. I always felt like an underdog or an outsider. I felt like I had to work twice as hard as everyone else. I would work very unhealthy hours trying to prove myself, and I ended up being way more productive than most of the students. At some point, I was sought after amongst the other professors as well, but I was very aware of the fact that my whole reason for this trajectory was because of this approach of assuming in my head that I was an outsider and they didn't want me to succeed. That was what I was telling myself. I kind of liked deliberately keeping them at arm's length, actually, and tricking my brain into playing that game. It was kind of a conscious thing, tricking myself into keeping thinking that they wanted me to fail, even though I knew at that point that they didn't. It helped me to be productive and really competitive. But because of that, I got a reputation for not being very collaborative.

Now, most of the people I collaborate with tend to be in my inner circle; they are often my students. I really like that close working relationship. I'm the sort of person who tends to build a few close relationships rather than lots of weak relationships. Maybe I am more of an introverted type of person. I have continued to avoid any big team collaborations, and tend to focus on working with just one or two people. If you look at my papers, it is just one or two authors generally that I collaborate with. I recognize, as I've gotten older, that it is not how really ambitious science happens. There is a lot of great science you can do that way, but sometimes there are things that just are not possible in small teams. If you really want to make those huge impacts, you have to reach across the aisle and you have to build a big network and work in those large collaborations. That is something I am aware is a weakness within me, and I try to work on that and push myself to be better at it.

With justice, I feel that because of my background — I'm a white male in science. I came from a middle-class family and went to a private school in the UK so I feel like I had an enormous amount of privilege in my career. That really blinded me to all of the injustices and inequities in my field. When you are very focused, as I was at that time, writing papers, doing the science, developing your career, you are not spending your time on equity and justice work. The only reason I could afford to do that is because of my privilege. There are people from other backgrounds who don't want to have to do that work necessarily, but have to. They can't navigate through this world without some part of their brain being occupied by the fact that they stand out in this crowd. I never really felt that way in terms of my identity, at least. I'm cognizant of the fact that I had this enormous advantage, a very unfair advantage, in terms of my progress.

You see it on YouTube as well. YouTube is dominated by white males, and so I'm trying to work on that. We created a Cool Worlds micro grant where we awarded $2,000 and had a mentorship session with our winner — Stephanie Okeyo. She is running a program called Under the Microscope in Kenya, where she is trying to build a network of African scientists, and also bring in creative people as well to help them with their science communication. I'm trying to support that project through the Cool Worlds work that I'm doing. It is just a small drop in the ocean with what we're doing, but it's something I actively want to do better at and improve.

This book is about developing, supporting, and promoting leaders with strength of character to tackle boundary-crossing grand challenges in society. Do you have any final thoughts on leadership, leader character, and astronomy as we are trying to create a better world?

One thing we certainly have to resist in academia that has been happening a lot is this kind of niche-ness, where we have become ever more specialized in our own areas. There used to be just a scientist — not even a scientist really, just a natural philosopher — who then became a scientist, then a physicist, then they specialized into a quantum physicist or an astronomer, and now you have people like me who study exomoons. It is getting ever more narrow. To some extent that is necessary to understand something really deeply and to push things forward, but the loss is the interdisciplinary benefit. I really do believe that all of us have ideas that could benefit other fields if we just talk to each other more. I certainly get wonderful ideas from hearing colleagues in other fields talk, and it really inspires me. There is a saying that there is no such thing as true creativity, especially in science, that it's really just borrowing ideas from different things and sticking them together in different ways. I certainly think of all of my papers that way. Whenever someone says, "You're so creative with your papers!" I say, "I'm not, I just found these two ideas and I put them together." But you can only do that if you are listening and aware of what is out there. I think this can be a challenge for all of us: to break out of the silos that we are in and to listen.

CHAPTER 12

BEN LAMM

Co-founder and CEO, Colossal Biosciences

Ben Lamm, the co-founder and CEO of Colossal, is a serial technology entrepreneur driven to solve the most complex challenges facing our planet. For over a decade, Ben has built disruptive businesses that future-proof our world. In addition to leading and growing his own companies, he is passionate about emerging technology, science, space, and climate change. Active in angel investing, incubators, and start-up communities, Ben invests in software and emerging tech, and is deeply engaged in the technology, defense, and climate change communities.

Prior to Colossal, Ben served as the founder and CEO of several companies, including Hypergiant, an enterprise AI software company focused on space and defense; Conversable, the leading conversational intelligence platform acquired by LivePerson; and Chaotic Moon, a global creative technology powerhouse acquired by Accenture. Ben was also the co-founder of Team Chaos, a consumer gaming company acquired by Zynga.

Ben is on the Board of Trustees of the Explorers Club, whose mission is to promote the scientific exploration of land, sea, air, and space by supporting research and education in the physical, natural, and biological sciences; serves as a member of the Planetary Society's Scientific Advisory Board; and sits on the Advisory Board for the Arch Mission Foundation.

Ben, you are a serial entrepreneur. You launched six start-ups and have been involved in areas such as mobile gaming, artificial chatbots, carbon capture, and space technology. Your sixth start-up is Colossal

Biosciences, a venture capital–backed start-up that supports Harvard geneticist George Church's work in the development of genetic engineering and reproductive technology.[1] You have been described as follows: "A straight-shooting, star-chasing ideas man who views the world as a place with infinite opportunities. And he often believes he's the one who needs to discover them."[2] Please describe for us the life experiences that contributed to your views, behavioral approaches, and successes. What are the defining moments that shaped who you are today?

I don't know if all that is true, but those are very kind words. I'm very curious and I really like to learn. While I'm fascinated by and passionate about technologies, I ultimately like to learn new sectors. At the time I got into gaming, it didn't really exist. At the time I got into conversational AI, it didn't really exist. I like to learn new technologies and new fields that intersect with technology.

I was very fortunate as a child to travel a lot. I got to experience a lot of different cultures and I got to understand a lot from the worldview perspective. Seeing so many different cultures at a young age furthered my curiosity. I've been fortunate to work with people much smarter than I am on these journeys. I think it's been driven by a sense of curiosity and a sense of exploration.

Speaking of drive, you stated: "I don't have that stillness in me."[3] How do you make sure that high drive does not overwhelm other aspects of leader

---

1   Catherine Clifford, "Lab-Grown Woolly Mammoths Could Walk the Earth in Six Years if Geneticist's New Start-Up Succeeds," CNBC, September 14, 2021, cnbc.com/2021/09/13/geneticist-george-church-gets-funding-for-lab-grown-woolly-mammoths.html. Church himself has had a storied scientific career. He initiated the Personal Genome Project, started more than twenty companies, and has more than one hundred patents to his name.

2   Danielle Abril, "Ben Lamm Has an Unconventional Approach to Business, and It Somehow Works," D Magazine, February 27, 2018, dmagazine.com/frontburner/2018/02/ben-lamm-has-an-unconventional-approach-to-business-and-it-somehow-works.

3   Catherine Clifford, "This 39-Year-Old Tech Exec Has Built 5 Companies, but There's a Price to His Ambition," CNBC, December 6, 2020, www.cnbc.com/2020/12/06/how-ben-lamm-started-five-companies.html.

character and hence effective leadership? For example, leaders with high drive but low temperance can make decisions that are reckless rather than well thought out, or may quickly lose patience with others.

I will say that I have made reckless decisions, but I always try to hire much smarter people than me. I try to learn from them very quickly, and then shift based on the feedback and input from my team. I have a pretty flat organization and I have pretty transparent communication. My colleagues can walk into my office, call or text me day, night, or weekend if there is a problem or if there is a decision that we need to make, or one that I've made that needs to be adjusted. I'm not one of those people that has to stick with a decision because I made it. I'm pretty flexible if better data come in. If you hire much smarter people than you in their respective fields, it's a travesty if you don't listen to that data. But, at the end of the day, somebody's got to make a decision, and a lot of times that's me. I definitely do make very gut-based decisions very quickly, because I think it is better to advance the ball than not, but at the same time, I always try to be receptive to the various ears in the field giving me feedback.

Being receptive suggests humility is a factor in your approach to leadership.

If you know everything, it would probably be a pretty terrible existence. I'd hate to be the smartest person out there, because then what else would I learn? The nicest compliment I ever received in my life was from George Church, who said I am the best student he never had. I'm not his student; I'm his partner and I do not have a PhD in biology. But, I do pick things up reasonably quickly, and I think the only reason I pick things up quickly and learn fast is because I'm so curious about them. Once I'm interested in a topic, I am obsessive about it.

In an interview with CNBC you talked about living in the tomorrow while struggling to be content in the present moment. You said: "It's more than just a longing for tomorrow, as in a longing to help push that company or people or market or society into tomorrow. . . . I sometimes do feel like it's a burden."[4] Why do you feel the forward-looking perspective is a burden? How do you cope with having that outlook if it places a weight on how you experience the present?

I am really terrible at being present. It is the biggest area of my personal and work life that I struggle with. I joke that sometimes I'm already in tomorrow and just waiting for everyone else to catch up. So, yeah, it's painful. I force myself to schedule very mindful and focused things, whether it is working out or meditation or just time off. For example, I am forcing myself to go on vacation next week for a few days. I am absolutely not looking forward to it, but I'm going to do it because I recognize the importance of doing it.

Maybe burden is too strong of a word; I think it is probably a bigger burden to everyone around me than it is to me. I feel like because we don't have unlimited cycles around the sun, I want to maximize them and create the things that I think should already exist but do not yet. I think de-extinction should exist, but it doesn't. A lot of technologies for conservation should already exist, and they just don't. It's more of a focus than a funding thing. I feel the strong desire to make those things happen because no one else has.

You talk about that difficulty being present, and yet you also talk about this big curiosity. Do you find that your curiosity can be a way of anchoring you to the present? Sometimes when you're really curious about something, do you find you become immersed in what is right in front of you in order to learn more about it?

I think that's a really good insight. I think that's an unintended consequence of my curiosity — the focus on the present around

---

4   Clifford, "This 39-Year-Old Tech Exec Has Built 5 Companies, but There Is a Price to His Ambition."

it. But then I quickly jump to, "Okay, what's possible with this?" So, I don't know how long-lasting that presence is. I think that may be a temporal distortion field for myself, and then I'm like, "I have to go out beyond it."

You are currently at the forefront of de-extinction. Colossal Biosciences raised $75 million in capital, and one of its objectives is to bring back the woolly mammoth, which has been mostly extinct for ten thousand years. You and your colleagues describe the vision of Colossal Biosciences this way: "For the first time in the history of humankind, we are in control of a science with the power to reverse and prevent biodiversity loss on a large scale. We can heal a hurting planet. We can protect the species living on it. We can ethically decipher and protect genetic codes. And we can begin to turn the clock back to a time when Earth lived and breathed more cleanly and naturally. This is not an option for us. It is an obligation known as thoughtful disruptive conservation."[5] What was the spark to found Colossal Biosciences and to support George Church's work?

I initially reached out to George about computational biology and how we could leverage AI and automation for faster discovery in science.[6] When George started talking about the extinction of the mammoth and the application of [technology], it completely blew my mind. I was shocked that we had the tools and the technology — it was really a surprise that no one had done it yet. We are going to lose up to 50 percent of biodiversity between now and 2050; it is a very pressing existential problem. I thought that if we could advance technologies for human healthcare, as well as advancing and subsidizing them for conservation, we could put better tools in the hands of

5   "A Better World," Colossal Laboratories & Biosciences, colossal.com/a-better-world.

6   Computational biology refers to the use of data analysis, mathematical modeling, and computational simulations to understand biological systems and relationships. An intersection of computer science, biology, and big data, the field also has foundations in applied mathematics, chemistry, and genetics.

conservationists so they could fight a better fight and prevent more loss of biodiversity.

Colossal is not going to save every species. We're focused on a couple of key species that are interesting, big attention-getters. If we can de-extinct the mammoth, and grow one thousand of them, those technologies can save a lot of other species. The area of marrying de-extinction with thoughtful disruptive conservation is one that we were very, very interested in at the get-go.

Once George and I decided to build the company, we went and recruited Brian Beard and Kent Wakeford and Andrew Busey and Peter Phillips and other executives who heard the story and decided that they would come be a part of it from day one.

You said that no one has done it. Why? The idea has been around for a while.

To achieve something like this — that is really hard and at the bleeding edge of technology — it requires focus and the latest and greatest advances in computational biology, cell and genome engineering, stem cell biology, embryology, protein engineering, and assisted reproductive technologies. And all of that takes money. To really push synthetic biology to the level that we are, we had to bring together the world's leading people, give them the best tools and technologies, and give them the support and leeway to do it.

That is what I feel my job is — an activator of that vision and of George's initial vision, and then a service provider to the team. My job is not to bring back the mammoth. My job is to build the infrastructure — give the tools and the freedom to operate within the culture — to enable others to achieve what is possible with these technologies.

Before now the barrier has really been a lack of funding and focus. We have had people say, "Oh, it's not possible," and they are just wrong. When we spend time, when we pull together some of the top scientific minds in the world that are telling us it *is* possible, then we internally and externally see that validation.

It's been really great to show some of the skeptics some early successes. But for us, it's not about proving a skeptic right or wrong. It is about learning from the feedback that we get from the community, including positive support as well as negative criticism. In feeding all that into our model, we ensure that not only are we achieving the goals, but we're achieving them at the level of transparency and in all the right veins that people are interested in.

The goals that you have set are audacious. One of your investors stated: "The path to de-extinction is now at hand, and leveraging CRISPR/Cas9 technology, to bring back extinct species and preserve those that we have, will have profound importance to humanity."[7] Another investor was quoted by CNBC as saying, "Synthetic biology will allow us to create new life forms that can address massive problems, from oil and plastic cleanup to carbon sequestration and much more. Solving tissue rejection and artificial wombs will go on to help improve and extend life for all humans."[8] How do you sustain momentum? How do you retain your determination and build resilience when the road to success is long and delicate?

I think it starts at the top, but then I think it also funnels up from the bottom. I think that we've done a good job of pulling together not just internal teams but also external teams of science advisors that help support the mission, as well as conservation-focused and future-focused investors. We judge everything through the lens of creation, impact, and inspiration.

Another principle along that line that I think we've done a really good job of is being radically transparent. As I have said, we have a very flat organization, so we make it very clear that anyone can come in — anyone at any time. Yes, there is

7   "Company," Colossal Laboratories & Biosciences, colossal.com/company.

8   Catherine Clifford, "Lab-Grown Woolly Mammoths Could Walk the Earth in Six Years if Geneticist's New Start-Up Succeeds," CNBC, September 13, 2021.

managerial hierarchy, but at the end of the day, if someone needs to be heard and it is really important, they feel empowered.

I think that as long as we maintain our north star of creating value for all of our investors and shareholders, while generating impact and providing an opportunity to do something as meaningful as de-extinction, we can be an inspiration for the world. And doing it all through the lens of radical transparency. We can maintain the ethos that we've set, really, by empowering other torchbearers of that ethos. I can say whatever I need to say to my co-founders or to the management team, but as the company grows, it's got to continue to trickle down. It's really about empowering that next level of torchbearer on this mission.

Many people, organizations, and government agencies have shown a keen interest in the work that you do and support your endeavors in biotechnology. However, there are also people who criticize the work that Colossal Biosciences is doing — for example, they label your work as "cowboy eco-engineering." They also point to the fact that the goals Colossal pursues push into ethically and politically fraught territory, operating on timescales that legislation can't keep pace with — territories such as gene editing, reproductive technology, animal welfare, conservation, and land management, to name a few. You practice the notion of radical transparency. Please describe to us what that means in practice, and why this is so important to you and your colleagues.

I think that, fundamentally, when you're doing anything big and bold, you are going to have feedback. People like things the way they are, even when things aren't great. People get very set in their ways, and so any time that you introduce new things, it causes friction. People forget that we don't really get anywhere without friction, because in a frictionless world, wheels don't even work. I fundamentally believe that it's okay to do things that are big and bold and complicated, and even things that are controversial.

I personally don't have any ethical concerns with trying to bring back species that humans had a hand in eradicating — in some cases, such as the Tasmanian tiger, humans fully eradicated them — and then leveraging those technologies to give better tools to folks in the field that are combating poaching and loss of habitat and everything else that is affecting populations of species. I don't have any ethical issues there.

We could have done all of this in secret and then had a big press event to unveil it. We didn't do that. We have been very transparent in our intentions and we have taken people on this journey with us. We don't see what we do as a Colossal-specific endeavor or an American-specific endeavor. We see our work as a worldwide endeavor.

I think it is our transparency that has yielded us 98 percent positive or neutral feedback. With that said, I also think it better informs critics, in a good way. I will listen to an informed critic all day long — someone who has done the research and that understands everything, or at least enough about it. I think that radical transparency not only allows us to make better decisions as an organization, but it also better informs the public, so it yields a higher result in favor of what we are working on.

To negative minds, it still better informs them so that they can have better feedback. If they have all the data, and we have all the data, and they have negative feedback based on that data, then maybe they are right and we should listen to them. We're very open to that. But sometimes they just don't listen or read all the data, and then we spend time with critics explaining things that we've already said publicly.

I think that radical transparency saves us time in the long run, because hopefully we'll either learn something really helpful from a critic, or it will make someone that is a critic not a critic, while allowing us to hire better people, hire smarter people. Smart people don't want to be hired and then be put in a little silo and not told anything. They want to be a part of it.

You are also committed to inclusion. For example, you work with bioethicists and conservation groups to guide your work. What is necessary on your part — and that of your colleagues — to make that collaboration truly work and still push your agenda forward and create momentum (and not be bogged down in disagreements)?

I think this again goes back to radical transparency. As long as you set and manage expectations, if people are unaligned, then they can come and talk to you about it. We've tried to build the right support with Indigenous groups, with conservation groups, with bioethicists and bioethics leaders, as well as with federal and local governments where we are working.

I just spent ten days in the Arctic Circle. I met with the lieutenant governor in Alaska. We held two public forums with people to share what we're doing. I met with some of the region's largest groups, one of which ended up investing in Colossal because they believe in our vision. That trip occurred because of some negative feedback we received that was important. We were told, "Look, all of this stuff works in theory and the advisors you have are amazing, but have you personally been to the Arctic Circle? Sure, people there have emailed you and you've talked to them on the phone and in Zooms, but have you had dinner with them? Have you talked with them? Have you sat down in their houses? Have you had these conversations?" We took that feedback and it took about six months to get everyone's schedules aligned, but I made it a priority to go up there and have those conversations. I like to attack those things when they come up so that negative feedback doesn't turn into bureaucracy and slow you down.

Also, I don't think enough companies have the right level of interdisciplinary and multidisciplinary groups behind them. If you look at Colossal, we've got everything from conservationists to technologists, genetic engineers to material scientists, AI experts to biologists. We've pulled together a very diverse group of people, with very diverse skill sets, which I think is really important and interesting.

Our research has shown that judgment is central to leader character: it's at the very heart of the constellation of the character dimensions. When you have good judgment, you make sound decisions in a timely manner, based on relevant information and a critical analysis of the facts. You appreciate the broader context when reaching decisions. You show flexibility when confronted with new information or situations, and you have an implicit sense of the best way to proceed. You can see into the very depth of challenging issues, and you can reason effectively in uncertain or ambiguous situations. How do you make critical judgment calls — and make sure you get the science and technology right? We believe this is an essential aspect of leadership, since many leaders confuse good intentions with good judgment.

For certain judgment calls, I don't know if it goes back to intellectual curiosity or that there are hard factors. For example, I have zero concern on the de-extinction of the species that we publicly announced and some others that we may announce in the future. I have zero concerns about that.

The hardest thing I believe Colossal will do is a placental interface layer. It is something that is solvable, something that humanity knows enough about from a development stage — how developmental biology works, how placentas work — but there are different types of placental animals. I spent a lot of time on our ex-utero development work. I don't view it as a science problem. There is obviously science involved in it, but it is really an engineering problem. I like systems, and at the core, I think I'm a systems designer, so I like looking at the entire system and how a system works.

Solving ex-utero development and generating full-term artificial wombs — going from an embryo to a living, breathing animal, and being able to do that fully ex-utero — that is the biggest game changer from a technological perspective. In the technology stack that we are building for extinction, it is the biggest game changer. It is not required for us to be successful in our journey. It is required for us to have the impact that we want to scale. That is the area where I worry the most and spend the most amount of my time ensuring that we have the right people.

In September 2021, a press release from Colossal stated, "Never before has humanity been able to harness the power of this [CRISPR] technology to rebuild ecosystems, heal our Earth and preserve its future through the repopulation of extinct animals. . . . In addition to bringing back ancient extinct species like the woolly mammoth, we will be able to leverage our technologies to help preserve critically endangered species that are on the verge of extinction and restore animals where humankind had a hand in their demise."[9] Why the mammoth? You could have picked other animals to jump-start the process of de-extinction. And what is the one misperception that people may have about bringing back the woolly mammoth?

First of all, Colossal is working on a handful of species that we have announced. There are multiple reasons we started with the mammoth. First, we have a wealth of specimens with well-preserved DNA. All our work and technology development on de-extinction directly benefits elephant conservation, including our biobanking, genome database, in vitro gametogenesis, assisted reproductive technologies, and artificial wombs.

Furthermore, we believe cold adaptation can enable elephants to survive the Arctic environments that favored woolly mammoths when we achieve trait engineering. And we also believe restoring the rich and diverse mammoth steppe ecosystem will benefit both the mammoths (restoring an iconic species to its lost ecosystem) as well as the environment, as mammoths are known to be geoengineers. In fact, peer-reviewed studies on African forest elephants have shown that they contribute to above-ground mass of vegetation over periods of time.

---

9   Colossal Laboratories & Biosciences, "Woolly Mammoths Will Walk the Arctic Tundra Again," press release, September 13, 2021, reviverestore.org/press-release/colossal-press-release-091321.

How will the mammoths help the Arctic environment? Peer-reviewed studies from our Pleistocene Park collaborators show that animals treading on snow during the cold winter months in Siberia lower the ground temperatures by as much as 8 degrees Celsius.[10] This slows down the thawing of the permafrost, which contains gigatons of organic mass trapped and released as methane when warming occurs. Arctic warming is more accelerated than any other area globally, and it is worrying to exacerbate the already saturated atmosphere through our carbon emissions.

The Arctic tundra is composed of slow-growing shrubs and mosses, and dark-barked coniferous trees (taiga) that absorb even more heat. Mammoths and elephants, being the incredible geoengineers that they are, disrupt this poor ecosystem by removing the trees and stepping on the slow-growing flora of the Arctic to favor a rich grassland ecosystem that supports even more biodiversity. Rewilding cold-adapted elephants will contribute to a higher albedo environment with more reflected light back to the atmosphere, keeping the surface cooler.

I think the biggest misconception that people have is semantic. What most people don't realize is that genetically an Asian elephant (which is endangered) is 99.6 percent woolly mammoth and thus is closer genetically to the mammoth than it is to the African elephant. Once people actually understand that, I think it changes their perspective. But there is also the case that when we say that we are taking the Asian elephant and modifying genes and inserting genes and up-regulating genes that already exist in the infrastructure of the Asian elephant to withstand the freezing temperatures of the Arctic, they are like, "But it's not a full mammoth."

So sometimes we get into these semantic arguments, which I think are a waste of time, because if you look at an animal and it looks like a woolly mammoth and it has all the core phenotypes, and it can function as a woolly mammoth and be in its habitat

---

10 Pleistocene Park is an Arctic ecosystem restoration initiative located in northeastern Siberia.

at −20 to −40 degrees Celsius and solve the ecosystem and geoengineering issues that we wanted to solve, such as climate change, how is it not a mammoth? Is my dog any less of a dog because it's not purebred and it was a rescue? I don't think so. We say Arctic elephants, we say woolly mammoth, we say functional mammoth. People call it the mammoth family . . . there have been a lot of these weird names. Whatever you want to say, we say.

There is tremendous upside to the work Colossal Biosciences is committed to. However, some people are opposed to the idea of de-extinction because they believe there may be risks associated with the process that scientists cannot accurately predict, such as diseases that could affect livestock or other species. How do you and your colleagues work through such questions and consider unintended or potentially harmful consequences?

These types of considerations are ones that are discussed on a regular basis at Colossal. We have assembled an amazing team of experts as well as an equally amazing set of advisors and partners. This network is integral for analyzing the entire scope of our projects to identify potential hazards and innovating amazing solutions around those hazards. We believe in radical transparency and success through partnerships. These internal and external viewpoints allow us to build strategies to address as many considerations as possible, both scientific and ethical. Using the wildlife disease example you mentioned, I can provide a brief case study into our thought process.

Along the roadmap of de-extinction, we have several steps that allow us to utilize various tools within our toolkit to ensure our genetic edits have the intended effects. These checkpoints include the ability to utilize AI for comparative genetic analysis that could highlight any disease susceptibilities.

Additionally, the method in which we edit extant species genomes to create extinct species genomes gives us the added benefit of understanding what diseases affect the extant species and therefore would be conferred into the restored animals' unedited regions of DNA. Then, the second layer of protections come into play when we actually restore individual animals from extinction. These animals would be managed in human care and "soft release" type of management settings that would allow us to study and evaluate these species in controlled settings before they would be considered for rewilding, whether that be studying animals' social readiness for release or understanding disease susceptibilities. This type of rewilding is happening every day with critically endangered species being returned to ecosystems they were extirpated from generations ago.

And finally, the rewilding effort itself includes many steps of research and analysis that ensure not only that the ecosystem is prepared for a species to return, but that the local communities and governments are prepared for that restoration, as well.

CHAPTER 13

GENNADIY MOKHNENKO

Pastor of the Church of Good Changes and Member of the Chaplains' Battalion, Mariupol, Ukraine

Gennadiy Viktorovich Mokhnenko is a Ukrainian chaplain and is the founder and senior pastor of the Church of Good Changes. Gennadiy was born in Mariupol on February 27, 1968. He studied at the bible school in Vilnius, Lithuania, and then later at the Theological Seminary of Reformers in Kyiv. In 1998, he graduated from the Donetsk Institute of Social Education.

In 2000, Gennadiy developed and founded the Republic of Pilgrim (also known as Pilgrim Republic) in Mariupol, a rehabilitation shelter for street youth, many of whom were orphaned and addicted to drugs and/or alcohol. Today, more than three thousand children have found refuge there and gone through its recovery programs, as well as been provided educational opportunities. Gennadiy also helms the national adoption movement in Ukraine called You Will Be Found. He himself is an adoptive father of over thirty kids and teens and has founded several foster homes, including one for HIV-positive kids.

A number of documentaries are devoted to the life and activities of Gennadiy including *Makarenko from Mariupol*, *One for All*, *Once Upon a Time in Africa*, and *Almost Holy*. Gennadiy wrote two books: *Execution Cannot Be Pardoned* and *Non-Pedagogical Poem*.

During the Revolution of Dignity that took place in Ukraine in February 2014, Gennadiy stated that he was an opponent of any revolutionary movements. However, despite early statements about apoliticality, Gennadiy took a decidedly pro-Ukrainian position with the beginning of the Russian invasion of Donbass. He took a direct part in the creation of fortifications around Mariupol and was one of the builders of Mariupol checkpoints. He joined the battalion of chaplains of the Armed Forces of Ukraine and founded his own "Chaplain Battalion Mariupol."

We interviewed Gennadiy via Zoom on April 26, 2022, just weeks into Russia's invasion of Ukraine. The fighting was heavy in and around Mariupol. Thousands of citizens had been killed in the Russian attacks, including one of Gennadiy's adopted children. Gennadiy's church became a safe harbor for as many women and children as could be squeezed into the basement, and Gennadiy and his colleagues risked their lives each and every day as they evacuated thousands from Mariupol.

Born into a hard-drinking family of factory workers in the industrial area of Donetsk, Ukraine, Gennadiy's destiny as a pastor seemed unlikely. We started our interview, therefore, by asking Gennadiy what inspired him to become a pastor and, more importantly, to start Republic of Pilgrim.

"This year, I will have thirty years from when I started my pastor ministry," Gennadiy began. He took a year's course in a bible school in Lithuania, then founded his own church, the Church of Good Changes, in 1992. The church is affiliated with the Pentecostal Church of God in Ukraine.

"Maybe twenty-five years since I started Republic [of Pilgrim], more than 3,500 children have gone through this rehab project." The project began as an outreach program for youth hanging out nearby the church. The youth were largely homeless, addicted to drugs, and lost, but neither Mariupol nor Ukraine had a strategy for dealing with homeless children. In need of a bath, nutrition, and a stable environment, some of the youth began asking Gennadiy if they could live "inside your church." Gennadiy felt it was impossible to say no to the youths, who then began inviting their homeless friends to join them.

Gennadiy was frustrated by the government's failure to address the problem of homeless youth, and he personally connected with their struggles with drug abuse. He witnessed his parents' and sister's struggle with alcoholism. Gennadiy credits divine mercy for saving his mother, father, and sister from the ravages of continuous drinking, and he feels compelled to step in where no one else is offering support.

"A Hobby for Life"

"Most of this decision had one root," Gennadiy said. "I have a hobby for my life: *I love saving people.*"

> During Soviet times, I was in the army; I served as a firefighter in Moscow. The first time me and my team went inside a burning building and saved a man, I had a special feeling, special experience. I think that experience has influenced all my life.
>
> When I saw how his family jumped and were joyful for his life being saved, me and my team understood it was a result of our job. We just came inside that fire at the right moment. It was such a critical moment for that man. If we didn't go inside that fire, he didn't have a chance.
>
> I think that day was very important in my life. From that day forward, I said I had a hobby — to save people. Every time, when I saw how life changed, and when I know I had maybe played a little part in it, I think it's the best. I have many amazing feelings.

He then described being on the frontline hours before our interview, continuing his efforts to evacuate people to safety. That day, he and his team of volunteers evacuated nearly five hundred people. By this date Gennadiy and his team of more than sixty volunteers had evacuated more than seven thousand people from Mariupol.

> I was in one big room and maybe fifty soldiers were there. I started talking with them, and I know all of them are real heroes. I don't think I am something special.

Maybe it's a Hollywood movie effect! Around me, I have so many unbelievable people.

My adopted son, he was a homeless boy with a long criminal story. For the last month, he was inside Mariupol, and he was shot at every day. He saved many, many people with huge risk to his life. He went under airplane attack to save somebody and took them to the basement of my church.

Some days ago, a friend of mine gave me a present: a very good car. I never dreamed about a car like this. A huge Nissan pickup truck. 2017. Very good for frontline right now. I was so happy.

That day, another friend of mine gave me this present. Can you see this gun? [*Gennadiy holds up the gun in front of the camera for our inspection.*] For me, this is better than the truck, because it is for saving lives. But still, the best of what I have in my life is when I saw people who were saved, and I know I had a part in that.

Today, we will save more people from that complete hell — from Mariupol. In the past several weeks, we saved more than seven thousand people. I know that I have a little part through all these seven thousand stories. Even today, we saved more lives.

I think this is a very important point for leaders. When I saw how former homeless children have changed their lives: they now have a family; they finished university; they are good people, good fathers. I think this — to save lives — is the best.

I'm sorry I [haven't been able to] preach the last few months. I've just preached one time in church.

Gennadiy described how his son and other volunteers took food packs to vulnerable families. The volunteers broke through the frontlines to take packs containing water, canned meat, vegetables, oats, oil, flour, and pasta to people who were sheltering in basements. Gennadiy's church basement was sheltering about three hundred people waiting for evacuation from Mariupol.

Gennadiy spends his time praying with Ukrainian soldiers on the frontlines and delivering humanitarian assistance to largely forgotten elderly Ukrainians. He described himself as "one little part of the big team" putting their own lives at risk to provide food and water and to help evacuate those they could to safety. "I saw so many unbelievable heroics around me," he repeated. "I'm not a savior. I don't think I'm something special in this world. I'm just a normal man.

"Right now, in my country, I have thousands, thousands of unbelievable heroes around me. They are more heroic than me, and they are everywhere around me."

Leaders Beget Leaders

We asked Gennadiy who, or what, in his life had shaped his principles and values, and his leadership. He described the people and events that led him to be who he is, not just a leader in his own community but also an international role model. He acknowledged that he had benefited from knowing certain people and experiencing certain events, but wanted "maybe now to tell [us] about just one man": "Me and my friends took him from hell, from Mariupol, just two weeks ago. He is my neighbor. He lives on the first floor, and my family was on the third floor. I grew out of an addicted family. My parents were alcohol-addicted, and my sister. My family was destroyed by alcohol 100 percent."

Gennadiy has been candid in the press about his experience growing up in a family ravaged by alcoholism. He has described those years as "like hell" because he loved his parents and needed them, but their alcoholism "destroyed everything." Gennadiy literally feared for their lives.[1] He said: "Nobody cared about me. My parents were drunk. Thank

---

1   Peter Hartlaub, "'Almost Holy' Explores Efforts of Impassioned Ukraine Pastor," *Austin American-Statesman*, September 3, 2016, www.statesman.com/story/news/2016/09/03/almost -holy-explores-efforts-of-impassioned-ukraine-pastor/10099169007.

goodness that later they came to find God. But my neighbor — his name is Yuriy — he was just one man in this world who asked me, 'Gennadiy, how many times can you do a push-up?'"

Because his neighbor showed an interest in Gennadiy's fitness, Gennadiy committed to developing his physical stamina. "Every time, I said, 'Twenty, forty, fifty . . .' and even now, at fifty-four [years old], my last record was one hundred. It's not a bad result, trust me."

Gennadiy also described how Yuriy introduced him to the game of chess:

> He played chess with me for the first time in my life. We had a big difference in age: twenty years. I was twelve when he was thirty-two.
>
> He played with me for the first time in my life, and after that, I started playing chess very professionally. I close my eyes and three people sit on that side, and I get three games in my mind and have competition with them.
>
> This man, he knew all of my friends. He knew what is the name of my friends. He was the man who . . . he gave me attention. He loved people, and he was interested in people's lives around him. He was a very good, big influence. Now, [Yuriy] is a deacon in my church, thirty years later.
>
> Yuriy taught me about good leadership. Leadership is not just about, "I must say direction. Everyone must go on this side or that side." It's not just about money. I have money; I have resources. Leaders, it is something about real love for people. If you love people, you have the biggest resource for influence. If you love, you can get direction. If you love people, you can push them on the right side. If you love them, you can say, "Stop, we don't do it." Real love gives power for leaders.
>
> I think this man — Yuriy — he is an amazing leader. All people who know him love him very, very much. He's an unbelievable man.

Right now, though, he is a refugee. Last month he was without water, without electricity, without food, without nothing, with his disabled wife. He stayed inside Mariupol under all the shooting, and he served people there. He was in such a critical situation, but he served for people there.

He is one of the best leaders, but nobody writes a book about him. Hollywood doesn't produce a movie about him. Not so many people know about him, but he is the strongest leader that I've seen in my life. We were able to send him to Germany with his wife. An amazing friend of mine gave him a place to stay.

Hope Is Natural

We shared with Gennadiy our experience of watching *Almost Holy*, the documentary profiling Gennadiy and his work with homeless and drug-addicted youth. The movie offers many messages, but we were interested in the message of hope in the face of hopelessness. "How do you maintain hope?" we asked. "What drives you to keep trying to change the seemingly unchangeable? People and politicians work against you, and the drug trade is a source of income to many and places a challenge on you as well. In a hopeless situation, what gives you hope?"

Gennadiy declared that "hope is natural": "Can you see this tree? Just two weeks ago, it was a tree without one little bit of green. It was like this tree was dead. But now, it looks like hope. This is the symbol of hope now. Everywhere you can see here, you can see this river.

"I think hope, it's part of my nature. It's part of the construction of this world. In the middle of tragedy, a friend of mine — a young boy here, twenty years old — his marriage will be in just one week. One more young man from my team, he will have a marriage two weeks later. In the middle of this war, in huge crisis."

Gennadiy described his philosophy of hope, explaining that life progresses in cycles of joy and despair: "I think life is not just growing. You have very good times, but sometimes you have crazy times. If you know the graphic of life, we go high and low, high and low. If you know it, when you go through terrible times, you understand: maybe just one or two steps more and you will have joy. Don't fall down today, because life will be better tomorrow. Or maybe in just ten minutes . . . a situation can change completely."

Reaching into his personal experiences, Gennadiy proclaimed the importance of understanding that joy will surely follow despair, even when despair seems unending: "When you cry now, and when you think life is finished — no more light, no more joy — I know what that is. I have had too much crying times these last two months. Just half an hour ago, I found the official paper about my adopted daughter, Vika. She was killed. Russians killed her."

Gennadiy had thirty-eight children at that time: three biological children with his wife, Olena, plus thirty-five children he and Olena had adopted. When the shelling began in Mariupol, Gennadiy made plans to evacuate his family. The youngest children were evacuated first. He planned to return to Mariupol for the older siblings, but his return was blocked by the frontline. Vika, who had been orphaned, had just moved into an apartment building that was shelled by a Russian tank. She was among those killed by the attack.[2]

It took a month and a half for Gennadiy to confirm that his daughter had been killed.

> Just thirty minutes ago, one and a half months later, I had details about it. I found a young girl who was close to my daughter. I cried for the last time just thirty minutes before this interview. But when you cry, you must know that in maybe two steps and you will smile. Something will happen and give hope for you.
>
> Short answer, I think that hope, this is a part of reality. We just must say, "Yes, hope is around us!" Spring will

---

2   Stephen Strang, "Russian Tank Kills Daughter of Well-Known Pentecostal Pastor in Ukraine," *Charisma News*, March 24, 2022; www.charismanews.com/world/88715-russian-tank-kills -daughter-of-well-known-pentecostal-pastor-in-ukraine.

come. The new family will have marriage. They will have little children; their children will have first steps some months later. Life goes on, and God is good. Hope is part of reality. This is my answer.

Justice Will Win

In December 2021, Gennadiy was awarded the Light of Justice Award by the Institute of Leadership and Management at the Ukrainian Catholic University. In his acceptance speech, Gennadiy stated, "Justice will rise. I believe that one day, justice will prevail [in Ukraine]. Today we have to stand by its side and nurture it."

We asked Gennadiy what challenge he would issue to others, especially when he is in such a challenging situation himself. "How do you nurture justice?" we asked. He responded: "I really believe that justice will have victory. When we read books for children, every time, the good man will have victory. But it's not just in children's books where justice wins."

Gennadiy has been nicknamed "Crocodile Gennadiy" or "Pastor Crocodile" — not for his rough and tough personality, which harkens to the movie character Crocodile Dundee, but for a cartoon crocodile from a Soviet animated TV show who saves youth from the forces of evil. Gennadiy is a fan of the character and shares his enjoyment with his own children and the youth of the rehabilitation center. But he is not naïve about the fight for justice:

> I'm sure it's not just children books. It's also the principle for life. If I stay on the just side, maybe people will win today. In the long term, justice will win.
>
> Eight years ago, when Russia came to my country and started this war, I started saying what I was thinking about it. So many people said, "Gennadiy, don't tell about justice for the people. It's not good for you. Some sponsors who like Putin won't give money to you. Some people who love

Putin's system don't invite you into their church. Pastor, don't tell about justice!"

I said to them, "Goodbye. I will stay true, and justice will win."

Now, nine years later, when Putin's systems show their evil face for all of the world [to see], the people who told me — many critical; they hate me! — but now they call me and say, "Pastor, let me say sorry about these eight years. I said so many bad things about your position and I hated you, but let me say please forgive me, because your position was true."

Maybe a little story about how justice wins. I think it's a good idea to be on the right side with justice and truth. Maybe you'll have many problems along the way, but the result will be victory of justice.

On April 1, 2022, after Russian forces withdrew from Bucha, photographic and video evidence emerged of a massacre of Bucha residents. Local authorities reported the recovery of more than 450 bodies, most of whom had been killed by weapons. Corpses showed evidence of summary executions, torture, and rape.[3] Gennadiy had recently visited Bucha and recalls:

> This is why I hope Ukraine will win through this crazy time, because I saw it. Just some days ago, I was in Bucha. In Mariupol, we now have maybe a thousand people from Bucha. When I hear that story about how those guys killed people, can you imagine? They killed one person for over one and a half hours. They can do it in a second,

3   CBS News, "CBS News Finds Evidence of Atrocities Near Ukraine's Capital as Russia Is Accused of War Crimes," April 5, 2022, www.cbsnews.com/news/bucha-massacre-ukraine -russia-atrocities-evidence; and Liz Sly, "Accounting of Bodies in Bucha Nears Completion," *Washington Post*, August 8, 2022, www.washingtonpost.com/world/2022/08/08/ukraine -bucha-bodies.

but Russians killed one man in one and a half hours. They torture him very slowly before they kill him.

Justice will win through all crazy stories. Truth will win, we just must stay on the right side of history.

Forgiveness Changes You

Given Gennadiy's talk of justice, we asked him what he thought about forgiveness. People had asked Gennadiy for his forgiveness when they realized that he was correct for speaking out about Russian actions in Ukraine over the previous years. We wanted to know what role Gennadiy thought forgiveness would play in achieving justice and a just world. He explained:

> I'm a pastor. When people say "sorry," it's like changing something inside you. I love forgiving people. Even my enemies. Even those who were angry.
>
> Forgiveness is not hard for me. I love it. Because I'm also a sinner, and I often ask God for forgiveness for things. All of us have done many wrong things in our life. But when we understand that what we did was bad — when we say, "Please forgive me" — I am sure God loves this. I try to follow him in this subject.

"I've Never Felt Myself So Destroyed"

Gennadiy and his large family were in constant danger. His daughter had been killed; his wife was ill. We wanted to know how he found the energy and vitality he needed to cope with the trauma and exhaustion of what he was experiencing and continue to do his good work.

Gennadiy acknowledged his exhaustion, especially over the previous two months, and described his family's current situation. He opened positively — "My family is great," he said — but then went on to describe the loneliness and separation he was feeling.

His wife of thirty years was ill and had been evacuated to a western region of Ukraine. Gennadiy saw her a few days earlier for the first time since the war began two months before that. They were together for a few hours. He didn't elaborate on his wife's condition, but indicated that his place was in Mariupol for the moment: "She is very sick now," he said. "I can't stay with her right now."

Gennadiy was also separated from his daughters and his youngest sons, all of whom were already living elsewhere or were evacuated when the war began. His grandchildren — thirty-five grandchildren through his adopted family and one biological grandson — were also living or sheltered elsewhere. It had been almost three months since Gennadiy had seen his biological grandson. "I am not sure if I will have a chance to give him one more hug," Gennadiy mused aloud.

Gennadiy's social circle extended beyond his large family to embrace friends and children of friends. Like many Ukrainians, Gennadiy had lost a number of friends in the fighting. He recounted stories of friends who sheltered inside a factory for sixty days while Ukrainian soldiers put up a resistance against the Russians. Children of friends and youth Gennadiy had coached through his Republic of Pilgrim program were fighting the war.

The burden of it all seemed to overcome Gennadiy. He did not know how he was finding the energy to continue to do what he was doing. "Right now, I don't have answers for these questions. I need good recommendations right now because I've never felt myself so destroyed. All my life, it's like . . . I don't know an answer for this question. Sorry. If you have ideas, send them to me very quickly!"

All in the Family

We pointed out to Gennadiy that there were not many women who would think it is a great idea to adopt thirty children. "Your wife must be someone exceptional, and your relationship must be very special," we said. "We're sure that's what makes it so hard right now to be separated. Can you tell us a little bit about how your wife supported your leadership or perhaps how she was a leader in all this too, and how the two of you came together to adopt these children and give them a new life?"

Gennadiy acknowledged that his large adopted family was only possible because his wife, Olena, was extraordinary, standing by him throughout his ministry with resilience: "My wife, she is really unbelievable. I'm sure God gave me just one lady from this world who was ready for life with a crazy man like me. This is not a good idea to adopt thirty-five children! We never had a normal life. Can you imagine? We live in a little home — five hundred square feet — and we get seventeen children inside."

Some of the adopted children were already grown and moved on to their own independent lives. Some of the older children lived in a neighboring family house.[4] All of them were children that no one else wanted — children with drug addictions, infections, disabilities, social issues, criminal records, and more. Gennadiy just couldn't say no to them.[5] He figured the children each had one chance, and he wanted to do what he could to make the best of their chance — to give them a home, a purpose, friends, family, and food.[6] Gennadiy elaborated:

> Not so many people want to adopt twelve-year-old boys who are criminals, drug-addicted, alcohol-addicted, already have many sexual experiences. Not so many people are ready for that. Yes, my wife is an unbelievably special lady.
>
> Let me say one last story. This is about my adopted son, number thirty-three. Many times, we would say, "It's the last adoption. Stop. No more. Enough."

4   "Interview with Senior Pastor of Church of Good Changes in Mariupol, Gennadiy Mokhnenko," Republic Pilgrim, no date, accessed January 15, 2023, republicpilgrim.org/en/intervju-pastora-gennadiy-mokhnenko-dlya-americanskoi-cerkvi.

5   Ciaran Varley, "Meet the Man Who Adopts Ukraine's Drug-Addicted Street Children," BBC Three, December 14, 2016, www.bbc.co.uk/bbcthree/article/ec1b151d-2185-42e2-8e9d-63101a2165a3.

6   Cynthia Fuchs, "'Almost Holy': A Controversial Mission to Save Kids in Ukraine," PopMatters, May 20, 2016, www.popmatters.com/almost-holy-a-controversial-mission-to-save-kids-in-ukraine-2495431966.html; and interview with a Senior Pastor of the Church of Good Changes in Mariupol, Gennadiy Mokhnenko.

The leader of my children's rehab center sent me pictures. There was a young boy, twelve years old, and he sat directly on his mother's grave. He was sitting and crying, and they got a picture and sent it to my family. They called me and said, "Pastor, he is so depressed. Is it possible that we send him to your home for one or two days?" I said, "Yes, please. Send him to my family."

Directly from his mother's grave, this boy came to my home. We cried together, we prayed together, and two days later, I had to shake his hand and say, "Goodbye, boy. Go to an orphanage."

I couldn't talk to my wife about one more adoption because she was sick. She is very sick now. She was a healthy woman before war came, but on that day when I must tell him goodbye, my wife told me, "Honey, I have to talk to you." I can't start that talk, but she told me, "No orphanage. We have a place in our home for one more boy."

The next day, this boy had a birthday. He told me later, never in his life had he celebrated his birthday. That morning, we sat together with my family and we invited him and said, "Roman, we have one little present for you: if you want to be a part of our family, welcome. We want to adopt you."

My wife . . . I am almost holy, but she is a real holy lady. Right now, today, Roman is sixteen, and today, when my wife is very sick, he sits with her in Ukraine and he cares for her. One of my youngest sons sits with mother for two days, and then another comes to sit with her.

Roman is an amazing boy. I want to send him to the United States for education. Now I'm trying to prepare papers to send him to the United States for college. He's a very talented boy and I love him, and I miss him.

My wife, she is an unbelievable lady. She is the leader; I just follow her. She's the real leader.

Leadership Vision

Early in our interview Gennadiy talked about his mentor — Yuri — who taught him about good leadership and exemplified being able to meaningfully connect with people. We asked Gennadiy, "What lessons have you learned about mobilizing people to facilitate positive change in communities? You work with people toward a particular goal, which is to save children, to save civilians. What lessons have you learned about bringing people together to make positive change?" Gennadiy referred back to his "hobby" of saving people:

> Around me here, right now, I came to this city with some of my friends two months ago. We don't have anything. We were homeless. I am a homeless pastor. I don't have a home, I don't have an office, I don't have my church. But, because I love saving people, we just do what we can.
>
> One week later after I was first here, I saw maybe ten people who stayed with me. They just started doing what I do. We recruit people; we bring some humanitarian help and go to the frontlines. We go under shooting to save somebody.
>
> After two weeks, I had maybe twenty people around me. After two months, I had too many people who stay around me here. So now we have a building here. People give me a huge place for humanitarian efforts, like a warehouse. A lot of humanitarian help goes through here, including care carrying goods and taking people to safer places. Many people are working together. Now, it's a big team around me.
>
> What's happened through two months? Maybe we must separate my team and send part of them to another part of the frontline because it grows so quickly.
>
> I think if leaders have that fire inside us, if we have this vision about saving people, helping people, serving for people, it's like fire. If you have little fires, it is going

to grow. Fire can grow. This is about leadership, I think. If you have fire and passion, it will grow and more, and you'll have more and more influence around you.

Right now, when I look back through these two months, I say, "Oh Jesus!" I came to this city and didn't have food for myself. Today, maybe 3,000 kilograms of food just today will be sent to people on the frontlines. We send thousands of pounds of food and medicine for the last few months to different critical places. Absolutely critical situations where people live in basements with nothing. We go through huge risks — shooting, under mortars, under Russian artillery — to give people presents.

It's grown. Maybe tomorrow I will separate my team into two or three parts and send them to other parts of the frontline because it's grown so quickly.

"The World Must Have Strong Leadership"

With time for our interview coming to an end, we thanked Gennadiy for that story and brought the conversation back to the war in Ukraine. "The invasion of Russia and the brutality shown by the soldiers must change people. How has it changed you in good ways and bad ways?" we asked. He replied:

> I think this brutality, maybe it sounds strange, but it is like a shake for our world. You know, a big part of the world is very comfortable, very safe, very rich. They have enough food, good medicine, they can travel and have adventure. They are peaceful, nice, joyful. I think that a crazy time like now, it's like a shake.
>
> I think Western leaders, they are like sleeping leaders now. Everything is so good, so nice, and people must be nice, people must smile, and just [*Gennadiy dramatically fluffs his hair*] . . . talk about good things.

Reality is sometimes very evil. I think this Russian story . . . now I saw Western leaders wake up. Just in the last few weeks, they say, "Oh, no, no," when they saw so openly the genocide. This is real genocide: my city, just in my city, they killed nobody knows how many. Maybe 20,000? Maybe 30,000? Maybe 40,000? Nobody knows. They killed people, they raped people, they torture people right now in my city. The twenty-first century! It's a shock! Sometimes we need shock therapy to get back to reality.

This world must have strong leadership to stop crazy guys who kill people like on computer games. It's not just about world leaders. It's about leaders in my country. Can you imagine eight years of war in Ukraine? Eight years, we've had war. But, let me say too, 95 percent of Christian leaders have never been on the frontlines through these eight years. Ninety-five percent of bishops or Christian pastors don't go to the frontlines for eight years.

The frontline is so far in the east part of Ukraine, and we are not talking about it in our church. The people have different positions. Everybody has a little piece of truth. We are done talking about it in our churches, even in Ukraine. But now, when all the masks fall down, they will show their crazy faces. It's unbelievable what's happened. All bishops from my country go to checkpoints, some of them with guns, like me.

Two days ago, we had Easter. I went to the soldiers, and one pastor joined me. He got guns. He said goodbye to his church, and he went with his son to the frontline. He gave me a present: this magazine [for a gun]. This is my Easter present for me from the pastor.

Let me say when I saw it, I said, "Many leaders in my country are waking up right now."

Many of them are sleeping so good through these years. That pastor told me, "Gennadiy, in nine years, war was so far from my home and I didn't think so much about it." Now, he had a leader's decision. He said, "I'm a man, I have a son, and me and my son will go to the army to stop this evil thing in my country."

This is the real leader's answer: go inside the problem and try to stop it. I think this is a good influence — this war — for leadership.

Get Inside the Problem

To wrap up our interview, we asked Gennadiy if he had any final thoughts that he would like to share about leadership and about leading people and communities. "How could we make the world a better place?" we asked. Gennadiy suggested that we share one of his slogans:

Through many years, very often I repeat this slogan to myself. It sounds like, "Leaders must be inside problems." If I see the problem, I must go in that direction, not run away from the problem. If I saw a problem — in my culture, in my country around me, it doesn't matter — if I saw it, the leader must go in that direction to the center of the problem and build a defense line. Attack that problem to change something.

It's back to my fire experience in the Soviet Army. On September 11 in New York, when people were running away from that World Trade Center — thousands of people ran away from fire, from danger — some hundreds of others, they ran in the other direction inside the World Trade Center. First of all, it was firefighters. You have a monument in New York remembering the over three hundred firefighters that died in those days.

The leaders must be like firefighters. They must go when people run away from a problem.

People ask me, "Gennadiy, why are you staying?" Because this is my principle. I am a leader, so I must be in the center of the problem. Right now, from here, it's twenty minutes to the frontline. Twenty minutes to the hell, to the fire, to the real frontline. When Russia tries to attack this city, the leader must be inside the problem. The leader must go to the epicenter of the problem. This is a short slogan in my life.

CHAPTER 14

MARIA RESSA

**CEO of Rappler, Journalist, Author, Freedom Advocate,
and 2021 Nobel Peace Prize Winner**

Maria Ressa is the CEO of Rappler.com, an online news organization in the Philippines. Maria's courage and work on disinformation and "fake news" culminated in her being awarded the 2021 Nobel Peace Prize in recognition of her "efforts to safeguard freedom of expression, which is a precondition for democracy and lasting peace." Her numerous awards include being named *Time*'s 2018 Person of the Year and listed among its 100 Most Influential People of 2019.

Her experience as a journalist and an entrepreneur in the digital world makes her a sought-after keynote speaker and panelist on freedom of the press, democracy, and corporate governance.

A journalist for over thirty-six years, Maria has had ten arrest warrants filed against her related to exposing the Rodrigo Duterte government's corrupt practices and was convicted of cyber-libel in June of 2022. She is out on bail pending her appeal but, true to form, Maria vows to keep fighting.

Maria was featured in the 2020 documentary *A Thousand Cuts*, which profiles her fearless reporting on the abuses of Duterte's presidency, while also illustrating social media's capacity to deceive and entrench political power.

Her newest book, *How to Stand Up to a Dictator*[1], was released in November 2022.

---

1   Maria Ressa, *How to Stand Up to a Dictator: The Fight for Our Future* (New York: HarperCollins Publishers, 2022).

Tell us about the early life experiences that contributed to your motivation to become a journalist.

I actually didn't set out to be a journalist. In fact, in college I was drawn to both the sciences and to the arts, and, quite frankly, just trying to figure out who I was. I fell into journalism when I returned to the Philippines after being away for thirteen years.

My family had left the Philippines in 1973, one year after President Ferdinand Marcos had placed the country under martial law, thereby changing it from a democracy to a dictatorship. When we landed in the United States, I could understand English, but I couldn't really speak it. But when I returned to the Philippines in 1986 on a Fulbright Fellowship, I was in search of my roots and wanted to study political theater. At that time, the People Power Revolution had just overthrown Marcos, and what I really found was "real-life theater." With so much going on politically, I somehow got roped into the government television station, so I used that opportunity as a way to discover and understand my country. I never felt completely American, and yet when I came back to the Philippines, I realized, "Oh, my gosh, I am so very American." Over time, trying to figure out who I was, bits and pieces of these two worlds showed me that when I was with Americans, I felt most Filipino, and when I was with Filipinos, I felt most American.

In a weird way, being a part of both worlds while also being part of neither pushed me into this observation zone. It was great training to be a journalist. I also became comfortable in a news studio. So ultimately, I learned about this country — my country — through news. I thought it was incredible that my job was to go and ask people questions, and that the way you govern that gathering of news is through a set of standards and ethics. That early experience in journalism helped shaped who I have become.

Can we please take a step back? In 1982, at age nineteen, you were voted "most likely to succeed" at your high school. Where did that drive come from?

I think from insecurity, strangely enough. I always used to joke that I'm really a mutt — like a dog that's a combination of different breeds. When I came to the United States, my teachers had told me that I was quiet that first year because I had no cultural signals; or rather, I couldn't interpret the cultural signals. I was learning the language and trying to understand what everyone else seemed to already know. Over time, however, I wanted to prove that I belonged. But, how do you prove that you belong if you're the shortest and only brown kid in a very white public school system in Toms River, New Jersey? I did it first through academic excellence, and then I began to play sports. I played basketball and softball. And because I was so quiet, my teachers gave me music lessons. During my second year — this would have been fourth grade — my public school system gave me free piano and violin lessons. I actually played up to eight instruments, all the way through school, because it was a way of communicating without language. When I was voted most likely to succeed, I had been class president three years in a row by then. That must have meant I was good enough to be in America, right?

I started by saying that I developed this drive because of insecurity. This was actually the topic of my college essay going into Princeton to study theater. In many ways, I aim to be the best, but why did I aim to be the best? Because I wanted to prove that I belonged.

This is my thirty-seventh year as a journalist. Every time someone asks me, "How do you have courage? How do you stand up?" It's layers and layers of motivation, values, and character that you build up over time. For me, it began with insecurity and trying to prove that I belonged through that search for excellence, the search for learning. Making the choice to learn made me grow as a person. It enhanced my personal toolbox. You never go wrong if you work really hard. The advice I always give to young people is to "build yourself." It is like going to the gym. You go to the gym so that you are physically prepared to run a race when you have to run a race but, more than anything, it prepares you to be ready mentally and spiritually as well. I think that is what I love about journalism. It tests every aspect of who you are.

You worked for CNN in Asia and wrote for the *Wall Street Journal*. You also co-founded the online news site Rappler in 2012. We know that your work as a defender of independent journalism and freedom of expression, and particularly in exposing human rights abuses, has resulted in death threats, rape threats, and doxing, as well as racist, sexist, and misogynistic abuse and memes. You've been arrested and put on trial. How do you deal with it all?

I was a television broadcast journalist with CNN for eighteen years and started both the Manila and Jakarta bureaus. I came of age during the golden age of journalism through reporting on air. When I was in a war zone and had to do a live shot, it provided the best training on how to not just focus, but to have clarity of thought. Even if bullets are whizzing by on either side of you, a journalist's task — my task — during those two minutes of live reporting is to distill everything into three points.

Those experiences provided the best leadership training that I could have because I was in charge of my team. It was a team of four people covering the violence in East Timor that then expanded to ten people. In Jakarta, at the end of almost thirty-two years of Suharto's rule, my bureau went from four people to almost forty people overnight. What does that mean? It means you have to lead. If you're driving into a conflict area, every person on your team has a task. You think ahead. You conduct drills on these tasks so it becomes muscle memory, because as a team, you are only as strong as your weakest link. I got used to thinking in a particular way that ensured I was prepared for everything. This approach still is with me today. Courage, to me, was drawn forth by planning ahead so that I was ready for the worst-case scenario. We did that . . . always.

So when you talk about these personal attacks, I go right back to being young and trained as a journalist. The personal attacks are not personal. I don't set out to be critical of Rodrigo Duterte or of anyone. I set out to get the facts, and to give it to you with context. That is how I was trained as a journalist. So when it came down to being personally attacked, I pushed it back. It wasn't about me. For me, it is the role and the mission of journalism that is so critical: to hold power to account. As an old-style broadcaster, our task was to take our egos out of the picture. That goes against the grain of what being on television is, right? If you can do that, then you do fantastic journalism.

Let me answer your question directly — what do the memes, the threats, the attacks, and the abuse mean to me? I tried very hard not to take those personally. However, when I got the data of what these attacks were on social media — an average of ninety hate messages on Facebook per hour — then I began to realize that they were meant to stop me from doing my job, to silence me. This just pushed me to tell a better story. For example, we were the first news organization globally to talk about Facebook, their algorithm's impact on democracy, and the weaponization of the internet to spread disinformation and, possibly, even dismantle democracy. We researched the social media campaign of Duterte — it took months to complete as it involved manual counting. We identified twenty-six suspected fake accounts which evolved into a vast information-gathering machine. We believe these twenty-six fake accounts, all supporting Duterte, influenced 3 million other accounts. That's when the scale — or in author [Joseph] Conrad's words, "The horror! The horror!" — hit me. Simply put, a lie told a million times becomes a fact; that's the reality of social media, and that's what authoritarian-style rulers around the world are now taking advantage of. We presented Facebook with our data but no action was taken, and I had even met with Facebook's co-founder and chief executive officer, Mark Zuckerberg, and chief operating officer, Sheryl Sandberg, personally. This was the time that I began to appreciate the critical role that social media was playing in undermining democracies.

Ultimately, though, a part of dealing with this kind of abuse is to not take it personally. But to do so you have to fully appreciate your why. That's the crucial question: Why do you do what you do? Why is this happening? If you can distill it, have the clarity of thought to sort through that, then you can keep going.

So for me, while broadcast journalism taught me how to control or ignore my emotions within certain contexts, it also taught me how to tap into my emotions so I can be empathetic, I can tell a story. What emerges is rational, logical analysis coupled with empathy, instinct, and emotion. That's the ability that reporting gave me.

Your responses suggest that the development of your character was a natural evolution. You weren't hit by lightning and all of a sudden young Maria Ressa is the iconic Maria Ressa you are today. What insights or advice would you have for young people (or anyone, really!) on actions they can take right now that will build character?

There are three insights that I learned when I was still in elementary school, and these three keep coming up in different parts and at different times in my life. The first is *make the choice to learn.* The second is *embrace your fear.* The third is *stand up to a bully.* These all connect to the bigger themes of the book that I just published, *How to Stand Up to a Dictator.*[2] So even though I learned them in elementary school, these insights took me all the way up to standing up to Duterte and his government allies.

---

2   Maria Ressa, *How to Stand Up to a Dictator: The Fight for Our Future* (New York: HarperCollins Publishers, 2022).

Making the choice to learn came from being an immigrant kid. When I arrived in America, I entered into a third-grade elementary class. After I had only been there for a few weeks and had just gotten to know everyone's name, my teacher tells me one morning, "Maria, I think you should go up to the fourth grade!" I didn't want to go, but she talked to my parents about it and also convinced me. I will always remember her saying, "You should always make the choice to learn, and you have nothing more to learn in my classroom." When I won the Nobel Peace Prize in 2021, that teacher was in Norway. It was the first time I'd seen her since my time at Toms River. Make the choice to learn. I will always remember her for that and it is advice that has really kept me company through the years. If you have two roads to take, choose the road where you learn. Learning strengthens you as a human being.

The second one is embrace your fear. I learned this again in third or fourth grade when, one day, the most popular kid in school invited me to a pajama party she was throwing. I didn't really know what that was so I asked my mother. "Mom, does that mean I wear pajamas to the party? It's a sleepover." She said, "Yes!" So I go and I put my pajamas on. We are in the car and my parents are driving around the cul-de-sac where her house was. It was four o'clock in the afternoon and I could see my classmates playing kickball, and none of them were wearing pajamas. We pulled up and when I say, "Mom, they're not wearing pajamas!" she then admits that she really didn't know what a pajama party was.

My classmates had seen me, so I had to get out of the car. It might seem trivial to adults but at that time, as a young girl, opening the car door took everything. I just wanted to sink. I opened the door and my friend who is hosting the party comes to the car, and I step out and she looks at me and she says, "Oh my god, you're wearing pajamas!" I said, "Yeah, I thought it was a pajama party!" She grabs my bag and says, "Do you have a change of clothes?" She quickly brings me inside the house to change. The lesson: When you take a risk, you have to trust that someone will come to your aid, and when it's your turn, be that aid for someone else. It is better to face your fear than to run from it, because running won't make the problem go away. By facing it, you have the chance to conquer it. That was how I began to define courage.[3] I was afraid to step out of the car, but if I didn't, it would have been worse. That actually works for almost everything in life. We can all be our own worst enemy. Whatever it is you're afraid of, you have to touch it, hold it tight, and then think through how you are going to deal with it. Because once you do that, nothing can stop you.

Getting shut down as the head of Rappler — not only did I make myself comfortable with that, I thought out a step-by-step workflow for the entire company, and we drilled it every quarter so that we were prepared for the worst. Embrace your fear. Be a person that stops you from letting your fears get in your own way.

The third insight is how do you stand up to a bully (and in my case, it was a dictator)? Again, I learned that in school. At the time, I remember I didn't yet speak English very well, but I was first violin in the orchestra. I remember there was a girl that everyone made fun of because of her polyester pants. I didn't understand what the issue was with polyester pants, but I didn't feel that I could ask the question because if I did, then maybe they'd make fun of me for not knowing. So I stayed quiet. Does this sound familiar? Think of how a dictator comes to power and pressures everyone — and no one stands up against him? We all stayed away and my classmate continued to get bullied.

One day I was in the orchestra room and she was crying. I passed by and I just thought about the situation. I reflected on the values my family holds as members of the Catholic faith. In Christianity, there is the notion that I believe is common in many world religions — do unto others as you would have them do unto you. I walked into the bathroom, got a tissue, and

---

3   This story was also shared in *How to Stand Up to a Dictator*.

brought it back and gave it to her. Then I started talking to her. I was still afraid that I'd maybe be targeted, but slowly we became friends. Then one day I asked her why she was being bullied about her pants. I learned that it was because polyester pants were cheap. Her dad had been in the hospital for a long time and her family was under stress. And indeed, because we became friends, her bully began trying to bully me.

But, interestingly, my friends stood behind me. That's part of what gave me hope in the Philippines. It was kind of foolish for us in Rappler to stand up against a dictator. To stand up and continue doing our jobs, despite these tactics of harassment and intimidation. I learned to move forward and trust that someone will be there.

After you were given permission to leave the Philippines for a Princeton trip, you sent out a tweet: "Lessons learned: hope is dangerous because it creates expectations, but life without hope means you become an automaton with no meaning or purpose. So it's really a balancing act: be prepared for the worst, but keep taking risks to make your world the way it should be."[4] How can we find this balance? Because it seems — for many of us — to be an either/or situation: hopeful vs. hopeless.

I love this question! Thank you for finding that tweet. I think it is important to know your "whys" in life, because if you don't then your ego takes over. Again, it goes back to being strong enough to be able to lead. Leadership is about knowing your strengths and weaknesses and being able to harness people to move. There is another great phrase that we used a lot at Rappler and it also has religious roots: "All it takes is one, but one is not enough." In a group, one dissenter or challenger actually makes a group better because they make the group rethink. But one challenger isn't really enough to effect or create change.

---

4   Maria Ressa (@mariaressa), "Lessons learned: hope is dangerous because it creates expectations," Twitter, February 16, 2022, twitter.com/mariaressa/status/1494093266501107712.

To answer your question, I think for me, it was finding this balance between trying to be the best at everything I tried to do while keeping my ego in check. I've always figured you put in 150 percent, which meant you worked really, really hard. Then, as I gained power, it wasn't about feeding my ego; it was about trying to use that power for a greater purpose, and for me, that was journalism.

There is a book I often talk about — *The Empty Mirror: Experiences in a Japanese Zen Monastery* written by Janwillem van de Wetering.[5] Oftentimes, when you look in the mirror, you look at yourself. How wonderful would it be if you look at a mirror and it is empty, and rather you see the world reflected back without your ego being in the way. You have to have enough confidence so that you are able to chart the way and lead people, and yet at the same time you have to control your ego so that you can take yourself out of the picture to make the right decision.

Journalism also gives you a set of principles. These principles (and the discipline to stick to them) are critical, because you are in places where you need ethics to make judgment calls. For instance, this goes back to the "whys" again. I'm very clear about my mission. The *why* — why I do what I do. My actions have always been guided through a set of clearly defined goals, standards, and ethics. But unfortunately, it is frustrating today that many people can't tell the difference between a journalist — mission-driven, critical to a working democracy — and an influencer. Frankly, in the age of social media, being an influencer is just taking the high-school popularity game into adult life.

So, how do I find hope? As a journalist, you get to see the best and the worst in the world — and that is a wonderful thing. Ultimately, through what I have seen, I believe people are basically good.

5 Janwillem van de Wetering, *The Empty Mirror: Experiences in a Japanese Zen Monastery* (New York: St. Martin's Press, 1973).

You were awarded the 2021 Nobel Peace Prize for your effort to safeguard freedom of expression, which is a precondition for democracy and lasting peace. This cannot be a burden you carry alone. What advice do you have so we all can contribute to the fight for keeping a free and fair press? How can we hold social media to account for the amplification of lies perpetuated by their algorithms? And what role does personal accountability play in this?

In the Nobel lecture, I spoke about toxic sludge: a virus of lies to infect each of us, pitting us against each other, bringing out our fears, anger, and hate. Social media is, by design, emotionally manipulative. I will give you an example: Russian disinformation in the United States since 2016. In this instance, identity politics was the target, the Black Lives Matter movement was the target, *but these Russian attacks were not trying to be pro or against Black Lives Matter.* They attacked both sides, because the goal of that campaign was not to make you believe one side or the other. It was to open a chasm, using your emotions, and to weaken the entire infrastructure of society by tearing it apart, thus making you distrust everything and taking away the shared reality.

Another example is that if you were marginalized in the past, you are actually further marginalized online today. In the Philippines, for instance, women were attacked at least ten times more than men because we had a president who encouraged sexism at best and misogyny at worst. It is unclear where this insidious manipulation, repeating lies a million times, and micro-targeting is all leading to. But consider this: we watched Ferdinand Marcos Jr. change information operations from 2014 to 2022. He turned from being a pariah to a hero, and from a corrupt leader to being the greatest leader. And now, today, he is the president of the Philippines. This is what corrupt information operations did. Our greatest need today is to transform that hate and violence; that is, the toxic sludge that is coursing through our information ecosystem.

You ask, How do we hold social media platforms to account? For me, in the long term, it has to be education. People have to understand that they are being insidiously and deliberately manipulated by design. For example, there is what Shoshana Zubov calls "surveillance capitalism," or the widespread collection and commodification of personal data by corporations, including those in the technology industry — all for the profit-making incentive. In her book, she describes how your personal information is captured by organizations and is being used by others to not only predict your behavior — through predictive algorithms or mathematical calculation of human behavior — but also to influence and change it through behavior modification. Zubov also discusses how such insidious, automated manipulation of behavior is undermining human dignity, freedom, and democracy.

Therefore, in the medium term, we need legislation. To be clear, social media is not a freedom of speech issue. Technology lobbyists keep saying it is a freedom of speech issue, but it's not. It is a freedom of *reach* issue, a distribution issue. The comedian Sacha Baron Cohen said it best in a speech at the anti-defamation league in 2019: "This is not about limiting anyone's free speech. This is about giving people, including some of the most reprehensible people on Earth, the biggest platform in history to reach a third of the planet. Freedom of speech is not freedom of reach. Sadly, there will always be racists, misogynists, anti-Semites, and child abusers. But I think we could all agree that we should not be giving bigots and pedophiles a free platform to amplify their views and target their victims."[6] We need guardrails.

How do we protect ourselves against manipulation? For instance, the soda I am drinking has certain regulated requirements so I can trust it is not poisoned. There are building codes for our

---

6   The full speech can be accessed here: www.theguardian.com/technology/2019/nov/22/sacha
-baron-cohen-facebook-propaganda.

homes and workplaces, and so forth. Do you not deserve the right to be safe?

And lastly, in the short term, it's just us. This is about a battle or defense of our values. We live in an environment where we are being manipulated to be our worst self, to use the worst of our humanity. We can choose to fight for a better world.

What actions should we be taking to ensure democratic speech exists in academic environments?

I think first is self-awareness. Students in college are at an age where they are going to define their own lines in the sand. This is something I've said all the time since we — in the Philippines and other civil societies — came under attack in 2016. You have to draw the line, where on one side you're good, and when you cross over, you're bad, if not evil. That's normally called values, right? And you must draw those lines, determine those values, before you move into the business world or professional realm, while you are still young enough to be idealistic and able to see the line between corruption and civic virtue. This is a critical thing. Corruption has a tipping point, and then it takes over a system. When I talk to students and young adults, I always say, "Before you get out in the real world, define the line where on this side you're good, and you cross over and you're evil. Make it that simple on every front."

You're responsible not just for yourself, for your honor, but also for the honor of the world you're in. When you turn a blind eye, silence is taken as consent. I believe these are important considerations as you build or define your identity, as you build or hold power. Be clear about who you are, why you do what you do, and what values you have so that you are not caught unawares within situational ethics when you have to make a tough decision. This makes sure you don't rationalize bad behavior.

In 2021, at Toms River North High School in New Jersey, your high school, you told the students and staff that: "Every single decision you will make is going to decide who you are and whether your life has meaning . . . It's not going to be how much money you make or how cool you are."[7] Please unpack this strong statement for us. What prompted you to say this? What is the message you wanted to send to the students?

It's quite simple, actually. Meaning isn't something that you can buy. It isn't something that falls from the trees. It is like your identity — it is something that you build layer by layer. I think this is why I worry about this generation, who are growing up in a very toxic, manipulative environment like social media. In my days or in pre-digital generations, we tried on identities and words and even clothes with only our family and friends. Today, our current generation of young adults and kids are trying to figure out who they are on global social network platforms such as Instagram, TikTok, or Snapchat. On these platforms you curate your life; it becomes performative — whether it is for popularity or clicks or whatever, your life becomes a performance for others that has to look just so. But that popularity, that crowd that is giving you what you crave, can turn into a mob real fast.

That has real consequences to our kids growing up today. Facebook's own internal documents show that young girls, for example, have a greater incidence of eating disorders. People on Instagram have a greater incidence of depression, of suicide. We know this because former Facebook product manager-turned-whistleblower Frances Haugen turned over thousands of internal documents to United States authorities. These documents suggest Facebook misled the public and shareholders about the harmful effects of its platforms on the physical and mental health

7   Bryan Ke, "New Jersey High School Names Auditorium after Nobel-Winning Filipino American Journalist Maria Ressa," Yahoo! News, May 24, 2022, news.yahoo.com/jersey-high -school-names-auditorium-172952826.html.

of its users. The lesson therefore is that meaning in your life is something you choose, and you have to fight for it.

Do not let someone else decide who you will become. Take control of that, and learn to build meaning in your life. Young people need to understand that life is all about making choices — small and big. Making choices is what we do every minute of the day. These choices come to define who you are. They define your character.

In 2018, you said, "You don't really know who you are until you fight for it, and it's been one big fight for my values and my profession since 2016. Nietzsche was right. What doesn't kill you makes you stronger."[8] What has made you stronger?

I've helped write standards and ethics manuals in four different organizations, including CNN and Rappler. It is easy to say you believe in certain values if you are not tested. It is much harder when you're tested, and you live in an environment like today. I think what I loved, strangely enough (thank you, President Duterte!), is that he forced me to define who I was. He forced Rappler to define who we were — that the mission was critically important and that we were not going to be intimidated, no matter how much we were harassed. These attacks not only came on social media; they came bottom up, and then they came top down through all of the legal cases. By 2018, there were fourteen ongoing investigations, and in 2019, I had ten arrest warrants issued against me in less than two years. I was facing jail for the rest of my life. It added up to what would be almost a century once the cases started coming.

These legal cases forced me to fight for journalism. It forced me to stand up when it truly mattered. It's a little bit easier now

---

8   Ben Cohen, "Nobel Peace Prize Winning Journalist Maria Ressa Unable to Fly to Toronto for Gala," *Toronto Star*, April 23, 2022, www.thestar.com/news/gta/2022/04/23/nobel-peace -prize-winning-journalist-maria-ressa-unable-to-fly-to-toronto-for-gala.html.

that the court acquitted me on four tax evasion charges. I would have faced a maximum sentence of thirty-four years if convicted. But I was prepared. I wasn't going to buckle [under]. And that is actually a good thing to know. I came out of it stronger — my beliefs are stronger, Rappler is stronger. I guess for me, I felt like if I buckled, then I was never really a journalist.

If I am who I say I am, then this is the only path. Ursula K. Le Guin was an American author, and in her book *A Wizard of Earthsea*,[9] she captures this reality perfectly in a passage where an old magician shares: "You thought, as a boy, that a mage is one who can do anything. So I thought, once. So did we all. And the truth is that as a man's real power grows and his knowledge widens, ever the way he can follow grows narrower: until at last he chooses nothing, but does only and wholly what he *must* do . . ."

You actually challenged all of us global citizens during your speech at the Nobel Peace Prize ceremonies in December 2021. You said:

> Democracy has become a woman-to-woman, man-to-man defense of our values. We're at a sliding door moment, where we can continue down the path we're on and descend further into fascism, or we can each choose to fight for a better world.
>
> To do that, you have to ask yourself: what are YOU willing to sacrifice for the truth?
>
> I didn't know if I was going to be here today. Every day, I live with the real threat of spending the rest of my life in jail just because I'm a journalist. When I go home, I have no idea what the future holds, but it's worth the risk.
>
> The destruction has happened. Now it's time to build — to create the world we want.

---

9   Ursula K. Le Guin, *A Wizard of Earthsea* (New York: HarperCollins Publishers, 1968).

> Now, please, with me, close your eyes. And imagine
> the world as it should be. A world of peace, trust, and
> empathy, bringing out the best that we can be.[10]

Do you see more people making the necessary sacrifices to pursue truth? Are you optimistic? Do you see forward momentum? What would you like us all to do going forward?

The incentive structure rewards the bad, it rewards the lies. I became a journalist because information is power. The basic assumption of journalism is that you're not going to lie and that the facts are not debatable. How can you have a healthy, well-functioning democracy if you do not have integrity of facts? Journalism helps to determine what our system is, right? For without facts, we can't have truth; and without truth, we can't have trust. And without trust, we have no shared reality, no democracy, and it becomes impossible to deal with our world's existential problems.

Now, because of technology, we reward lies. We need to get the checks and balances back, and I feel like it is finally starting to come in. For me, the court decision acquitting me of tax evasion helps me believe that. Otherwise, it is quite lonely to keep believing in the good when everyone else gets rewarded for lying. Therefore, the first thing I ask the reader to do is, as I said before, to please define where your lines are now. Think about it like this. The tobacco lobby knew smoking was bad for people. It's the same thing with social media right now. The technology companies are doing their greatest harm in countries where institutions are weakest. How do they justify it?

They justify their actions because of profits and the creation of shareholder value. I continue to be amazed that so many people are complacent. They seem to be okay with the fact that our freedoms are taken away by technology companies' greed for

---

10 Her full speech and text can be found here: nobelprize.org/prizes/peace/2021/ressa/lecture.

growth and revenues. I don't know why we are not panicking. It is important that we bring together multi-stakeholder alliances, because technology organizations do not seem to believe they have any obligation to serve the public interest. But we must achieve a balance and focus on the greater good.

The second thing I'd like people to consider is that life isn't all about money. Moderate the green. The reason I became a manager in news, why I led this company, is because I believe principles rule above all, and that money will follow. It is the way I built my life. Money was not what I pursued. What I pursued was meaning. So, draw your lines now. What is important to you? Find what gives your life meaning.

What is the last leadership-related lesson or insight you would like to share with the audience, those whose ambition is to lead people and communities to a better world?

I want people to remember this phrase: "the present moment of the past." This is a quote taken from "Tradition and the Individual Talent," an essay written by poet and literary critic T.S. Eliot. He said that the fact that you read the works of William Shakespeare will impact the latest novel you've read. But, the latest novel you read will also have an impact on your appreciation of Shakespeare. It suggests that the past and present coexist, and both create the future. That's really part of building identity. The present moment of the past. For example, I can go all the way back to when I was ten years old and became an immigrant kid. This experience affected part of what gave me the courage to stand up to Duterte. These are some of the things that you don't forget. The person you are today has been shaped by all your past selves and associated experiences. However, you can also seize the past and transform all that you have learned into something new. That is how you find meaning. The present moment of the past. Who you are, and who you are becoming, is a work of art.

CHAPTER 15

MARY ROBINSON

Chair of The Elders, Former President of Ireland, and Former UN High Commissioner for Human Rights

Mary Robinson is Adjunct Professor for Climate Justice at Trinity College Dublin and chair of The Elders. She served as President of Ireland from 1990 to 1997 and UN High Commissioner for Human Rights from 1997 to 2002. She is a member of the Club of Madrid and the recipient of numerous honors and awards, including the Presidential Medal of Freedom from former US president Barack Obama. Between 2013 and 2016 Mary served as the UN Secretary General's Special Envoy in three roles: first for the Great Lakes region of Africa, then on climate change leading up to the Paris Agreement, and in 2016 as Special Envoy on El Niño and Climate. Her foundation, the Mary Robinson Foundation — Climate Justice, established in 2010, came to a planned end in April 2019.

Mary's memoir, *Everybody Matters*, was published in September 2012 and her book *Climate Justice: Hope, Resilience, and the Fight for a Sustainable Future* was published in September 2018. She is also co-host of a podcast on the climate crisis called Mothers of Invention.

In July 2009, you were awarded the Presidential Medal of Freedom, the highest civilian honor awarded by the United States. President Barack Obama said, "Today, as an advocate for the hungry and the hunted, the forgotten and the ignored, Mary Robinson has not only shone a light on human suffering, but illuminated a better future for our world."[1] Where did your relentless focus on human rights come from? How has your deep sense of justice evolved over time?

I come from a very close family, but I often joke that my early sense of justice came from being wedged between four brothers in the west of Ireland — two older and two younger. I had to learn about gender and human rights and use my elbows from a very early age.

My first sense of justice was to open up Irish society by taking court cases as a barrister that would particularly affect a wide number of people on issues like civil legal aid, gay rights, equal pay for women, etc. Then, I went from Ireland to Europe and took part in the referendum debate in 1971 [which would decide if Ireland should amend its constitution to allow it to join the European Economic Community, later the European Union]. I held the strong view that if Ireland joined Europe, it would help our relationship with Britain. This was because, up to that point, the relationship between Ireland and Britain was always an unequal, post-colonial relationship; but, if we became a part of a wider group of countries, I believed it would help our culture, it would help our identity; and it would help our morale, which, of course, it did. That was a learning curve.

And then, finally, when I became UN High Commissioner for Human Rights and I began to see the need to address human rights globally — which frankly, at the beginning, connected to places I had never heard of! — I found myself being asked questions about countries or communities that I didn't know anything about. With this role, however, I didn't have any big stick, did not have any power at that time, so I decided the best way to address these issues was to be close to

1   The White House, Office of the Press Secretary, "Remarks by the President at the Medal of Freedom Ceremony," August 12, 2009, obamawhitehouse.archives.gov/the-press-office/ remarks-president-medal-freedom-ceremony.

the victims. My colleagues in my office would always describe me as coming back energized from being in some of the worst and most dangerous places in the world. And I was indeed energized by those I met — by the bravery of the people who were on the ground fighting for human rights — because I was in and out, [but] they were there permanently. That really taught me a huge lesson in the fact that human rights are defended all over the world by people who would describe themselves as ordinary. That was a big learning curve for me.

When referring to the first article in the Universal Declaration of Human Rights, which states, "All human beings are born free and equal in dignity and rights," you have often said that you "love that 'dignity' comes before 'rights'" in its phrasing. Can you please explain why this is important?

I've often talked, particularly with the students, about this. In my view, dignity means that a person is afforded a sense of self-worth. Yet if you're homeless and lying in a doorway with people ignoring you, how can you cultivate that self-worth? If you are living in absolute dire poverty and can't feed your children, how can you be provided with a sense of dignity? I think that by placing dignity first, it brings out far more compassion and empathy in the approach to human rights. Very often, to a fault actually, human rights can be judgmental or finger-pointing, but if you place the need for people to have dignity first, suddenly you're into thoughtful compassion.

In terms of how we relate to one another as human beings, are things getting better?

This is not a good time in our history, and it is mainly a problem top-down. Many leaders are becoming more authoritarian, more populist. What is happening on the ground, however, very often continues to be courageous and resilience-building. It is those who are in positions of leadership that are mainly the problem.

As a young Senator, one of the first bills you intended to introduce was a repeal of the Criminal Law Amendment Act of 1935, which banned contraceptives. You shared that you were unprepared for the vitriolic opposition with which it was met. You received hate mail, condemnation in the press, and were denounced from pulpits across Ireland, including your hometown of Ballina. How did you remain resilient through that experience, especially considering how young you were and that this was your first major political act? What advice would you have for others, especially women, who receive this kind of backlash for standing up for what is right and just?

I wasn't resilient to start with! I was very shocked, taken aback, and, you know, completely depressed — so much so that my (then new) husband, Nick, burned the letters I had been sent. Of course, we now regret that very much because we are natural archivists. He did that though because I was not coping very well. I remember walking down the main street in Dublin — Grafton Street — and being afraid that people would jump in front of me and say, "You are a witch from hell!" because that was what they were writing to me. But, it forced me to have to say to myself, "No, I need to become more resilient, and I just need to be ready to pay the price of being unpopular." I literally remember saying those words to myself. But it was not pleasant at all, and I have every sympathy for those who face social media. I only had snail mail letters, and that was bad enough.

Because of that potential for viral hatred, it is easy to envision how good people, people with leadership potential, don't or won't actually run for leadership positions. And unfortunately, these are the very people who could make an amazing difference to communities and societies. How do we deal with this?

I think people just have to have the courage to put up their hand. Very often, if you really feel passionate, if you care enough, you'll find the courage. I think it is a question of motivating young people to know that they can make a difference.

Before I ever had to cope with the hate mail, I should explain about why I wished to get elected to the Senate in the first place. In short, it was because I had spent a year in the Harvard Law School — I have no doubt about it. I was in the class of 1968, and that year — from 1967 to 1968 — was extraordinary. My contemporaries were condemning an immoral war and trying to avoid being drafted to go to Vietnam. Martin Luther King was assassinated in April, and just after I graduated, Robert Kennedy was assassinated.

But that wasn't what affected me. It was that young people were taking responsibility. I saw them going into the poverty program or into the civil rights program in the south of the country when things were really, really bad. Where people were being killed, schools were being blocked, and so on. All of that meant that I came back to Ireland with what Nick calls my "Harvard humility," meaning the opposite! But without that, I would not have dreamt of going against the system where it was male, elderly professors who got the Senate seats. It also helped me to cope later on with the problem of media. I think, though, that the way to motivate yourself is not to focus so much on "Can you cope with hate mail?" but "Are you driven enough by your own passion for change?"

In taking up your post as UN High Commissioner for Human Rights, your goal was to be a bridge-builder, but at the same time you had no hesitation about speaking out and standing up to bullies. How did you learn to do this effectively and build workable relationships to tackle problems? It seems that today we often provoke for the purpose of political grandstanding — and then move on without building bridges. How did you learn to be a person who doesn't just cross the divide, but spans it so others may too?

I think I always did — and still do — find it easy to stand up to bullies. I hate bullying; standing up to bullies means you are helping those who are their targets. It lets their voices and thoughts come out. I think that is where the bridge comes in.

But, it is not just about standing up to bullies; it is actually about standing up because you want the voice of the bullied to be heard. It is about wanting people to have a place at the table and an opportunity for others to understand what their situation is. For example, when I was president of Ireland, I made a visit to Somalia when there was a problem [with] two warlords stopping the food from getting to feeding stations. So, I met both warlords and at one stage, I poked one of them in the tummy because I was so angry with him! Our foreign minister was very worried about what the repercussions would be, but I knew that I had to tell them that what they were doing was not acceptable. It just went on from there at the UN. It just was very clear to me that if I was in a position to stand up to bullies, I would — but always with the purpose of opening up space for others, for those who were fearful.

What would you tell the younger generation on how to bridge differences? Especially as we will not progress or make the necessary changes that the times are calling for without a deep sense of collaboration and without bridging our differences.

Interestingly, in recent times, especially as an Elder and now as Chair of The Elders, we have learned the value of the intergenerational dialogue and the collaboration that comes out of that. Frankly, I am very impressed with how collaborative the young people fighting for climate action are, and how much they care for those less privileged. They talk about love quite a bit. There is a real sense of collaborating within a broad movement; and now, we are talking about an intergenerational movement, focusing particularly on women leaders and young people. That is my frontline work at the moment.

You have said that human rights must inhabit the "small places" of our world because, as you quoted Eleanor Roosevelt as saying in your book *Everybody Matters*, "unless these rights have meaning there, they have little meaning anywhere."[2] In your view, what is the state of human rights in today's small places, and how do we ensure that rights and equity inhabit them, especially when so much energy seems to be dedicated to large, global issues?

I actually think that the state of human rights within small places is quite good; we just don't know about it. There are a lot of people working for human rights even though they might not call it that — they are working for resilience in their community. They are working for land rights, water rights, standing up to mining companies — whatever it may be. As I said before, it is at the top level that we tend to have bad leadership. I'm very keen on hearing the voices of the frontline people on any issue.

Currently, I am mainly involved in planet conferences. It is critical that we hear those frontline voices as they will bring home to us the reality of what is really happening much more rapidly. When I had my foundation, which wound up in 2019 because we fulfilled our objectives, we linked women leaders top-down and bottom-up. I also belonged to a network of women ministers and we could determine who would be in the delegation and participate in the climate dialogue. It became really important to open up space for grassroots, Indigenous young women in particular, to come and tell about their reality. I literally saw the largely male negotiators, who had negotiated so vociferously on the small print of their own points, put down the pen and listen when they heard that reality and it somehow affected them. They realized they weren't actually the experts; the frontline people were the experts on what was happening.

Is progress fast enough?

Well, unfortunately we are not making much progress. We are in a time of short-term populism and authoritarianism. There

2   Mary Robinson, *Everybody Matters: My Life Giving Voice* (New York: Bloomsbury Publishing, 2012).

used to be a time — especially in a Western context — if a leader didn't robustly uphold human rights, they would suffer for it. We have seen it with Trump in the United States, with Orbán in Hungary, that now you can actually gain. That is sad. Frankly, short-term populism needs to be combated with education and understanding, which is slow and longer term, but badly needed.

You have previously talked about the Irish phenomenon of *meitheal*, which relates to a sense of neighborly helpfulness — people working together to provide cooperative support and aid to one another. What can we learn from the spirit of this word? How would the world change if we adopted a global spirit of *meithal*, in both a literal and figurative sense?

Well, interestingly, related to the small places, there is a Mary Robinson Centre being developed in my hometown of Ballina. It will be located in what previously was our family home on the River Moy and immediately opposite the cathedral, which is how I learned about the symbol of the light in the window. Because our house was directly across the river from the cathedral, my mother used to put candles in our home's windows — and she wouldn't put just one candle, she would put at least three, and sometimes five! She wanted to make sure that nobody would feel alone at Christmas. That was where I got the idea of placing the ever-burning light in the window of Áras an Uachtaráin [official residence and workplace of the president of Ireland] for the Irish diaspora.

When I have talked to the design firm for the centre, we actually talked about *meithal*. I encourage them to link it with *ubuntu*, which I learned about from Archbishop Tutu and means "I am because you are." *Meithal* and *ubuntu* stem from the same idea: we are connected. For instance, when I was young, my father would talk about how he would see the one tractor and all the local farm workers in a field on one day, and then they would move to the next. If a farmer was sick, his fields would still be done. That is *meithal*, that is *ubuntu*. This idea is found in a lot of cultures in different ways, but we aren't paying enough attention to that local culture of community, of generosity, especially in times of trouble.

Why do we seem to lose that?

The spirit of *meitheal* was something I observed when I was campaigning in Ireland in 1990. Ireland was benefiting significantly from our membership in the European Union, in particular from the common agricultural policy which helps small farmers in Ireland to have reliable prices for their products. This is incredibly important because Ireland was constantly squeezed by the UK and their cheap food markets. There was money in the country, but the government still didn't have enough to provide the facilities that were in the city, so people just literally banded together. I remember talking then about the spirit of the *meitheal* community.

After my term of presidency, however, Ireland entered into the Celtic Tiger era, where people behaved as though we were going to have growth forever. It was foolishness — things like 100 percent mortgages for young people — and greed, frankly, and we lost that *meitheal*. Of course, we had our terrible crash — self-inflicted, and helped along by German and other banks lending us too much money. Once we experienced the fiscal crisis, the spirit of *meitheal* bloomed again; it was also very notable during the COVID pandemic. It is in our DNA and in the DNA of a lot of countries, but what we don't do is recognize it enough.

Many women cried when you became president, and you have stated that you were aware of how much it meant to them to see the first woman elected to the highest office in the country. You said, "I knew I had to be a woman who, as the first woman president, did it proudly as a woman. I wasn't trying to be an honorary man, not at all. I felt the value of being a woman and the way women make decisions."[3] What did you mean by that? How have you seen women's leadership manifest differently?

At the time, what I was determined to do was walk tall as a woman. I was going to work as hard as I could, and told myself, "I'm going to do this job better because I'm a woman." I had the trust of the people. I believe that leadership is about serving those who trust you by electing you, but I also felt that, as a woman, I was more equipped. One of the first appreciations I had, particularly during the election campaign itself, over the many months traveling around the country, and in particular when I had the bully pulpit as president, if you like, was to recognize those women who undervalue themselves — domestic women or women in the home. That's why on the night of the election itself, I talked about *mná na hÉireann* [women of Ireland] who, instead of rocking the cradle, rock the system. I was very deliberate to use that denigrating phrase — *mná na hÉireann* — to twist around to refer to women we value. That was a big point I wanted to make.

I do think women's leadership is going through quite a positive phase. In fact, I was speaking at a conference where we were discussing the need for Europe to shift to clean energy more quickly, and a point was made — it was made by a woman, but it was made — "We need to go where the energy is, [and] that's women leaders!" I think that's true now. Also, during the pandemic, women leaders were more successful at responding to it. Overall, there is a sense that women who have come into leadership today are less likely to be a populist, ego-driven, hierarchical, or autocratic leader.

In your view, why does leadership matter? And not just leadership at the top, but at all levels? Could you share some recent examples where

---

3   Mary Robinson speaking during an appearance on the UK's *Late Late Show* hosted by Ryan Tubridy, November 20, 2020.

leadership at all levels is making an impact? And, where is leadership failing in our world today?

I have always felt that leadership matters and gave the example of women ministers who linked with grassroots, Indigenous young women — getting them onto the delegations — so that they would be at the table and be a voice in the climate space. I have also learned a lot about valuing leadership from Mo Ibrahim, who is a very good friend of mine. He invited me to go on the board and the prize committee of his foundation, which is focused on African leadership. Mo said to me, "Leadership is priceless. That is why we have to have a $1 million award for Africans who lead well and don't break their constitution so they can serve for another term, for life, and so on. Those of us on the board questioned him about the size of the award, saying it didn't need to be so large. His response was "Yes, it does. Not to bribe, but to value the leadership."

We've been going for about seventeen or eighteen years, and we have given the prize to six African leaders now who have become exceptional statespersons for their continent. One of them is Ellen Johnson Sirleaf of Liberia, who also won the Nobel Peace Prize. The other award winners are less well known globally, but they are working in Africa and known for going into difficult places to talk about leadership. That convinced me that it really does matter. His foundation is not only about the award either; another important element is the Ibrahim Index of African Governance, which monitors and measures governance performance in Africa's fifty-four countries. Mo Ibrahim is an incredible champion of leadership and democracy.

You are also an inspiring leader to many. Which leader inspired you with their character? What aspect of their leadership do you try to emulate?

I feel very lucky for having the opportunity to meet outstanding leaders, and the most outstanding being, of course, Nelson

Mandela. I met him when I was president of Ireland and I attended his inauguration. Afterwards, I made a state visit to South Africa, which is when I learned about his great capacity to tease, his great humor. We also interacted with each other when I was the UN High Commissioner for Human Rights, and then, when he brought The Elders together, I was one of the founding Elders. He had an immense capacity to inspire, even though he often used humor to try to stop people from putting him on such a pedestal — he was constantly self-deprecating in that sense! I greatly admire his ability to forgive his enemies, as well as his resilience — he was in prison such a long period, and yet came out with this great sense of compassion and forgiveness. Amongst many others, I also had the privilege of getting to know and work with Archbishop Tutu, whom I have already mentioned.

Earlier in my life, our family included some exceptional women who were nuns and from whom I learned a great deal. One of my great aunts in particular, who at one point was the Reverend Mother General of her order in the UK, was great fun. She was quite a forthright woman in her own way and I learned many things from her. Another aunt, my father's sister, was a nun in India for about thirty years and she used to write long letters to my father about her work in educating girls from impoverished areas. Now, Irish nuns are a dying species in a way, but you still find them in obscure, little places throughout Africa. For instance, when I was High Commissioner I visited Goma and traveled into a remote place where, sadly, women were being raped and experiencing violence, and then I heard an Irish voice and it was literally one nun on her own out there trying to help.

I also wrote a book — *Climate Justice: Hope, Resilience, and the Fight for a Sustainable Future*[4] — and that was about my heroes. The book contains eleven stories, and nine of them involved women, but there are also two very good men featured.

---

4   Mary Robinson, *Climate Justice: Hope, Resilience, and the Fight for a Sustainable Future* (New York: Bloomsbury Publishing, 2018).

One of the men was former president Anote Tong of the Republic of Kiribati, who talked about his islands and fighting for the future of his people. I've learned so much from the work people do on the ground and in difficult circumstances. That is what I find so admirable.

On July 18, 2022, you articulated that leadership has too often become associated with dominion, control, and avarice, and has little regard for the essential goodness that flourishes in kinship and the generous accommodation and kindness Nelson Mandela spoke of when he first founded The Elders in 2007. A main objective of The Elders is to share their wisdom in an effort to help solve some of the world's toughest problems — problems in the areas of peace, justice, and human rights. In these realms, the world is often described as a dark place — a place that is broken. And yet, in the aforementioned speech you said, "And it is the light, and it is the hope, that will prevail in the end!"[5] Where does your hope — or inspiration — come from? Also, can you share with us some positive changes or impacts that were facilitated by The Elders?

I have no choice in the matter! When Nelson Mandela brought us together, he made it perfectly clear that we had to be a force for hope in the world. He told us that wherever we went to be humble, to listen to the local people, who would most certainly know more about the help we could provide in their area than we ever could know coming from the outside. He said, "Listen to them and then help them to get their voices out."

Following Mandela, our first chair of The Elders was Archbishop Tutu, who was a wonderful champion of hope. I was on a panel with him during the 2011 Social Good Summit in the United States, which was a gathering hosted by the UN Foundation as a way of bringing young people together to

5   See Robinson's full speech, delivered on Mandela Day 2022, and her reflections on the passing of Archbishop Desmond Tutu: theelders.org/news/marking-mandela-day-2022-mary-robinson -reflects-global-state-hope.

discuss the world's greatest challenges. At that time, it was kind of new and trendy because they now had phones and iPads, and they could create a social media buzz. We were supposed to be trending, which was all completely new to Arch and myself — "Arch" was the name we were encouraged to call him. In front of young people, Arch showed his love, his hope, and his belief in them.

As he was doing this, an American journalist who was moderating our panel asked us why he was such an optimist, and he said, "No, I am not optimist, but I am a prisoner of hope." That struck me enormously at the time, and ever since I have thought a lot about it and tried to harness that perspective ever since. For example, when I discuss the climate issue, I could describe it in such a way that would frighten the hell out of people. If I did that, all the energy would go out of the room and people will put their head down and feel helpless to do anything about it. Whereas if I approach it as a prisoner of hope, I say, "Yes, it is very clear that we have a small window that we are up against. We're not on course for a safe world, but we have a choice! We can choose this best world which is just right in front of us, or we can have the worst world. It's our choice. Come on, let's do it!" Then you galvanize people's energy and that is really what hope is about. It's about the energy to make the difference. The small difference, the tiny difference, the individual difference, the collective difference.

Is that something that can be developed in people or was Archbishop Tutu such a unique human being that we would be lucky to have more people like him around us?

I think it would be good if we had more people like him. But, if we continue to explore this through the climate lens, I do think that we need to change the narrative on climate completely into one that is more positive as quickly as we can. Only a positive narrative will help us get to where we need to be, which is this

best world that is still possible — a world free of fossil fuel and
has access to clean energy, and a more equal world.

You have referenced five layers of climate injustice, with the fifth layer
being injustice to nature herself. How do you think we can cultivate a
more holistic perspective on and relationship with nature? How do you
suggest we change our behavior towards nature from being extractive to
generative, from dissonant to harmonious?

I think this is extraordinarily important. If only we would
listen more to the Indigenous wisdom. We are nature. We are
part of nature. We are connected in a profound way with the
mountains, with the rivers, with all human beings, all animal
species. Any harm to them is harm to us. We have had it all
wrong. I don't think the Bible has helped in this because its
approach saw men as masters of a world we were given by
God. But, actually, we are deeply a part of this world and we
are harming ourselves when we harm nature. I think the more
we can educate ourselves about that, the better. Indigenous
wisdom can teach us so much about this in so many ways.

I had an experience that really brought this home to me
more profoundly and viscerally than anything else. In August
2019, I was lucky enough to be a part of the last scientific
exhibition to Greenland until post-pandemic. I was given this
gift because I had served on the European Climate Foundation
for nine years. Towards the end of the trip, we went by boat to
a remote place where we would stay in a pretty primitive camp
overnight so we could then wake up in the morning and go out
on our own and listen to the glacier that was quite close to us.
Everybody else went off in different directions, but because I was
one of the older ones I took advantage of the seat right at our
camp. As I sat, I could feel the heat on my Irish skin — it was
17 degrees Celsius and the sun was shining in a blue sky. I was
too hot. But more than that, I could hear the noise of the calving
of the glacier — it was like thunder. Suddenly there would be

sounds like rifle shots when smaller bits fell off. I began to cry because I knew, to the core of my being, that this is not right, what we humans are doing! I could feel Mother Nature hurting. I mean I really, really felt it and it was a very profound lesson of something we all need to realize. We are profoundly hurting her and ourselves if we go on like this.

What important leadership questions have we not addressed during our conversation? What is the last leadership-related lesson or insight you would like to share with the audience — those whose ambition is to lead people and communities to a better world?

I will share with you one last phrase, that is not mine but was said by Kofi Annan, the former secretary-general of the United Nations. It is a phrase I heard him say over and over, and that I use myself more and more now: "You are never too young to lead, and you are never too old to learn."

CHAPTER 16

THE HONOURABLE MURRAY SINCLAIR

Former Senator of Canada, Chief Commissioner of Canada's Indian Residential Schools Truth and Reconciliation Commission

The Honourable Murray Sinclair, LLB MSC IPC, is Anishinaabe and a member of the Peguis First Nation. He is a Fourth Degree Chief of the Midewiwin Society, a traditional healing and spiritual society responsible for protecting the teachings, ceremonies, laws, and history of the Anishinaabe. His Spirit Name is Mizhana Gheezhik (The One Who Speaks of Pictures in the Sky).

He graduated from law school in 1979. He has been involved with the justice system in Manitoba, Canada, for over forty years — as a lawyer, an Adjunct Professor of Law at Robson Hall, as Associate Chief Judge of Manitoba's Provincial Court, and as a Justice of the Court of Queen's Bench. He was the first Indigenous Judge appointed in Manitoba and Canada's second.

He served as Co-Chair of the Aboriginal Justice Inquiry of Manitoba and later as Chief Commissioner of Canada's Indian Residential Schools Truth and Reconciliation Commission (TRC), culminating in the TRC's widely influential report in 2015. In 2017 Governor General Julie Payette awarded him the Meritorious Service Cross (Civilian) (MSC) for service to Canada.

He has won numerous awards, including the National Aboriginal Achievement Award, the Manitoba Bar Association's Equality Award (2001), and the CBA President's Award (2018). He has received Honorary Doctorates from fourteen universities and became the fifteenth Chancellor of Queen's University in July 2021. He was appointed to Canada's Senate on April 2, 2016, from which he retired on January 31, 2021.

In interviews, you speak in calm and measured tones, even when the conversation may suggest that you have every right to be upset and angry. How did you develop your temperance and restraint?

I think it's probably because those are the characteristics that I most benefit from personally, and those which I always felt are the most important in the situations I find myself in, going back to my earliest upbringing. It was the way that my grandfather behaved. It was the way that those people I admired the most behaved, those who were responsible for leadership positions that I was engaged in. There were others, of course, who didn't behave that way, but I found that by observing the impact of the way they were doing things, I could see the downside of their loud, more abrasive behavior. I felt that the one important thing to understand was that if people are going to listen to what you're saying, then you need to be careful about what you say, and you need to say those things that are going to have the most impact upon them.

From the time that I was little, I always responded a bit differently than my siblings and cousins in the family did. My grandmother, Catherine Sinclair, always made it clear to me that I was responsible for taking care and showing better behavior for the benefit of the other boys and girls in our neighborhood. It wasn't that she held me accountable for that — she just said it was what I *could* do. She recognized that ability within me, so she pulled it out.

Most people don't know that my grandmother was raised in a Catholic residential school, and she was very taken by the teachings of the church. She only gave up on the school because, when her mother died, they wouldn't let her leave to go to the funeral, so she was quite disheartened by that. She was going to be a nun, but she decided to leave the convent. In order to do that, she was required to get married, and so she married my grandfather, Jim Sinclair. She was also told that, in leaving, she was expected to dedicate one of her family members to the Church. My uncles and aunts were not interested, but from an early point she saw something in me and thought that I should become a priest. She directed my involvement with the Church, but also talked to me about the responsibility that went with a position like that.

From my earliest time, I was also taught to be observant by my grandfather, who was a hunter and a fisherman and a trapper. You can't be successful at that unless you learn to be observant, be quiet, not talk out of turn, and not make noise. From my grandmother's side, of course, it was about belief. Believing in yourself, believing in the people, and believing in a more inclusive relationship with the spirit world.

Anybody who knows me will know that I have always been very spiritual. I still take a lot of enjoyment in listening to teachings, listening to stories about the creator and creation, listening to the teachings about just about every religious denomination around the world. I have friends who are Muslim, and they have shared their stories and religious teachings with me. I have friends who are Christian, of course, and I myself studied Christian teachings for the longest time while I was thinking of becoming a priest. I always believed that there was a "one-ness" about all of it that needed to be understood.

Eventually, I had to disappoint my grandmother and recognize that priesthood was not for me. Early on in my youth, I grabbed on to our own teachings as Anishinaabe people, and I chose to embrace those for the benefit of my children as well as myself.

You are known as a patient man. However, in 2017, there was a moment of seeming impatience on your part when you responded to a colleague in the Senate who defended residential schools and members of our society who wonder why Indigenous people don't just "get over" the trauma of residential schools and move on. You said to Anna Maria Tremonti, the then-host of CBC Radio's *The Current*:

> My answer has always been "Why can't you always remember this? Because this is about memorializing those people who have been the victims of a great wrong. Why don't you tell the United States to 'get over' 9/11? Why don't you tell this country to 'get over' all the veterans who died in the Second World War, instead of honoring them once a year? Why don't you tell your families to stop thinking about all of your ancestors who died?"
>
> It's because it's important for us to remember. We learn from it. And until people show that they have learned from this we will never forget. And we should never forget, even once they have learned from it, because it's part of who we are. It's not just a part of who we are as survivors and children of survivors and relatives of survivors, it's part of who we are as a nation. And this nation must never forget what it once did to its most vulnerable people.[1]

I think of the heaviness that it really does create for all of us. We, who are the descendants of the survivors; and we, who are the descendants of those who were here at the time; those who may have had a connection to the ones who did this in government, or who worked in the schools; and even newcomers — we must all feel the weight of this process of reconciliation. Because even if you weren't here, you still have a responsibility to the future of this country. Therefore, you need to understand this. We do need to remember.

---

1   CBC Radio, "How Senator Murray Sinclair Responds to Why Don't Residential School Survivors Just 'Get over it,'" *The Current*, April 4, 2017, www.cbc.ca/radio/thecurrent/the -current-for-april-4-mmiwg-ottawa-public-forum-1.4053431/how-senator-murray-sinclair -responds-to-why-don-t-residential-school-survivors-just-get-over-it-1.4053522.

I keep thinking back to the time when we were beginning the work of the Truth and Reconciliation Commission, and one of the staff who was working on drafting the report and putting together the beginnings of the report said, "How do we make people care?" I said, "We make them care because we want them to know that this is their story too." I think we did that.

If we do move forward without remembering, then we are not the people that we should be. We are not the people that history really fashioned us to be, and we are doing things without realizing why we're doing things, or understanding why we are who we are. I know that for young Indigenous people today, for example, their question often is "Why are things like this? Why are things the way they are? Why is my family in so much trouble and hurting so badly? Why don't we have better economies? Why don't we have a better sewer system? Why don't we have better housing?" When they learn this history, they know why. One thing they learn is that this is not their fault. They are the victims of this history, and they now need to learn how to turn it around.

We hear the word "reconciliation" a lot. What does that word mean to you?

Reconciliation is about establishing a respectful relationship. A relationship of mutual respect, in which we respect each other. I've often said reconciliation implies a very simple concept, which is "I want to be your friend, and I want you to be mine." So, when you need my help, I will be there to help you. When I need your help, you will be there to help me. Because that's what this country should be about: being respectful of each other.

One thing I have also pointed out is that Indigenous people have so long been oppressed and victimized by this history that we need to understand it before we can have mutual respect. We have to ensure that Indigenous people are given the opportunity to develop self-respect. That's a first step to the mutual respect relationship we're going to have to have. We do see young, angry Indigenous people out there. It's often reflective of the philosophy of people like Frantz Fanon, who articulated that one of the impacts of colonialism is that the victims of colonialism take it out upon themselves first, because they begin to believe the stories they are told about their inferiority and their lack of rights. They begin to see themselves in a bad light, and then they take it out on their neighbors. Then they take it out on people who are around them, and people who come from other places too. Eventually, they will take it out on their oppressor, and that's when things will really change. But they won't necessarily change for the best.

How do we recognize those concerns in very concrete ways so that the anger and the frustration that a new generation feels, and is talking about, and is trying to act on, can actually be answered in a constructive way going forward — not only for them, but for all of us?

Indigenous youth are really looking for answers from their own Elders and from their own community leaders. It is their grandfathers and grandmothers and their community Elders who need to be the ones to share wisdom about what their responsibility is to the future. That will come from understanding their teachings. I often tell people that when I was a young lawyer, I quit law. I said, "I'm not going to do this anymore, because I don't want to work in the system that is doing bad things to our people."

I went to see an Elder shortly after I made that decision. He said, "You can do that if you want. You can go become a carpenter or become a mechanic. If you do that, you will be a mechanic who knows the law, and people will know that you know the law, and they will still come to you to ask you for advice and help. It's not like you can run away from that. What you need to learn, really, is how to be the best lawyer that you can be. In order for you to be able to do that, you have to learn what it means to be Anishinaabe, and to learn what it means to be a husband, to be a father, to be a son, to be a grandson. You have to learn what it means to be a leader in your community, because then you will be the best human being you can be." That's what everyone's responsibility is, but for Indigenous people, it comes from knowing who they are.

You have worked inside and continue to work with the very institutions that systematically work against Indigenous people. Please tell us more about that inner struggle you went through when you thought about leaving the law.

My temptation was to walk away from the legal profession because I didn't think there was room for me. I didn't think that I would be able to make myself fit, and I didn't want to try to make myself fit into that. I wanted to do what I thought was right.

However, I had a talk with my Elder — a good friend at that time, Angus Merrick, a respected Elder in the Long Plains First Nation, who has long since left us. The one thing that he convinced me of was that you don't have to change for this system to work for you. You can make the system change, and you need to figure out where you can do that. I didn't set out to change the system, to be honest with you. I set out to be a lawyer within the system. That was my initial ambition. As I flipped my thinking in that way, I began to see that there were certain things that the system was doing that were wrong, that needed to be changed. I thought, "Well, maybe if I start to draw attention to those things, they will become things that can be changed."

I have made a number of observations or recommendations. I've chaired two different major inquiries: I was Co-Chair of the Aboriginal Justice Inquiry of Manitoba and I was the Chief Commissioner of Canada's Indian Residential Schools Truth and Reconciliation Commission. I have to say that change has been slow, but the negative creation of this particular situation has been slow too. It took 150 years for us to get into this mess and, as I've often said, it may take us that long to get out of it.

The real key in the long term is the way we teach our children, so that when they are relating to each other, they will relate to each other better.

You have done incredibly important work — work that is on the nation's record.

My grandmother always wanted me to be a priest because she saw the priest as the one who took care of the people. When I told her as a young teenager that I didn't want to be a priest — I finally got up the nerve to tell her that — she said, "What do you want to do?" I said, "I want to go to university."

And she said, "If you're going to do that, you have to promise me that you will not just become an educated bum, and that you will do something with that education, and you will do the best that you can with it." Every time I wonder about whether I'm doing the right thing, I can hear her voice in my head. She's either saying, "Yes, that's the right thing," or she's saying, "No, no — you've got to change that. You've got to do better than that." There is that voice that still talks to me.

However, I've learned that it's going to take us many generations in order to achieve reconciliation, because there will be those that will constantly work against us. There will always be those who will be not just deniers, but people who are going to try to undermine and destroy what we're trying to build. We have to be ready for that, and we have to be prepared to fight against it in whatever way we can.

The Seven Grandfather Teachings (also called the Seven Sacred Teachings) are rooted in Anishinaabe traditional knowledge, but many other Indigenous communities follow or adapt them as well. The Seven Grandfather Teachings are a way of being, a holistic set of teachings that can serve as guiding principles to living a good life — both individually and collectively. How do these teachings guide your life? And how do you consciously strengthen these teachings?

I open each day with a prayer and Pipe Ceremony if I can. I like to be outside with my pipe, around the fire. Whoever comes to visit me, that's where we talk and visit. I find it meditative and a place that is more in tune than a square room to being able to think holistically about things, and to think about what's going on around me. Two of my daughters live with me, and they make way for that, and participate in that with me. I always kid my daughter that she can sing our ceremonial songs better than I can. She certainly dances far better than I can.

More importantly, I wanted my children to embrace their culture, so that they would feel not only validated but proud of who they are. I wanted them to be able to come to terms with everything that they had been taught in public school about Anishinaabe people, so that they would be able to challenge what they were hearing from their teacher: that we were wild, savage and uncivilized — inferior to other people. I wanted them to be strong in that way.

They've all grown up to be like that. If you know my children, you know that they are all courageous when it comes to challenging racism, challenging misogyny, challenging anything that is not consistent with what we have taught them about our relationship with humanity, with creation, with all of the animals of the world. I have a granddaughter, Sarah Fontaine-Sinclair, who is probably one of the most engaged environmental activists in the city of Winnipeg, and has been since she was nine years old. She used to demonstrate outside of Jim Carr's office — he was the former Minister of Natural Resources — because she didn't think he was doing enough to protect the environment. She's now sixteen and she's still very much involved in environmental activism.

I wanted all of our children to understand the teachings and to be able to not only stand up for themselves and be themselves, but to stand up against racism and misogyny and all the things that they would face as they were growing up. They have to have the inner strength to be able to resist going over to the dark side, so to speak, and at the same time to call it out when they see it.

I used to tell them when they were growing up, "I'll spend any amount of money for anything that you want to do, but I have only a limited amount for bail money. Be careful."

What were the important moments in the development of your leadership? What were some of the defining moments that helped you to cultivate leader character and the Seven Grandfather Teachings within your own life?

One of the stories that I tell, and one of my favorite stories of my young life, is about when I was coming up to my twelfth birthday. My aunt Josephine was responsible for my upbringing. My grandmother was sixty-two when we went to live with her, so she was too old to take care of four young children, and she assigned one of our aunties to take care of us. The auntie who was assigned to me was a teacher. Wherever she went to teach in her career, I would go with her and perform tasks like a son would. I'd cut her wood; I'd carry her water. Of course, every break from school, whether it was Easter break or Christmas break or summer break, we would come back to my grandmother's house. My birthday happened to fall during the Christmas period, and so they were going to have the celebration before we went back to the community where my aunt was teaching. Auntie Josephine said to me, "What do you want for your birthday?" I said to her, very clearly, "I want a bicycle. It's very important because we live in the country, and sometimes I want to go into town. All of the kids that I go to school with all have bicycles, and I'd like to have one." She just said, "Okay, I understand."

On my birthday, when I got up in the morning, there was this huge box in the living room. I just knew it was my bicycle. It was all gift wrapped and had a ribbon and everything. After dinner that evening, and when we had gone through those parts of the festivities — including the birthday cake and the singing of songs and small gifts that I was given — it came time for me to open the big box. I opened up the very heavy box, and inside was a complete set of *The World Book Encyclopedia*. My aunt, of course, who was the teacher, said to me, "I know you wanted a bicycle, but this is more important." My grandmother said, "Yes, it is." My aunt said to me, "You are going to read one of these books every month, and I'm going to test you."

I was a little taken aback. I was a little chagrined. My aunt was serious. Every month from that point forward, I had to read one of those volumes of the encyclopedia. And I did. Very quickly, I became intrigued by what I was learning, by all of the information that was in those books. By the time I finished reading through the complete set, which took me a couple of years, they started calling me "the Professor" because I could answer any question that anybody asked me about anything in the world. One time my grandfather asked me, "What's the difference between an ape and a gorilla?" So I told him!

I have often said that this was the most influential act a person ever did for me in early childhood. That gift taught me the importance of knowledge, and also the beauty of it. The beauty, to me, is that really wonderful way of expanding my mind, expanding my knowledge base, and wondering about things. There were a lot of things that were not in the encyclopedia that I had to find elsewhere. I remember when I was fourteen or fifteen, just as I was graduating, somebody mentioned the writings of Frantz Fanon, a political philosopher from the former French colony of Martinique. I found one of his books in the school library — nobody had ever taken it out of the library — and I read it. His thinking and books were influential in the field of post-colonial studies. From that point forward, I became a political and social activist.

Ultimately, I got my bike. I actually had to buy it myself. I took a job in a grocery store, and as part of my responsibilities, I had to have a bike in order to deliver the groceries to old ladies. My grandmother took me to the store where they sold bicycles. I told the owner I needed a bike because of my job. He let me buy a bicycle on credit. Here I was, sixteen years old, and incurring my first debt. I had it paid off within a short time.

How may the Seven Grandfather Teachings help us in the fulfillment of ambitious societal goals, the mitigation of crises, or the creation of new ways of seeing or being in the world? How can we bring them from the communities in which they reside and which they informed, and from which you've drawn wisdom, out into the wider world?

The Elders never actually said, "The Seven Teachings are wisdom, love, respect, bravery, honesty, humility, and truth." Instead, what they would do is tell you a story. Sometimes it was a funny story, sometimes it was a serious story, and sometimes it was something that happened in their own lives. They would tell you a story, and then at the end of it, they would say, "And that's why it's important that we love people, because then they will love you back."

I remember a time when we invited a number of Elders to come and talk to us about leadership. One of the Elders talked about things from when he had been young, what he had heard about how things had happened back in the former times, and how people behaved with those who were strangers and considered the enemy.

One of the things that would come out of that story was that often the success or the survival of the people depended upon the leadership that they received from somebody, or from a number of people. That was his teaching about leadership — it was not to say that leadership is good. It was to say this was how leadership works, and this is why it works that way. And then he would bring in the teaching of love, because ultimately he said, "You have to be prepared to love the people, because they will not always love you. And you still have to love the people." The teaching of leadership was the teaching of love.

That's how they used those Grandfather Teachings. They would use what the Bible calls parables. I would equate that to the stories that Jesus used in telling his people about how to behave and how to treat each other. That's the way the Elders who have been raised in a traditional way utilize this technique to tell a story and then bring it back to one of the teachings. That's what I do with my grandchildren — I tell them a story. The benefit of a story is that you have the listener's attention while you're telling it, and they are really enjoying the story, and they are enjoying the relationship with you. Then you can tell them something that will help them.

In my reconciliation talks, one of the things I learned early on was that it was important for us to connect to the people who were listening, for them to understand why reconciliation is important. So, what I would do is, at the outset, I would encourage them to open their phones and look at their photos. I asked them to pick a photo of one of their babies — everybody has baby photos on their phone, whether it's their baby or somebody else's baby. This request is actually contrary when you go to a presentation and you've got 2,500 people in the room, because the one thing we're always telling people is to put their phones away.

So, I used to say, "Open your phones! Pick a picture of a baby in your family, or someone who really has touched you in your life." And then I would say, "Tell the people at your table, or the people on either side of you, about that little baby. Take five or ten minutes. I'll give that to you." You hear a real buzz in the room, and of course people are laughing, and people are crying — and they're looking at their phones. Then I would say, "Show me the photo." I would ask them to hold up their phones and show me the photo. For a moment, I would have 2,500 people all showing me their photos. Then I would say to them, "Delete that photo from your phone." Of course, they can't do it. I would say again, "Please delete the photo. You don't need it. Delete it!" They wouldn't. I've had people swear at me in those large gatherings! They'd say, "No way! I'm not going to delete this!" I said, "Okay, I understand. But imagine what it would have been like for the parents of the children who were taken away, and who never saw their children again. Deleting those pictures would be like deleting those children. Not just from the phone, but from their lives." And then I've got them. And then they are listening. I've got their attention, and that's why it's important to think about what it is that you need to do in order to have an impact on people when you're talking with them.

If you want to have an impact, you have to make a connection. I know that from my understanding and my receipt of traditional education through the use of teachings. The Elders who have done that have always ensured that they connected with me through story, and then they connected me to the teaching. They connected me to what they wanted me to know, what they wanted me to learn. It was important, whether it was wisdom, honesty, love, respect, kindness . . . whatever it is, there is always a story that you can use to help bring that home.

Many Indigenous worldviews include the understanding of the impact of decisions on the next seven generations. In the corporate world, a lot of people just look to the next quarter. In the political world, many officials just look to the next term. In the social world, the buzz lasts only minutes. How might non-Indigenous leaders and aspiring leaders learn from Indigenous beliefs and practices about how to make decisions that have substantial impact on communities and societies?

To a certain extent, it's circumstantial, in the sense that it depends on what kind of decision-making process you need to engage in. Some decisions in the business community are about immediate needs and immediate actions, and so those require a different approach than the long-term planning. I think part of the problem is that we don't do enough long-term planning and long-term thinking about what it is that we're going to do. What are we doing to the people? What are we doing to the environment? What are we doing to the animals? What are we doing to ourselves, as human beings? The questions that I think we need to ask ourselves are: How do we plan properly, and how do we think things through properly? How do we find our balance as individuals within this overall competitive world that we are thrust into?

Finding our balance is key to all of this. Finding our balance at a personal level is one thing, and finding corporate balance as an institution is also very important. That means also making space for those institutions and organizations that are dedicated to doing what they can to speak up for the environment, for the animals, and for those elements without a voice. We do know that in the long run, our children are going to benefit from it. It is about understanding what those teachings are and understanding what the Elders are saying.

Consider the Haida people on the West Coast of Canada. Every summer they hire a group of young people to go out on the land. Their job is just to go out and stay on the land and live on the land and travel around on the land, and then to come back and meet with the Elders on a regular basis and tell the Elders what they see. They were the first ones to actually see the spruce beetle infestation that was destroying the trees in northern British Columbia. They told the Elders and the Elders then reported that to the environmental forces in the province. But government officials did nothing with the information, because these were just kids wandering around in the bush as far as the environment department was concerned. They were speaking the truth, and they reported the infestation at least two years ahead of the issue becoming as prominent as it is.

I have a good friend back home who runs a lodge in which he invites corporate leaders to come and sit with him and just talk with him and ask questions. He is glad to respond to their questions, but it's always based upon what he says, which is "These are the teachings of our people about that." I think that kind of conversation would be very helpful to every leader. Those who have been there have always had very high assessments of the utility of that process.

Are there some guiding principles you can share when it comes to finding that balance?

The first thing is how you treat your people. The people who work for you, the people who work within your organization. Treat them as you would treat your relatives, as you would treat your mother, as you would treat your father, your brothers, your sisters, your cousins, as you would treat people who are part of your circle. I think the first thing that the corporate world needs to learn is how to treat its people. Treat them well. We are driven by a capitalist philosophy which says it is important to be successful by earning lots of money and to centralize that money into as few hands as possible. Whether we admit that or not, that's the way the process is inclined to push us. It's a systemic bias within the system — that's how the system works. Yet, if we reorient our thinking so that we are more considerate of those who are helping us to gather that income and gather those profits, and share more with those who are helping to pull it together, then I think that's a worthwhile endeavor.

There are other things to learn about respecting your community, respecting your environment, respecting the places where you have an impact. Recognizing that in the long term, you should be asking yourself, "What am I going to do to this place, and what is that going to do to my children's relationship to this place?" Not only my children today, but my grandchildren and their grandchildren, and the children seven generations from now. That's the Teaching of the Seven Generations. Think about them when you make those big decisions. You'll be long dead by the time they're here. But they'll care and they'll think about you.

What do you think is the greatest challenge for Canada right now? What should we be thinking about?

I think our greatest challenge in this country is the environment and environmental change. Indigenous people and Indigenous Elders will tell you that too. They are more concerned than they ever have been about the fact that they are seeing the land being so devastated. Not only by economic activity, which concerns them, but also just by the changes in temperature. The Inuit people in the Churchill region around Hudson's Bay tell you that they now see polar bears walking around the bay, through their communities, whereas before, the polar bears used to walk across the ice and go north. Now they don't see that as much because the ice doesn't form until later in the year. The bears start wandering through their communities, and that presents significant challenges. First, it presents a danger. Second, it creates an impact upon their local food supply and things such as that.

Indigenous people are, of course, concerned about the issue of reconciliation, and I think that's important. Changing the relationship that Indigenous people have with this country is important, because Canada has come through a significant period of suppression and what I'm not shy to call white supremacy. They need to atone for that, but they also need to recognize that we have the opportunity and the means, now, not just to bring an end to it, but to repair it. That's important too. I think they can go hand in hand, because Indigenous leaders will tell you that their people are still eager to learn, to teach, and to show others how to live off the land properly.

Early in your career you worked as a social worker and administrator at a Friendship Centre in Selkirk, Manitoba. Friendship Centres were created to deal with a large influx of Indigenous people who moved from their home communities into urban centers as a result of government programs. You are quoted as saying: "That social activism period at the Friendship Centre taught me that if you want to effect some change, you better be willing to involve somebody at the political level or have some political

power . . . and so I thought becoming a politician would be the answer."[2]
What other advice would you like to share with the reader that helps them
to become an effective activist in creating a better world?

One thing that I've learned as a grandfather is the importance
of engaging the children, engaging them in understanding what
activism is all about. It's a huge political force in and of itself, a
powerful force of children. As I said, my granddaughter is a very,
very committed environmental activist. She not only dragged her
friends into the conversation and led them in demonstrations,
but she also spoke at rallies with five to six thousand people at
the legislative building here in Winnipeg when she was twelve
years old. She's not afraid to do that. She's brought the family
in too. The family knows that we better have a recycling box in
the kitchen, right? And we'd better be involved in protecting our
property so that we're not leaving garbage all over the place.

I think the important thing for people to remember in terms
of their activism is that it's really about the children. It's really
about what it is that we can do today to ensure that our children
are better than we are. That they do better than what we have
done. That's a significant responsibility. We can't leave that
to others; we have to do that ourselves. We rely too much on
believing that the public school system is doing the right thing
by our kids, without really monitoring that, when in reality they
could be impeding our children significantly in their ability to be
the kinds of citizens that we want them to be.

I was just talking yesterday with a young woman from
Florida who wants to move from Florida back to Manitoba
because of the new laws that they passed in Florida — for
example, laws that prohibit classroom instruction on sexual
orientation or gender identity in kindergarten through third
grade, and laws that increased scrutiny of school libraries,

2 Ian Austen, "He Almost Quit the Law. Instead, He Reset Canada's Indigenous Dialogue,"
New York Times, February 5, 2021, www.nytimes.com/2021/02/05/world/canada/canada
-indigenous-people.html.

classroom bookshelves, and book fairs. She said, "I can't stand that. I don't want my grandchildren to grow up in that environment." I said, "I understand that. You want to give them the best possible world. But if you leave and others leave, who is going to change those laws? Who is going to make it right?" That's what we have to think about. We have to ask ourselves that. She's very successful, and her husband is a very successful doctor, so they are people of influence. I said, "Who is going to do that important work?" We have a responsibility to do that work if we can. We have a responsibility to our children.

You have famously said, "The road we travel is equal in importance to the destination we seek. There are no shortcuts. When it comes to truth and reconciliation we are forced to go the distance."[3] We believe that, in addition to truth and reconciliation, this wisdom can apply to many of today's crises: climate, inequality, etc. How do you feel we can collectively be better travelers on the road right now, so we reach that destination of a better world?

Keep in mind that reconciliation is not a spectator sport. This is not something you can sit back and watch other people do. You have to figure out where your spot is in that parade and go to it, because it is a social movement that requires societal involvement. We're not at the stage yet where people have totally embraced that concept. There are many people out there who think that somehow, magically, mystically, reconciliation is going to come about. When in reality it's going to take us a long time and a very concerted effort to undo the mess that we have created. We need people to understand that.

That's why that quotation takes on a significant meaning for me and for others. We always have to bear in mind that there is a rationale about why we're doing this, and that rationale is

---

3   Justice Murray Sinclair, Chair of the Truth and Reconciliation Commission of Canada, to the Canadian Senate Standing Committee on Aboriginal Peoples, September 28, 2010.

the history of what the Canadian government did to a very vulnerable group of people in society. We should think about this as similar to a situation of family violence where if the perpetrator — whether it's the husband or the wife, father or the mother, or the grandparents — if the perpetrator of the violence suddenly realizes what they have done and announces, "I'm sorry! I won't do it again. I will change," that's good. They might even apologize and say, "And I'm sorry for what I did to you." That's okay too. But then, what about the children and the damage that the perpetrator has done to them? What do we do for their mental health and their mental wellbeing? What do we do about the pain that they feel? What do they do about the fear that they have about getting into relationships with others? What do we do about their distrust of adults? What do we do about their distrust of society? What do we do about their anguish? What about their tears at night? What about their inability to sleep? What do we do about that? We can't simply say, "That apology was good enough." We also now have to try to fix what we have done.

We need to understand the importance of that, too, because we have a whole population of people who have been negatively affected by what has gone on, and we're not taking care of them. We're not addressing their needs. They often call them healing programs, but it's not just about healing. It's about relearning how to live, and how to be. I once had an Elder tell me that life is not about what you do. Life is about what you are. How can we let them be what they are when what they are is so badly damaged by what has been done to them? That's what we need to understand: that it's part of the journey. It's part of the responsibility as a society we have going forward.

It's a very challenging aspect of our collective future. That's what makes it difficult — this is damn hard work. The biggest single impact that the Indigenous population has experienced coming out of this long history of oppression is not the pain and the suffering and the anger towards others and society who did this to them. It is their sense of dependence. They believe that the only people who can fix it are the government. My message to them is that the only person who can truly fix this is you. Now we need to figure out how to get you the tools so that you can be better parents, better grandparents, better aunties, better uncles, better sons, better daughters. You need to understand that this is our challenge. We can't look to the perpetrator to fix the damage. We have to look to ourselves to fix the damage. I don't know if that answers your question, but it's a damn good answer to some question [*smiles*].

We can certainly understand why you want to continue to do that, but we also wonder how hard that is for you. How many times do you have to tell those of us who are not Indigenous to sit up and pay attention?

Some days I wonder too. I have to say that. I have a very supportive family. I have discussions with my family members all the time, because when I retired as a judge, I said, "Finally, I get the chance to stay home; I'm pulling back from public life." Eight days later, Prime Minister Justin Trudeau called and asked me to go to the Senate. When I talked to my family, I said, "Do you think I should do this?" because I had promised my wife I would stay home. She said, "You've been home for a few weeks and you've organized the cupboards three times now. I was going to tell you to get a part-time job."

I realized that there was more out there that I still needed to do, and that's what they said: "There is more out there that you need to do." The reality is that we must never give up the responsibility of doing what we can, when we can. The teaching that I learned when I was a young boy is that at the end of my life, I will be turned around on my spirit journey. They will turn me around, and they will make me look back at the trail that I created in this world, and they will ask me to account for everything I did, but also everything I didn't do that I could have done. I have to be prepared to speak for that. I want to be able to speak about this thing when I'm ready to go.

Do you have any final words of wisdom for those who are interested in leadership? What do they need to understand as they embark on their own journey?

No matter whether you operate in the public, private, or not-for-profit sector, your role is going to be a challenge to your sense of right and wrong. There will be situations that will make you wonder whether or not you agree with something. I always say that there is no part of this world that is totally inflexible to allowing for difference. If you feel the need to express yourself in a different way, you should. In particular, if you see injustice, you should right it. If you see something that needs to be fixed, you should fix it. If there is something good that you can do, you should do it.

It's as simple as walking down the street and when you see somebody who is homeless, you should always ask them if they are okay. I do that all the time. The reason I do that is because my dad lived on the street for much of his life. I always wondered what it was like for him when people just kept walking by while he was suffering as he was. When I see young girls who are sitting on the side of the street who are looking helpless, I always ask them if they are okay and whether there is anything I can do to help them. Sometimes it's just to give them money. I know that sometimes people criticize me for giving money to people who are homeless on the side of the street, but I always say to them, "If that was my daughter, I hope that someone would give her money so at least she would have a chance to buy some food." It's important to feel. It's important to have empathy. It's important for you to look upon every person as though they were someone you loved.

If you were to ask me now, "How would you like to spend the rest of your life?" I'd tell you I'd like to spend the rest of my life reading to children. In fact, if I could find somebody to pay me to record books all the time, that's all I would do.

CHAPTER 17

NEIL DEGRASSE TYSON

Astrophysicist, Author, and Broadcaster

Neil deGrasse Tyson is an astrophysicist and the author of the #1 best-selling *Starry Messenger* and *Astrophysics for People in a Hurry*, among other books. He is the director of the Hayden Planetarium at the American Museum of Natural History, where he has served since 1996. He is the two-time host of the beloved TV series *Cosmos* — rebooting the original 1980 series hosted by Carl Sagan. Neil is also the host and co-founder of the Emmy-nominated popular podcast *StarTalk* and its spinoff *StarTalk Sports Edition*, which combine science, humor, and pop culture. He is a recipient of twenty-three honorary doctorates, the Public Welfare Medal from the National Academy of Sciences, and the Distinguished Public Service Medal from NASA. Asteroid 13123 Tyson is named in his honor. He lives in New York City.

Can you help us understand whether the science of astrophysics contributes to the betterment of people's daily lives?

I had a physics professor in college named Ed Purcell. He specialized in astrophysics and studied what hydrogen atoms do in space. He studied their nuclei and the electrons that surround them, and in so doing discovered a new way to detect hydrogen in space. It is famously known as the "21-centimeter line," or the "H1 line," which is the electromagnetic radiation spectral line created by a change in the energy state of neutral hydrogen atoms. The discovery of this method of detection was very important because hydrogen gas, essentially, just sits there doing nothing, so how are you going to know it is there and how much of it there is? There is more hydrogen in the universe than anything else — it is the most common ingredient — but we couldn't tell where it was until Ed Purcell made this discovery.

Now, because of his interest in atomic nuclei, he and a colleague discovered a new nuclear phenomenon called magnetic resonance. They found that, *oh my gosh*, if you pass radio waves across a nucleus, it will resonate! The magnetic vector will resonate with it, and it is detectable. This was a new phenomenon that came out of his love for thinking about things from space. He and his colleague, Felix Bloch, won the 1952 Nobel Prize "for their development of new methods for nuclear magnetic precision measurements and discoveries in connection therewith."[1]

But wait a minute! A clever medical engineer then looked at that and said, "Oh my gosh! I can make a cavity that exploits this fact between one nucleus and the next. I can distinguish what kind of atoms are in your body using this magnetic resonance technique." And now you have magnetic resonance imaging, or MRI, which has become, arguably, the most potent machine available to a medical doctor other than the scalpel. It allows doctors to find out what is going on inside your body without needing to perform surgery or cut you open. None of that would have happened unless Ed Purcell did exactly what he wanted, what made him happy, what made him want to explore the unknown.

And so, I will say to you, I have no idea in advance whether anything that any astrophysicist does will improve life on Earth. I do not know this in advance, but I know after the fact that, historically, it has done so ever since we've had astronomers walking among us.

The role that astrophysicists, those people who look up, have played in society's growth — and to be clear, I am not placing

---

1 See www.nobelprize.org/prizes/physics/1952/summary/.

a value judgment on it or saying it is better or worse, I am just calling it "growth" — the advance of our technological powers to control our environment in the interest of our health, our wealth, and our security, has fundamental taproots into astrophysics. But I can tell you that no astrophysicist is doing it with that goal. It is a side consequence of it.

Another example is the navigations systems or GPS that we all use. Obviously, longitude and latitude are not pre-written on Earth's surface; it is an observation and a calculation of where stars are relative to Earth as Earth rotates. So, I would not say to you, "Fund what I do because here is how it is going to benefit you." I would broaden that ask and say, "Fund any science, any activity that steps in places where people had never stepped before, because that is where discoveries occur." Up front, how is it going to help us? I don't know, but the history of this exercise says it will, and for me that is good enough. I realize I specifically spoke about astrophysics, but I think my observations can be extrapolated to encourage people to contribute to the world by learning about whatever they feel a passion for.

This perspective reminds us of a quote by the civil rights leader Howard Thurman: "Don't ask what the world needs. Ask what makes you come alive and go do it. Because what the world needs is people who have come alive."

So our next question is about how you often talk of our place in the universe and how we as individuals are connected to the space around us. For example, you stated: "We are all connected. To each other, biologically. To the Earth, chemically. To the rest of the universe, atomically"; and, "Not only are we in the universe, the universe is in us."[2] We would consider this to not only capture a scientific view but, in essence, a spiritual one. If we truly appreciate this — if we really recognize and value deep connections

---

[2]   Sierra Schubach, "The Best Neil Degrasse Tyson Quotes to Increase Brainpower," *The Daily Shifts*, August 27, 2021, www.thedailyshifts.com/blog/the-best-neil-degrasse-tyson-quotes-to -increase-brainpower.

with others and the space around us — what might be possible? How might such interconnectedness benefit humanity?

It turns out that probably the most profound connection found among humans, and all life on Earth, was Darwin's theory of evolution — evolution by natural selection, captured in his book *On the Origin of Species by Means of Natural Selection*. I would have hoped, naïvely perhaps, that the publication of his book in 1859, and then later his 1871 publication of *The Descent of Man*, would have had everyone turn around and say, "We're all the same! We all have common ancestry!" You're taller, I'm shorter, you have darker skin, you have lighter skin, you worship a different god, you love different people — people would take all these things that we have, things we usually cite to divide us, and they would put them in a bin and say, "In fact, we're all together."

So that quote of mine stating that we are connected biologically, that is, in four words, what Darwin was saying. I was just restating it in a different way. And it is not just to each other, it is to all life on Earth. When you realize that the elements or atoms of our bodies are traceable to the stars then — yes, we are connected to the universe and the universe is connected to us. The stars manufactured those elements and then exploded and scattered them into the galaxy; that galaxy then creates new star systems and new planets, and on at least one of those planets, we have life. Those stars made us. It is not just a figurative truth, it is a literal truth: we are stardust. So, I was naïvely thinking that once we realized this and saw that we are all in this together, that it might diminish the forces of division that drive geopolitics, and even domestic politics, today. For me, if that does not work to bring peace and harmony in this world, I do not know what will.

I have thought that maybe an alien invasion could bring people together, because if aliens wanted to kill all humans, all the warring factions of humans would want to just defend humanity against the aliens. But we already had that exercise with COVID-19. COVID, a virus, is philosophically equal to an invading alien species, right? It attacks all humans. It doesn't care where you live or what your skin color is. I thought we would all band together, drop our weapons, and fight this common enemy. That did not happen. This gives me less confidence than I previously had in whether humans are, in fact, wise enough to be the shepherds of our own fate, and of the future of civilization.

I make a special effort to constantly assess what today looks like versus yesterday. When I say "yesterday," I mean it metaphorically — so, ten years ago, or twenty, fifty, one hundred, one thousand. I do this all the time, so that I never find myself saying we live in special times. Hardly ever is that true, because we are human and the people who lived before us were human, and the people who lived before them were human. They had leaders and they had technologies. We are not special.

Here is an example to show you how it is I know this. We live in one of the most peaceful times in the history of civilization, and I can give simple evidence of that. For instance, if a van plows through protesters and kills a dozen people, that is world headlines for a day or two, and then it is regional headlines for the weeks to follow. It is tragic. However, between 1939 and 1945, an average of one thousand people were killed per hour in the Second World War. One thousand people per hour, for every hour, from September 1939 to September 1945. Who are we to say we are living in especially violent times?

We are not especially violent. Of course, anyone who is a lover of peace and harmony would rather it was different. But there is no time in the past about which I could say, "Let me go back to the 1960s, when we were at peace." We were not at peace, because the whole world was held hostage with a nuclear arsenal, with two warring factions who could not get along at a conversation table. They thought, "Let's build more bombs, so that we feel safer." That is a disturbed state of mind that I don't want to return to. I don't want to go back to the American Civil War, to the so-called bucolic South, where one-third of the southern population were Black African slaves. There is no romanticized South without the slave economy. So no, I'm living for today and tomorrow, if we can make tomorrow better.

So, how do I think we can make society better by lessening resistance to science and accepting objective truth? The school system is an easy target, but I'm going to take a shot at it anyway. Today, the school system teaches things to know, and you are tested on them during your exam period or the end of the unit. But, it doesn't really teach you how to think, how to process information, or how to assess the likelihood of information being true or not. It doesn't teach you about bias of any kind.

I recently gave an entire masterclass on bias. How do you know you're not fooling yourself into thinking something is true when it is not? Or that something is not true when it is? That ability to think critically is the entire foundation of the methods and tools of science, but that is not what I was taught in school. I was taught "what is mitochondria" and "what is DNA" and what is this, and what is it that? I was taught to memorize words because they were in boldface in the textbook and then listed in the back. And the end goal of that is to have a vocabulary test so you can load up your head, take the exam, and then move on with a compartmentalized understanding of what science is — when, really, science is an exquisite method of querying nature that aims to establish what is objectively true.

Unfortunately, that is not how it is taught. But, in my view, if it were taught that way, you wouldn't have 90 percent of the idiocy that rises up out of the school system and ends up being in charge of other people's freedoms. So, in closing, my point is simply this: education needs to teach critical and holistic thinking rather than rote memorization and the compartmentalization of knowledge.

Your answer leads to another question: Is lack of education, ignorance, fear, or a limiting belief system undoing the hard work of science? Mistrust in governments, the media, and scientists has flourished in the pandemic. It can seem that many people have lost the ability to judge what is true and what is not, what is reliable and what is not, and what we should believe and not believe. In many communities there is widespread denial of what science is. However, as you have put it, "Science literacy is an inoculation against charlatans who would exploit your ignorance."[3] How can we get people to become more scientifically literate, to arrive at better judgments, and become ready to make sound, well-informed political decisions?

If you know what science is and how and why it works, then you know the progress of science. First, you get an early result that is intriguing, but you want to get it verified by other results. When you have something like a pandemic, where day by day the virus is spreading exponentially, you must use whatever you know at the time. But you need to be open to further scientific evidence as better data become available.

But what happens is that people think a base of knowledge is something ossified and does not change. They don't realize that science is a process. So you get a scientific organization that says, "Don't wear masks," and then later, when they have more information, they say, "Now wear masks." And people say, "Well, I don't know what to believe!" People have to realize this is science at work and this is how it works.

You certainly are entitled to ignore everything science says and listen to your palm reader instead. But if you look at and truly understand what scientists do, there is no way you will put more confidence in any other system of knowing than in what the Center for Disease Control or other reputable bodies of scientific research provide. Again, this is a challenging point in people's capacity to think in this world. Science and knowledge evolve constantly and changing your mind based on the assimilation of new information is not a weakness, but a strength.

---

3   "From a Universe of Wonder to the Politics of Earth," *Moyers & Company*, aired February 3, 2014, on CUNY, tv.cuny.edu/show/moyers/PR2002727.

To this end, it is important to seek out perspectives different from your own and be open to your belief system being destabilized.

You said in a *New York Times* article that "it's the absence of curiosity that concerns me."[4] Why do you think people no longer wonder or marvel at the world and the cosmos or engage with a sense of awe? How can we remedy this? And if we did, how do you see this shift in consciousness benefiting humanity?

I actually think the awe is still there. I don't think it is missing, and it may be as high as ever. I believe this because there is no other real explanation for me to have had a book titled *Astrophysics for People in a Hurry* on the *New York Times* bestseller list for eighty-two weeks, other than that people are curious about the universe. You could say, "Oh well, you just have a fan group." However, I wrote books before and after *Astrophysics for People in a Hurry*, none of which had that exposure. The book came out in 2017. It would fall down in the charts a few notches, and then bob back up again. It was like a cork on the tidewaters of what was occupying people's thoughts and emotions over those years. That is one bit of evidence in favor of awe.

Then there is the success of the *Cosmos* science documentary television series — not only dating back to Carl Sagan's original series, but right on up through the other two — *Cosmos: A Spacetime Odyssey* and *Cosmos: Possible Worlds* — that I had the privilege of participating in.

Also, the interest that was expressed in the total solar eclipse of 2017 went clear across the continental United States; I also consider that an indicator of awe. It was "America's eclipse." It didn't touch any other country but the United States. People flocked to locations to view it.

---

4   David Marchese, "Neil deGrasse Tyson Thinks Science Can Reign Supreme Again," *New York Times*, April 17, 2021, www.nytimes.com/interactive/2021/04/19/magazine/neil-degrasse-tyson-interview.html.

I have a very positive outlook with regard to people's curiosity. If you expose them to science, they are usually interested, but maybe they simply didn't know to look up. This is the entire foundation of my podcast, *StarTalk*. It is scientific food for people who didn't know science could be tasty. More than that, it is food for people who thought science was definitely bad, who dig their heels in and resist science. *StarTalk* is an attempt to fan the flames of curiosity. Maybe the ember of curiosity within you has lost its flames and it is just a dull glow. But I think if you fan it, it can flare back up and be manifest once again. All people have this curiosity within them.

You have said that children are never really your target audience because they still have that sense of curiosity. It is the adults that have curiosity driven out of them. What advice would you have for adults to increase their curiosity, other than finding people like you to fan the flames?

I can't say how often I get questions about children. Parents say to me, "How do I get my kids interested in science? How do I get them to be curious?" and my advice is "Get out of their way. You are in their way." You know how I know this? Because your toddler at age three or four crawls into the kitchen and your pans are always in the bottom cabinets and they pull the pans out, especially the heavy ones, and then they take the wooden spoon or the ladle and they start banging on it. And what is the first thing you do as a parent? You say, "Stop doing that, you're making a racket and you're getting all the pots and pans dirty!" And by doing that, you have thwarted an experiment in musical acoustics. That's how I see that activity of the child.

The child is excited because everything is new to them. Yes, you want to keep them safe — but there are lots of things they can do that won't harm them, but will just make a messy home. You didn't have kids to guarantee a clean home; that's not why we have kids. Kids are our entropy centers of the universe. Wherever they go there is a mess, but the act of having created the mess, the mess itself, is the consequence of their exploration. Let it be.

The lesson here is to have free-range kids, so that going into adulthood — or more specifically middle school age, puberty age — they can go in with deep foundations in what it means to be curious and evaluate things. Maybe they'll continue it forward into high school.

If you had a curious world, then you wouldn't have adults stuck in their ways. We would more often say, "I wonder if there's another way of thinking about this?" Our curiosity would manifest not necessarily as "I want to be a scientist and make a discovery," but more like, "This is the way I think. Is there another way to think? Is that better or worse than how I'm currently thinking? I'm going to find out." Is it by watching a video? Is it by reading a book? Is it by going to talk to people? There are lots of way of finding out.

And you know what else I think curiosity does? It destabilizes long-held views. I was once asked by the *New York Times*, "What books are you reading now?" I gave them a list of books on my bookshelf. It included a thirtieth printing edition of Barry Goldwater's *The Conscience of a Conservative*. Barry Goldwater was a conservative politician in the 1950s and early 1960s. I also had a book on astrology. The next thing that happened was that I received a lot of comments: "Why are you reading books by Goldwater? I thought you were a liberal," and "Do you believe in astronomy or astrology?" Based on the reactions that I got, it was as though people required me to only read books that agreed with my philosophies. A curious person will read widely, not just to confirm what they already think.

Many people have questions for me about religion. They have asked, "When you are in space, can you see God?" and, "What was around before the big bang?" People often kept going back to God and the Bible, and so I said that I needed to read up on this — I couldn't just wing it. So, I built three shelves of religious texts: the Quran, the Torah, the Bhagavad Gita, and other systems of philosophy. And even the pamphlets you get from Jehovah's Witnesses on the street corners. I have all this, and I've read it. Not every word of every document, but I've read enough to get a sense of where these points of views are coming from, so that when I encounter someone on the street, I can basically recite chapter and verse. My point is that by reading what they read, or what they claim to have read, I was equipped and empowered to have a conversation that didn't discount them, because now I've walked a mile in their shoes. It enabled me, as an educator, to not only see where they are coming from but to shape a message that could maximize the likelihood that their receptors would absorb it.

We read some mind-boggling numbers, including the following:

- There are about 125 billion galaxies in the universe.
- There are about 70 sextillion visible stars (within range of telescope), each with its own planets. (Seventy sextillion is about ten times greater than the estimated number of sand grains on all the world's beaches and deserts.)

We can safely conclude that we are smaller than we can ever truly comprehend. We are perhaps the smallest of the blips on the cosmic canvas. But you have offered an alternative perspective that can be paraphrased as, "If you look up into the universe and feel small, it is because you started out with an ego unjustifiably large to begin with. A cosmic perspective is ego busting. We are participants in the great unfolding of this cosmic story. People like to think they are special because they are different, but maybe you are special because you are the same. Maybe we are special because our ingredients are traceable across the universe." How would you suggest we reduce our focus on our fragile egos and replace it with an understanding of our active and intrinsic participation in this grand cosmic story?

I'll give you a cavalier answer and then maybe I'll have a more thoughtful one. My cavalier answer is to send everyone to the moon and have them look back to Earth. During COVID, I wrote a book called *Starry Messenger: Cosmic Perspectives on Civilization.* The book is about what civilization looks like when you are scientifically literate and folded within a cosmic perspective. And so much of what divides us just evaporates, because the perspective reorders how you think about the world. It is kind of like a firmware upgrade to your outlook, and you end up seeing beyond that which divides us.

I am not talking about warring factions going to the middle and having everybody compromise. I am talking about warring factions finding that there is a point of view they didn't even know was there — maybe because the direction is up instead of towards each other. And when you have that view, you have changed.

I am going to read to you the opening quote in the book, which establishes the tone and the mood for everything that follows. This is a quote from Apollo 14 astronaut Edgar Mitchell: "You develop an instant global consciousness, a people orientation, an intense dissatisfaction with the state of the world, and a compulsion to do something about it. From out there on the moon, international politics look so petty. You want to grab a politician by the scruff of the neck and drag him a quarter of a million miles out and say, 'Look at that, you son of a bitch.'"

That kind of perspective changes you. You can see how different the world looks from your school room globe, with its color-coded countries. It made me wonder, "Why did we color code the countries?" and I realized, "Oh, it's so you know who your enemies are, and where your friends are and where the line in the sand is drawn." It is a tactic, in a way, developed over the history of civilization, to ensure that none of us will ever get along. But when you see Earth from space, adrift in darkness, all you see is ocean, land, and clouds, you don't see the color-coded boundaries that define our maps of the world. And, there is no hint of anyone coming to help us and rescue us from ourselves.

I have often said that the objective of the Apollo missions was to explore the moon. But in doing so, we looked back over our shoulders and discovered Earth for the first time. People changed. But thinking about all of Earth as a holistic ecosystem had not yet — and has not yet fully — become a focus.

In this book, I introduce an alien who comes across Earth for the first time. The alien says, "Well, how come people are having wars?" and the explanation is "Oh well, because they live in different parts of this landmass." To an alien we all look identical, right? Everything we say to them to explain our divisiveness would just make them say, "What the fuck is wrong with you? Aren't you the same species?" "Yes." "Isn't that a contiguous landmass?" "Yes." "Don't you all live on one Earth?" "Yes." "And you're doing *what*?" And then I conclude that, when the alien rushes back home, it reports that there is no sign of intelligent life on Earth.

We believe that humility is foundational to learning. As someone who is extremely accomplished, how do you try to cultivate humility in yourself?

Often humility is manifested by someone who has things they believe but is not aggressive about them. If you tell them something that is different from their beliefs, they embrace it. They thank you for it. But I see the world a little differently from that, in a more abstracted way. I push my belief according to how much evidence supports it. If it is not confirmed with multiple sources of experiment and observations, then my belief is floating. It just floats, and I delight in that.

I don't invest emotion in my beliefs. That would be the trivial investment of an ego. If you do not invest your identity in whether or not something is true, and you embrace all those things that are not yet confirmed to be true, then there is no ego to reckon with. This is because you didn't build anything up that then has to be dismantled. Ego happens when people's emotional profiles get folded together with their belief systems. And we admire the people — well, *some* people admire people who change their mind. That shows that they are grown-ups, that there is an adult in the room.

What I am really saying here is that *I* don't change my mind — the *evidence* changes my mind. It is not about me. Therefore, there is only a dismantling of ego if you think highly of yourself. But what would justify such an opinion of yourself? I believe that no astrophysicist can think highly of themselves, because we fundamentally know that we are too small in time and space, and in everything.

And here's a quick one for you that I learned out of biology books that described humans in the tree of life. Those books stated that we, humans, are especially evolved — that we have complex brains and this is to be praised. We say we are smart, but who defined us as smart? "Oh, we did." Let's keep going. Okay, we said we're smart, but do we have the biggest brains? No, we don't. Whales, dolphins, and elephants all have bigger brains, so we are not really at the top of that list.

Let's look at another measurement and divide how much our brain weighs by how much our body weighs and see how we do on that scale. Hey, okay, it seems we're at the top of that scale. The ratio of brain weight to body weight is highest for humans. So, there we go, we're at the top of that list. When I first learned that, I said, "Okay that's interesting." It wasn't until later that I realized that was restricted to mammals.

Do you realize that midsize birds have a higher brain-to-body weight ratio than humans do? There's a video of a magpie — a very beautiful black-and-white bird — a midsize bird, not big but not little. There's a bottle of water in an open park, and it puts its beak in, and the beak just barely reaches the water level. The magpie, seven times — *seven times!* — walks away, gets a pebble that is small enough to fit through this hole, and drops it into the hole, which raises the water level. It drinks until it can't anymore, and then it goes and gets another pebble. This is the Archimedes Principle in action. It's a bird, and the bird has a "bird brain," which we historically discounted. But in fact, their brain-to-body weight ratio is higher.

You know what has a ratio even higher than birds? Ants. Our brains are two and a half percent of our body weight. Some ants have brains fifteen percent of their body weight. You can see this. Ants are in how many sections? Three! The first section is all head! Entirely head! They're always busy, and always building stuff, and they don't need us for anything.

So, we have formed our ego based on who and what we are, and what we have accomplished, especially our intelligence, which is what we think is unique among the animal kingdom — but even that is challenged. Every time we study animals we come to observe that they are smarter than we ever thought they were! So maybe we are not as separate and distinct as we think we are.

If the Olympics were open to all animal species, there is almost no event that humans would win. The high jump, long jump, the sprints? We might win the triathlon, just because most animals don't know how to ride a bicycle. So, an astrophysicist can't really walk around with an ego of the kind that people typically reference.

You know what I would say humility is? I would say it is compassion. Compassion allows you to question: Are you so into what you're doing that you will discount someone else's long-held beliefs? Or rather, how will you encounter those beliefs? Will it be with a tone of understanding? If someone says, "Jesus is my savior and I love him, and I know he loves me, and I'm going to meet my family in heaven." For me, I'm not going to take that from them. It's not my place.

What we need, I think, is a little more compassion for those who are deeply embedded in a belief system. Like I said, the problem comes when you have your belief system, and you rise to power and then try to impart it on others.

So ultimately, it seems as though you view humility as simply a rational act because of how you perceive and understand the universe.

Yes. So much of our ego is believing that what we think is true in the face of what anyone else says. There's an old saying: If an argument lasts longer than five minutes, then both sides are wrong.

You are a vocal, passionate believer in science and you clearly see the benefits of science for humankind. What is your great ambition, audacious vision, or big dream to inspire people to create a better society? What do you want your legacy to be?

I'll tell you right now, I don't care about legacy. I just care that the world is better off for me having lived in it. I don't need credit for that. If it happens, then it happens. I have been asked if I would allow a biopic to be made about me. My thought on that is "A whole movie about just me? No!" I don't care about me. I care about the enlightenment of other people. That is what I care about. I don't need to be remembered. Bury me in an unmarked grave and let the worms eat me, as I've said many times. Give back to the flora and fauna that I've dined upon for my whole life. There is no legacy here.

PART III

Character
in Action

CHAPTER 18

OUR NECESSARY AND URGENT WORK

We set out to write a book that would help to challenge the belief that character is a subjective construct and something innate, but a critical component of leadership and being that can be observed, measured, and developed in each one of us every day.

Our hope is that by reading and reflecting on the dimensions of character illuminated by our interviewees, you will have gained a deeper understanding of the importance of character in leadership and life, and be able to recognize its tangible, observable behaviors within yourself and within the leaders you encounter in all realms of your life. We hope you have been engaged and enlightened, but also inspired and called to do the necessary and urgent work that is so critical for human and planetary flourishing.

While you may have come to an understanding of the work you will commit to, let us reflect upon a few final questions. Do your leadership behaviors:

- consider our obligations to one another, to the generations to come, and the caretaking of our home — Earth — and all her creatures?
- build a regular practice of both introspection and exercising character?
- consider how each of us can raise the bar in our respective personal and professional lives by recognizing, measuring, fostering, and being leaders with good character?

- prepare you to do what you can to contribute to tackling global challenges in any large or small way you can: climate and the loss of biodiversity, health and well-being, social and economic justice, national and international conflict, nationalism and authoritarianism, women's rights, racism, Indigenous reconciliation, and so forth? No one remains untouched by these (and other) realities and, consequently, no leader in the public, private, or not-for-profit sector can ignore the intersecting effect of these challenges and crises when making decisions, especially if we hope to create a more just, prosperous, and sustainable future.

These challenges — if they are to be truly addressed and overcome — will require all of us to contribute. So, let us not allow pessimism or despair to become entrenched, or to subscribe to the belief that these problems are too large for our individual choices and actions to matter. Our actions do matter, and always have. As Erika Cheung reminded us, "Never underestimate the power of your own and other people's voices. Believe in your own and others' ability to say or contribute something truly remarkable, and never take that for granted." The shaping of our collective future is a responsibility that we all share because, as Maria Ressa said, "All it takes is one, but one is not enough."

Neil deGrasse Tyson harkened to elements of this when he shared, "When you see Earth from space, adrift in darkness . . . there is no hint of anyone coming to help us and rescue us from ourselves." It is up to us. We created these problems and it is now our responsibility to engage our transcendence, our spirit of collaboration, and our humanity and humility to solve them. This is because, as stated by former astronaut Edgar Mitchell, "Transcendence gets you beyond ego. If you go beyond ego, you see all of this in a more decent perspective and you can start to put all the pieces together. We haven't done that yet. Not as a civilization."

It is not only members of our human family that will suffer but all of Earth's creatures, and of course, the Earth herself will be impacted in a way that stagnates flourishing. This is why it was key for Unilever to acknowledge and act against both climate change *and* the long-term destruction of nature. This is also why Ben Lamm and George Church launched Colossal Biosciences, and outlined their ambitious vision as custodians and defenders of the nature which sustains life on Earth:

> For the first time in the history of humankind, we are in control of a science with the power to reverse and prevent biodiversity loss on a large scale. We can heal a hurting planet. We can protect the species living on it. We can ethically decipher and protect genetic codes. And we can begin to turn the clock back to a time when Earth lived and breathed more cleanly and naturally. This is not an option for us. It is an obligation known as thoughtful disruptive conservation.

As David Kipping articulated, even though the Earth is 4.5 billion years old, "We are living in a very unique moment, at this apex of bio-productivity. Earth is probably the most beautiful it will ever be. Well, maybe rewind the clock two hundred years, before we started screwing things up."

How extraordinary! Take that in for a moment. In this small blip of time that humans are inhabiting the Earth, we are — not witnessing — but are *a part of* its most exquisite phase. It would be incredible if the work of an organization such as Colossal helps us to rewind the clock to that time, just moments ago in the grand timeline of the universe, before we started to damage our home.

This alignment must extend into all areas of our lives, whether spiritual or emotional, logical or professional. We need to transform how we do politics and business.

Yvon Chouinard is the founder of Patagonia. He turned his passion for rock climbing into one of the world's most successful sportswear brands. In September 2022, Chouinard announced that he was giving away all of his shares in Patagonia — worth over a billion dollars — to a trust that will use future profits to "help fight" the climate crisis and defend nature.[1] In a message to staff and customers, he said: "Earth is now our only shareholder . . . Instead of 'going public,' you could say we're 'going purpose.' Instead of extracting value from nature and transforming it into wealth for investors, we'll use the wealth Patagonia creates to protect the source of all wealth."

Julia Hoggett was unflagging in describing her purpose in transforming the business model of the London Stock Exchange: "To bring together those who have capital with those who need it, in service of an objective. Today, one of the most important objectives is the just transition to net zero."

Similarly, the shareholders of Unilever adopted the Climate Transition Action Plan to reduce emissions to zero within its own operations by 2030 and to net zero across their value chain by 2039. Unilever's former CEO, Alan Jope, believes in a multi-stakeholder model towards which many companies are shifting because "it is impossible for us to do our fiduciary duty without considering climate change, the destruction of nature, and social inequality."

Collaboration too plays an essential role in addressing social inequality as explained by the Honourable Murray Sinclair. While his words and wisdom with respect to Indigenous reconciliation were expressed in a Canadian context, they are universal. He reminded us that we should never forget about the extreme harm wrought by colonialism and its destructive impact on Indigenous people, their languages, and their culture. Murray also said: "If we do move forward without remembering, then we are not the people that we should be. . . . We must all feel the weight of this process of reconciliation. Because even if you weren't here, you still have a responsibility to the future of this country."

In Canada, the Truth and Reconciliation Commission outlined ninety-four calls to action needed to move the country towards reconciliation. Globally, we can look to the articles within the UN Declaration

---

1   A richer description of this story can be found at www.theguardian.com/us-news/2022/sep/14 /patagonias-billionaire-owner-gives-away-company-to-fight-climate-crisis-yvon-chouinard. Observers noted that Chouinard has been consistent in his approach to leading a purpose-driven, compassionate, and committed company, with the core value of environmental consciousness.

on the Rights of Indigenous Peoples.[2] By activating our humility and our humanity, we can engage in the often-uncomfortable conversations necessary to bring about the learning, understanding, and action required to address the systemic abuse, genocide, and injustice experienced by many Indigenous Peoples. By holding the space for those who have been oppressed to speak their truth — and to be truly heard and believed — we can acknowledge the realities of the past and begin to build a path towards healing. In fact, many Indigenous people believe that, without truth, there can be no reconciliation at all. Therefore, whether one is a new immigrant or a descendant of settlers on lands and/or in nations where systemic colonialism continues to be present and maintained, we can exercise accountability and transcendence by making a commitment to remember — to not only acknowledge the trauma and abuse inflicted in the past, but to co-create a vibrant future.

This engagement in truth-telling and deep listening by activating our humanity, humility, justice, and collaboration can contribute to creating a culture of respect and dignity for all those involved. It is important that we remember, as Murray states, that "reconciliation is about establishing a respectful relationship ... [but] one thing I have also pointed out is that Indigenous people have so long been oppressed and victimized by this history that ... we have to ensure that Indigenous people are given the opportunity to develop self-respect."

This mirrors Mary Robinson's belief in the importance of dignity coming before rights within the phrasing of the Universal Declaration of Human Rights. Not only does "placing dignity first" affirm the right to self-worth and self-respect for those whose circumstances have stripped them of it, but "it brings out far more compassion and empathy in the approach to human rights. Very often, to a fault actually, human rights can be judgmental or finger-pointing, but if you place the need for people to have dignity first, suddenly you're into thoughtful compassion." Again, it invokes the character dimension of humanity, which leads to

---

2   The United Nations Declaration on the Rights of Indigenous Peoples was adopted by the General Assembly on Thursday, September 13, 2007; see social.desa.un.org/issues/indigenous -peoples/united-nations-declaration-on-the-rights-of-indigenous-peoples.

the activation of our sense of justice and collaboration, specifically our interconnectedness. Recall Mary Robinson's discussion of *meithal* and *ubuntu*, which stem from the same idea — we are connected.

The work of Adam Kahane also echoes this as he explores love as being the drive to reconnect the separated. This was captured when he shared, "People experience joy when they recognize that they are connected to and are a part of the same larger whole as people whom they thought of as their opponents or enemies. Relationships and interdependence — that's the expression of love."

The confidence and drive to tackle complex and large problems are rooted in character. This is combined with the wonderful potential for people to constantly learn, modify, adapt, and experiment as they make their way in life — and for all of us to develop our character throughout our lives regardless of age, role, rank, or status. It has been said many times before that leadership is a journey — and many leaders go through personal transformations as they mature and deal with personal and professional challenges that, in many cases, make them even better leaders. Remember, as Maria Ressa said, that "who you are, and who you are becoming, is a work of art." It is critical, therefore, that we bring awareness and intentionality to the development of our character in order to strengthen each dimension and maximize their individual and collective effectiveness.

Nanea Hoffman is the founder of Sweatpants & Coffee, a popular lifestyle brand, social media platform, and online community focused on comfort, creativity, inspiration, and fun. She sent out a social media post in 2015 that said, "None of us is getting out of here alive, so please stop treating yourself like an afterthought. Eat the delicious food. Walk in the sunshine. Jump in the ocean. Say the truth you're carrying in your heart like hidden treasure. Be silly. Be kind. Be weird. There's no time for anything else."[3]

For too long, the development of our character has been an afterthought. It feels, at times, that we treat character as though it is a residue,

---

3   Nanea Hoffman, "None of us is getting out of here alive . . ." Facebook, May 19, 2015, www
    .facebook.com/SweatpantsAndCoffee/photos/a.507797995941166/818817198172576/?type=3.

rather than the main substance of our lives. Why are we leaving this vital part of ourselves to chance? Or why are we, as Tracy Edwards phrases it, being a bystander in our own lives? Why aren't we taking part in our character's development? It is critical that we stop treating the cultivation of our Self — that is, who we are — as secondary to what we do or even how we appear to others. We need to be an active participant in our own becoming — being passive or performative when it comes to character limits our ability to live deeply and deliberately. Like Hoffman encourages, we should speak our heart's truth (be candid and brave), be silly (vulnerable), be kind (compassionate and considerate), be weird (curious and creative).

And consider how empowering it is to see how youth have found meaning in becoming leaders of influence. Leaders such as Gitanjali Rao, Malala Yousafzai, Greta Thunberg, Mirko Schedlbauer, Mariam Nourya Koné, and many others have already harnessed a global network and use it effectively. These young innovators, activists, and entrepreneurs are helming international movements and are seeking solutions to manifest a more inclusive, sustainable, and resilient world. As a *Forbes* article put it: "As the most outspoken, informed, and empowered generation of youth to-date, they have spent the last years honing their messages and abilities, building resources and networks, and improving their activism. They pair raising their voices with taking direct action. Youth have become leaders occupying top-level positions that enable them to improve lives and protect the planet."[4]

Meaning is also very personal. Our experience of interviewing Pastor Gennadiy Mokhnenko brought home in a deeply immediate, emotional, and visceral way the abject horror of war and it remains with us to this day. The impact of that interview was not only created from hearing his story, but by vicariously experiencing his life within those very moments of our discussion. Within that hour, missiles had just rocketed over where he was camped, and the destruction of Mariupol and its citizens was

---

4   Natalie Pierce, "Davos: A New Era for Youth Activism and World Leaders Must Listen," *Forbes*, January 10, 2023, www.forbes.com/sites/worldeconomicforum/2023/01/10/davos-a-new-era-for-youth-activism-and-world-leaders-must-listen/?sh=63e2e5b27a70.

happening only a few miles away. We were completely unprepared when Gennadiy shared with us that only thirty minutes prior to the start of our interview he had learned of the death of one of his daughters, herself a young mother, by Russian tank fire (a neighbor managed to find a piece of her body and bury it in a small grave). It was utterly heart-wrenching, and we could not even fathom the resilience he possessed to conduct the interview under such circumstances.

As he spoke to us, however, and recounted his experiences as a fire-fighter in Moscow, in creating an orphanage for homeless teenagers and personally adopting so many of them, and then his actions in the war with Russia, what struck us as one of his most incredible acts of courage was his embrace of forgiveness. "Forgiveness is not hard for me. I love it," he said. Gennadiy has the self-awareness to know that he, and indeed all of us, will need forgiveness in our lives, as none of us are without faults, mistakes, or biases.

As the incomparable Nelson Mandela once said, "Forgiveness liberates the soul, it removes fear. That's why it is such a powerful weapon."[5] How would our lives change if we strengthened our own capacity for forgiveness — to both ask for it and grant it — since we will each need to forgive and be forgiven at many points throughout our lives? How would conflict change if one of our powerful weapons was forgiveness rather than violence? And, how would our understanding of courage expand when it is supported by elements such as compassion, vulnerability, open-mindedness, fairness, and patience? We believe it would remove elements like bravado or recklessness and return the *cor*, Latin for heart, back into courage.

David Kipping pointed out that we humans are a rare phenomenon: "We are a collection of atoms that can think, that can talk, that can feel, that can dream, that can have abstract thoughts — that is an extremely rare phenomenon as far as we can tell. I think it is important for us to realize and understand that this experience we are in — of possessing

---

5   Nelson Mandela did not come to forgive his torturers effortlessly. See the short article by
     Alessandro Gisotti, "Forgiveness Will Liberate You: The Lesson of Nelson Mandela," *Vatican
     News*, July 18, 2022, www.vaticannews.va/en/world/news/2022-07/alesssandro-gisotti-lesson-of
     -nelson-mandela-pardon.html.

a conscious sense of awareness — is certainly an extremely rare phenomenon. Therefore, so are you and so is each and every one of us." He went on to challenge us: "But on a human scale, all we have is about one hundred years, if we're lucky, to live on this planet. Your time is finite. There is a finite amount of time to engage in the things you want to accomplish. You should wake up with a sense of urgency, a sense of how every moment is important and you have to live it."

In many of the conversations with our interviewees, hope and optimism were central to their drive and commitment to trying to create a better world. A number of our interviewees referenced finding inspiration in Bishop Desmond Tutu and being a "prisoner of hope." Sister Joan Chittister stated that hope "is neither magic nor naïvete . . . It is something that you experience through your life. It is the result of experiencing and surviving the necessary struggles of life: pain and sorrow, depression and darkness, stress and suffering. With every experience, you get stronger. Your hope gets deeper, and your ability to deal with difficult challenges grows." Gennadiy described hope as natural and pointed to the new buds on the tree overhead of him, a tree sprouting new life in the midst of death and destruction in Mariupol. Maria Ressa said that "life without hope means you become an automaton with no meaning or purpose."

As a final reflection, advancing a nation's social, political, and economic development and well-being depends on character. We believe that no level of competence or commitment will fully work to potential without strong, well-developed character. Thus, it is critical that we develop, support, vote for, and promote leaders with strength of character to tackle boundary-crossing grand challenges in society. This will require actions on many levels involving numerous actors — parents, teachers, professors, bosses, coaches, mentors, board chairs, friends and colleagues, and many others — and what has been the goal of this book: an inspired, conscious, and deliberate focus by each of us to strengthen and develop our character.

We hope this book has encouraged you to become a beacon of hope. Being a beacon, a lighthouse in the dark, is not only the first job of a leader — it is the everyday job, through to the last job. In these stormy times, picture yourself as an ever-present, always visible lighthouse illuminating the shore to your constituent "vessels" on the open seas, reassuring them that solid ground is near.

There is no alternative to leader character that makes sense to underpin our social, political, and economic survival, development, and well-being. Your destiny depends on it. Our collective destiny depends on it. The Earth's destiny depends on it. We will close with more wisdom from the Honourable Murray Sinclair and David Kipping, respectively:

> No matter whether you operate in the public, private, or not-for-profit sector, your role is going to be a challenge to your sense of right and wrong. There will be situations that will make you wonder whether or not you agree with something. I always say that there is no part of this world that is totally inflexible to allowing for difference. If you feel the need to express yourself in a different way, you should. In particular, if you see injustice, you should right it. If you see something that needs to be fixed, you should fix it. If there is something good that you can do, you should do it.

> You are a rare phenomenon in the universe.

INDEX

Note: Page numbers in italics indicate a figure.

ABOUT THE AUTHORS

Gerard Seijts is professor of organizational behavior at the Ivey Business School at Western University in London, Ontario, Canada. He was the inaugural executive director of the Ian O. Ihnatowycz Institute for Leadership. Gerard received his PhD in organizational behavior and human resource management from the Rotman School of Management at the University of Toronto. He is the author of several books, including *Leadership on Trial: A Manifesto for Leadership Development* (2010) (with Jeffrey Gandz, Mary Crossan, and Carol Stephenson), *Good Leaders Learn: Lessons from Lifetimes of Leadership* (2013), *Developing Leadership Character* (2016) (with Mary Crossan and Jeffrey Gandz), and *The Character Compass: Transforming Leadership for the 21st Century* (2024) (with Mary Crossan and Bill Furlong). His award-winning research on leadership and leader character is published in top management journals, and he has authored numerous articles in practitioner journals. Gerard has designed and led executive education programs for public, private, and not-for-profit sector organizations around the world.

Kimberley Young Milani is the director of the Ian O. Ihnatowycz Institute for Leadership at the Ivey Business School at Western University in London, Ontario, Canada. Prior to joining Ivey, she was the director of the Circle Women's Centre at Brescia University College (Canada's only women's university) and also a founding member and director of Brescia's Institute for Women in Leadership. Kimberley received her Bachelor of Arts from the University of Toronto and a Master's Diploma in Organisational Leadership from Saïd Business School, University of Oxford. She has authored practitioner articles on leadership and has conducted extensive public speaking and workshop facilitation on character leadership and women's leadership in Canada and the US.

THE IAN O. IHNATOWYCZ
INSTITUTE FOR LEADERSHIP

Since its inception in 2010, the Ian O. Ihnatowycz Institute for Leadership at the Ivey Business School, Western University, London, Canada, has been at the center of leadership thought, inquiry, and education into what makes a better leader through its focus on leader character. The Institute's research is integrated into Ivey's degree and executive education programs and it conducts a wide range of outreach activities with the public, private, and not-for-profit sectors. Through its work, the Institute elevates the importance of character alongside competence in the practice of leadership and supports the development of global citizens who have strength of character, strive to make a difference, and contribute to the flourishing of teams, organizations, communities, and societies.

For more information on the Institute's research, teaching, and outreach, visit www.ivey.ca/leadership or email leadership@ivey.ca.

This book is also available as a Global Certified Accessible™ (GCA) ebook.
ECW Press's ebooks are screen reader friendly and are built to meet the needs
of those who are unable to read standard print due to blindness, low vision,
dyslexia, or a physical disability.

At ECW Press, we want you to enjoy our books in whatever format you like.
If you've bought a print copy or an audiobook not purchased with a subscription
credit, just send an email to ebook@ecwpress.com and include:

- the book title
- the name of the store where you purchased it
- a screenshot or picture of your order/receipt number and your name

A real person will respond to your email with your ePub attached. If you prefer
to receive the ebook in PDF format, please let us know in your email.

Some restrictions apply. This offer is only valid for books already available in the
ePub format. Some ECW Press books do not have an ePub format for us to
send you. In those cases, we will let you know if a PDF format is available as an
alternative. This offer is only valid for books purchased for personal use. At this
time, this program is not offered on school or library copies.

Thank you for supporting an independently owned Canadian publisher with
your purchase!